Journey Through Fire and Ice

Shattered Dreams Above the Arctic Circle

Deanne Burch

JOURNEY THROUGH FIRE AND ICE
Shattered Dreams Above the Arctic Circle
By Deanne Burch
1. BIO026000 2. BIO22000 3. BIO28000
ISBN: 978-1-949642-59-9
EBOOK: 978-1-949642-60-5

Cover design by LEWIS AGRELL

Printed in the United States of America

Authority Publishing
11230 Gold Express Dr. #310-413
Gold River, CA 95670
800-877-1097
www.AuthorityPublishing.com

For my Children and Grandchildren

And in memory of my husband Tiger,
who introduced me to the people of Kivalina

As a child growing up, we referred to the Inuits as Eskimos. When I arrived in Kivalina in 1964, many of the natives referred to themselves as Eskimos. I have taken the liberty of using Inuit words and often do not know the spelling and could not find it anywhere.

Enuchen is pronounced *E nu ken* and is the Inuit word for the wild people they believed existed.

Nanuktoque: I have no idea the meaning of this or the spelling but it was the Eskimo name of my dearest friend in Kivalina. Our oldest daughter Karen was given this Eskimo name in honor of Ruth Adams. Our daughter Sarah was given the name Appolinia. This is probably misspelled and I don't the meaning of it but her Eskimo name was for Amos Hawley, who was Tiger's best friend. David, our son, was named after Charlie Jensen, who does not appear in this memoir. His Eskimo name is Sagaluuzaq. This is the proper spelling but I don't know the meaning of it.

CONTENTS

PART II

ACKNOWLEDGEMENTS

I would like to thank the following people who helped me through this process:

My partner, John Skiba, who helped me in countless ways as I wrote this. Without his help and patience, this would never have been completed.

My editor, Suzanne Sherman, who taught me so much about writing and edited this memoir.

My granddaughter, Naomi Karmel, who also helped edit this as well as proofreading it.

Chela Hardy, who helped me put this book together.

My writer's critique group at the Fredrickson Library who cheered me on and encouraged me to finish this.

Peggy McLeish, who I was able to bounce ideas off of and who reminded me of certain things that happened that I had forgotten about.

And last but not least, the people of Kivalina. This memoir would not have happened if I had never had the opportunity to become part of their life.

PART 1

SUNRISE

Last night, I dreamed I was back in Kivalina, Alaska, with my husband, Tiger. We were young, in our twenties, with a bright future ahead of us. It was late spring, when the sun never set and people wandered from house to house at all times of the day and night. The country was awake with tiny wildflowers, though the temperature rarely rose above forty-five degrees Fahrenheit. The sea ice was the color of aquamarines and sparkled in the sunlight. Sometimes, the sky turned white as the fog rolled in, obscuring everything for miles around.

The scene quickly morphed into a winter painted in muted pastels—dove-gray hills in the distance, snow reflecting pinks and mauves when the sun was low. A perpetual glow toured the horizon for a few days in late fall, but by early December there was no light at all. The colors of Kivalina were an echo of my life there: The grays mirrored my loneliness and isolation, the soft whispers of pinks and mauves offered me fragments of hope.

Shaking, I struggled to light the kerosene lantern, our only form of light. What if it ignited in my face? I was worried. I gave this job to Tiger when he was home, but he wasn't around. The room was cold as the wind howled through the cracks and crevices of our wooden house. I didn't want to be here for another winter.

Despite being wrapped in blankets, when I awoke, my teeth were chattering, and my feet felt like ice. I reached over to touch my husband and instead was met with an empty place and a sense of overwhelming loss. He wasn't there.

I climbed out of bed and stepped out onto the deck at our cottage in Ontario, Canada. The sun was rising and the lake reflected the bright pinks, violets, and blue of the sky. This is where, more than fifty years ago, my life with Tiger began, and how I ended up on a journey that changed my life forever. Fifty-five years after I lived in Kivalina, I think about our existence there almost every day. It changed me from a young girl with hopes and expectations to a mature woman with knowledge and understanding.

Before I left for Alaska, my mother used to say to me, "Deanne, it's only a plane trip away." In reality it was so much more than that. Kivalina, Alaska, was four plane trips away. There were no phones. Our contact to the outside world was by mail. The mail plane came twice a week but by the time letters arrived, the news was ten days old.

We were two people with very different expectations. Tiger thought he could take his twenty-three-year-old wife to a remote Eskimo village and she would adapt to a way of life totally foreign to her. I naïvely thought love would conquer everything. In the end, it could not conquer loneliness, isolation, culture shock, and primitive living conditions. Now, looking back, at that time so long ago, I realize what a great adventure we had. Yes, it was full of hardship, but we also had some incredible experiences that I am so grateful for.

We lived in Alaska for less time than we had planned. It was more challenging than we'd anticipated and in the end, it defined who we were and what we did, long after we left. It stole my innocence and my belief that we could have a fairy-tale ending. Tiger, despite his tragic accident, loved Kivalina. It lived in the very fiber of his soul until the day he died.

I walked back into the cottage, still shaken by my dream. For a long time, I wished the memories of Kivalina would fade, but decades later, they are as vibrant as ever. Tiger would say what happened to us was bad luck. I would say it was destiny.

I am inviting to you to take the journey I took fifty-five years ago.

I

THE PROPHECY

My grandmother (fondly known as Goggy) was prescient. She seemed to know things before they happened, or she dreamed about them after they occurred, even when she wasn't present for them. One day, my grandmother said to my mother, "Ruth, I don't want Elizabeth living with the Eskimos." (My grandmother often called me by my middle name, Elizabeth.)

I was fifteen at the time, and still in high school. I was about to enter our small kitchen when I overheard their conversation. They were sitting at the metal table and as I watched from the doorway, I could smell the smoke from the cigarette Mom always lit when she was agitated, which was most of the time. My grandmother was drinking tea and eating her lunch at eight in the morning. For reasons unbeknownst to us, she started her day at three a.m.

"Don't be ridiculous, Mother," my mom replied, flicking her cigarette, "Deanne wouldn't do that. Whatever gave you this idea?"

My grandmother was adamant as she responded, "I know it's going to happen, and I don't want her going there."

I wanted to shout, "Mom's right! Don't worry about it." But I didn't. Why bother? Living with the Eskimos was the last thing I would ever do. I learned enough about that northern area in grade school to know I didn't want to be a part of it. I would never live with the Eskimos, not even in my wildest dreams. Bundling up in a thick parka and heavy boots in order to ward off the winter chill was not in my repertoire. It was cold here, in Toronto, but it was frigid in the north. No, the cold was not for me. I wanted to ignore what she was saying, and I decided this was one thing she predicted that would never come true. At least I hoped it was.

And yet, eight years later, I was living in the small village of Kivalina with my husband, Ernest Burch, who was known by all of his friends as Tiger. We married in 1963 and in 1964, our great adventure to Alaska began. I was terrified to leave the safety net of family and friends and I soon learned living with the Eskimos was more challenging than I ever dreamed of. Looking back, I wondered if my grandmother had a premonition of what was going to happen there. By the time we arrived in Alaska, Goggy was in a nursing home and never knew her prediction had come true.

II

THE PRINCETON TIGER

My husband's proper name was Ernest Suhr Burch, Jr. His father had gone to Princeton, and Tiger was the first son born to a member of the Princeton graduating class. Coming into the world at a little over nine pounds, it was fitting for him to be nicknamed Tiger, Princeton's mascot, by friends of his father. The name stayed with him the rest of his life.

I was fifteen the summer I first saw Tiger. Ironically, this was the same year my grandmother had made her prophecy. My family belonged to a club on Muskoka Lake, where my two brothers and I took swimming and tennis lessons, and occasionally attended the dances held there. During the last dance of the summer, I looked across the room to see a boy whose eyes reminded me of Paul Newman's. They were a piercing blue color, and I was immediately attracted to him, although we never spoke. Who was he, arriving with his family so late in the summer? Years later, I was reminded of the song, *Some Enchanted Evening*. I looked across the crowded room to see a stranger and somehow, I knew this person would be important to me.

The following week, I asked about the family and learned they had inherited a summer home at the end of Tondern Island from a bachelor who wanted it to be filled by a family. It was the most imposing summer home in the vicinity, sitting high on the hill dominating all the places around it. Our cottage, by contrast, was small.

Like my own family, there were three children in the Burch family. Tiger was the eldest, eighteen, the summer I first laid eyes on him. He was a few months younger than my brother David. His sister, Lynn, was the middle child in the family, and Johnny, the youngest, was the same age as my younger brother, Robert.

Over the next few days, I drove past the Burch home in the boat hoping to catch a glimpse of Tiger or his family. A couple of times, they were sitting on the dock and I waved hello, but we never spoke. August ended too soon, and it was time to return to Toronto for school.

The following summer, I met the boy who had impressed me the year before. We both taught swimming at the club—he taught the boys; I taught the girls. Tiger was sophisticated, intelligent, and fun. I liked him, but I heard the crowd he traveled in partied all the time. Alcohol flowed freely. I knew I wouldn't fit in, even if I had been older.

The same summer, Lynn, who was a few months younger than I, became a close friend of mine. She seemed to look at the world through rose-colored glasses and was perhaps the loveliest person I had ever met. Lynn was quiet like me and we soon became fast friends. We wrote letters when we were apart every winter and I knew Lynn could be trusted with anything.

Although the Burches lived in Harrisburg, Lynn was attending Miss Hall's School in Pittsfield, Massachusetts. She told me Tiger had attended the Hill School but was now a freshman at Princeton. When I wrote Lynn, I told her about things I never shared with my friends at home. Lynn in turn wrote me about her life at Miss Hall's School and sometimes, would tell me about some of Tiger's escapades. One time after drinking too much, he loaded himself into a shopping cart and flew down one of the hills in Princeton. I took vicarious pleasure out of these stories and thought he would be a lot of fun to be with. Later, after Tiger and I married, Lynn and I had a ceremonial burning of the letters I had written to her, and my life before Tiger went up in ashes.

Lynn sent me an invitation to her coming out party in Harrisburg, Pennsylvania, in mid-June, 1960. I heard of these parties, but never expected to be invited to one. I attended public school and came from a different background from Lynn and her friends. The trip would be paid for out of my meager salary from my job at the Department of Education in Toronto. Taking a bus was the least expensive way to travel.

The twelve-hour journey by bus from Toronto to Harrisburg was dreadful, and I arrived dirty, hot, and sleep-deprived at the bus station one day before the party. I was thrilled to be there and eager for all that was ahead. Lynn told me Tiger wanted me to be his date at the party, and I couldn't wait. We never had the chance to know each other at the lake but apparently he remembered me. Tiger had, by the time of Lynn's party, just finished his senior year at Princeton and although I had a serious boyfriend at home, the thought of seeing Tiger again was an exciting one.

The Burch's home sat at the end of a long road with a circular driveway leading up to it. Walking into the front hall, I could see the spacious living room with a spectacular window overlooking a rolling meadow. The dining room, with deep red wallpaper that brought to mind Victorian times, had a table large enough to hold twelve people. The bright and cheery breakfast room seated six around a circular table. The first floor also had a sunroom and library. Both the living room and library had fireplaces and original oil paintings hung on the walls. Upstairs, the bedrooms had their own adjoining bathroom. In Lynn's bedroom, a dressing table and three-way mirror flanked one of the walls. The room held twin beds with a brass headboard, but also a coffee table and chair matching the décor of the room, as well as a chaise longue. Lynn's room was fit for a princess.

My home was different in many ways from the Burch home. A modest house, it had only one bathroom shared by six of us. Both of my brothers had rooms of their own, but I shared a small room with my grandmother, known as Goggy. My mother had decorated the room in a green and yellow floral pattern to make it appealing for both of us. Apart from the twin beds, there was a small dressing table and a bureau. My grandmother used the latter, decorating its top with some of her memorabilia. She had a portrait of my grandfather there who had died when my mother was two. She also had a silver brush set given to her from my grandfather on their wedding day. Inside its drawers, she kept bits of poetry she had written or wanted to remember.

There was one problem with this arrangement. My grandmother went to bed at seven and she was up at three in the morning, long before the rest of the family stirred. I loved and worried about her, and so I woke when she did, listening, until she had made it safely down the stairs.

Since Goggy went to bed so early, there was no place to study, and so I lay on the bed in my parents' room with books piled all around me. It was a place to daydream, not to do schoolwork, and I wished there were another place where I could study.

This special occasion gave me a chance to have a peek into another way of life, one so different from my own. The day before the party, I listened to the chatter of some of Lynn's friends. Their voices rose and fell like a warm summer breeze as they spoke. The lives of these girls fascinated me.

"What are you doing this summer?" one girl asked the others. "I'm going to Europe for six weeks." She would be going to Smith in the fall and looked forward to having this playtime before beginning her studies.

"It's summer as usual on Martha's Vineyard," one of the girls replied. "You know, sailing, swimming, and relaxing." She would be attending Vassar.

The girls were full of confidence and they all dressed alike, in Bermuda shorts, Shetland sweaters, knee socks, and penny loafers. I felt them looking at my white pleated skirt, blouse, and sandals. What did they think of me? I wouldn't be traveling. I had a summer job to help pay my tuition for university in the fall. My parents provided well for my brothers and me, but money didn't stretch far enough to allow for everything.

The Country Club of Harrisburg was the venue for the party. The party was upstairs in the ballroom and there was a live band. Any dance I attended had music played by a DJ. I had never been to a place like this. The room opened onto a deck outside and sometimes, I found myself wandering there when I wasn't dancing and was tired of watching the others. The girls whirled around the dance floor in soft blues and pinks, floating from partner to partner with grace. Although I loved my gown, I had worn it several times, too late to realize it was out of style. My dress thankfully withstood being packed in my suitcase because it was made out of an under fabric overlaid with netting. The dress was a cream colored strapless with small gold bows holding it up. A wide satin sash matching the bows adorned my waist. It didn't compare to the dresses worn by the others.

Studying Tiger on the dance floor, I was reminded of how handsome he was. He had brown hair cut into a crew cut, and his blue eyes sparkled. His tuxedo was accompanied by a plaid cummerbund and matching bow tie. Tiger was a fabulous dancer, but he was obliged to dance and wanted to dance with others. He performed the Charleston with one of the guests. Their arms were in constant motion and their knees knocked together. Everybody stopped dancing to watch them and clapped when they were finished. Observing him with his partner made me envious. Dancing like that was not something I could do. Occasionally, I found myself standing on the sidelines watching while the others danced. Everyone seemed to know each other, and I longed to be part of their world.

After the dance, Tiger took the guests staying at his house back home. We had stayed at the dance until it ended, but most of us stayed up talking long into the night about the wonderful time we had had. As I sat with the other girls, I wondered if it was a wonderful evening for me. It had been a new and different experience and that in itself made it something I will remember forever. But I knew nobody there and I often felt out of my comfort zone. One by one, the girls drifted off to bed. I was about to join them when Tiger grabbed my hand. "Let's watch the sunrise together."

We walked out to the end of the driveway and watched as the sun painted the sky with lavenders, pinks, and deep blues. The evening had come to an end and as we greeted a new day,

I thought the experiences I'd had since my arrival made me feel as though I was opening new and exciting Christmas presents, one after the next.

Secretly, I hoped Tiger would be at the lake in a few weeks. I wanted to find out more about him and have a chance to get to know him better. But his mother's conversation with a visiting friend quickly dashed my hopes.

"Tiger's just graduated from Princeton," Mrs. Burch told her friend, "and he's going to school in Germany for the summer. He wants to speak German and says this is the best way to learn. Last summer, he went to France because two languages are needed in order to complete a PhD at the University of Chicago."

I tried to console myself. It was nice while it had lasted. Tiger would make a great catch for some woman in Chicago next fall.

I was dreading the return bus trip to Toronto, but Mr. Burch surprised me before the weekend came to an end. "Deanne," he said the Sunday morning I was leaving, "Lynn was delighted you made such an effort to be at her party. We all were. I'd like to fly you to Buffalo in my plane. You can take the bus from there."

I could hardly contain my excitement. This was to be my first time flying. As it was, I turned out to be a white-knuckle flyer and vowed that if we landed safely, I would never fly again. Many years later, flying into Kivalina in another small plane, memories of my first flight came rushing back. Still consumed with the fear of flying, I gripped the armrests and planted my feet firmly on the floor. Looking out at the snow-covered land, I prayed that we would land safely on the windblown runway.

The weekend in Harrisburg had been incredible. Nevertheless, I quickly drifted back into the life I knew. The evening with Tiger had been like a dream, but my relationship with Bob, my first love, was my reality. The magical weekend became a memory.

My horizons were limited, but I was happy to live in a cocoon of familiarity. Family and friends were an integral part of my life. Toronto was an exciting place to live and had a lot to offer. The university I attended was one of the best in Canada. My friends and I studied at the library and then spent hours in the coffee shop talking and playing bridge. Occasionally, I thought about the world outside my safety net and all it had to offer, but most of the time, I was content.

The summer I was twenty, I wanted to spend a final weekend at the lake. My relationship with Bob had soured, and it seemed appealing to get away from the city and from him. Working all summer at a dull job, time at the lake, promised adventure. Much to my disappointment, however, it turned out our cottage was full of relatives and there was no room for me. There wasn't even room there for my parents. I ran into Mrs. Burch at the club one weekend earlier in the summer, realizing this would probably be my last weekend at the lake. She asked if I would be coming back later this summer and I told her that unfortunately, I would not be back again. She surprised me with an invitation to stay with them.

"Lynn's away at volunteer camp," Mrs. Burch said, her tone convivial as always. "Why don't you come and stay with us next weekend? Tiger and Johnny will miss having a sister around the house." Years later, my sister-in-law, Peggy, would tell me she thought the Burches had me in mind to marry Tiger the weekend that they asked me to the lake. I told her they were probably afraid he would marry a native in Alaska and live there the rest of his life. Maybe it was their way of reintroducing him to the outside world.

"Oh my gosh, are you sure?" I said, smiling at the thought of another weekend at the lake. "I don't want to inconvenience anyone." I was flabbergasted—and excited by Tiger's parents' offer and the thought of seeing him again.

I arrived at their place on the lake exhausted from working all week but happy to be there for what was to be my last weekend of the summer. My job was over and my final year at university would be starting in mid-September. Despite being tired, I revived quickly when Tiger asked me to walk down the road with him to the dance at the club. During the mile walk, we chatted, and suddenly, he grabbed my hand. My heart started to beat a little faster.

Tiger was twenty-three by then, newly returned from a year in Alaska, where he'd worked for the Atomic Energy Commission. The last time I saw him, he had recently graduated from Princeton and was planning to go to graduate school at the University of Chicago. When the chance came to work in Alaska, he jumped at it. Chicago never happened. This explained why no girl had caught his attention. Now could be my chance.

I asked him to tell me about his time in Alaska. I figured his experience must have been fascinating.

"I loved every minute," he told me. "I lived in a little village called Kivalina. I hunted and fished with the Eskimo men and raised dogs for a team. It was the best year of my life."

"Would you go back?" I asked.

"I would. I liked the natives and their simple way of living. I always thought I wanted to study the Eskimos but living with them made me sure. I need two more years of graduate school for my degree, and then I'm going back." He told me his PhD dissertation was going to be on Eskimo kinship. "Actually, I can hardly wait to go back. The affluent lifestyle here and the city existence are not especially appealing to me." He let go of my hand and looked at me as he said this, almost waiting for me to reply.

I was hypnotized by his words. Then a shiver ran down my spine, as I remembered my grandmother's words from a few years back: "I don't want Elizabeth to live with the Eskimos."

Tiger and I seemed to have much in common. We enjoyed swimming and playing tennis together. Tiger was much better than I at tennis, and I was frustrated when he'd tell me to watch the ball, but then I'd hit a great shot and he would have to keep his mouth shut.

Both of us were interested in social sciences. I was majoring in psychology and planned on becoming a social worker. I wanted the people I worked with to have a better life. Perhaps they would have to change the way they were living. Later, this would be a stumbling block for us as a couple. Tiger wanted to become an anthropologist and study the way things were—not change them.

After Labor Day, I stayed with friends of my family, who had a place next door to our cottage. My mother told them to be sure I was home by twelve o'clock every night. When the clock struck twelve each night, I felt like Cinderella. I had met my Prince Charming. Playing tennis, swimming, and taking moonlit boat rides with Tiger made the days pass quickly. I knew that I was falling in love.

During the day, Tiger often sat on the porch to study the journals and other readings he had to do for school. I sat quietly beside him, wondering why he felt this was necessary. The weather was beautiful, and summer was quickly ending. We didn't have much time to be together before we both went back to school.

Our time at the lake ended too quickly. Tiger went to the University of Chicago for his first year of graduate school, and I returned home for my final year at the University of Toronto. We promised each other we would write often and see each other as much as we possibly could.

I hadn't seen Tiger for several weeks and one weekend, made the twelve-hour drive from Toronto to Chicago with a group of students I barely knew. This was our first time together since we said goodbye at the beginning of September. I was eager to see Tiger, and had butterflies in my stomach when he picked me up at the home of one of the women I had driven with.

I looked forward to walking around campus with him to see what it looked like and breathe in the air of an autumn day after being cooped up in a car for so long. Most of all I wanted to hold his hand and just walk around, talking. Right away, he hit me with a surprise.

"Did you bring your stuff for class with you? I have to go to the library and finish some things that I'm working on."

"God, no, Tiger; I hadn't planned on studying while I was here. Aren't you even glad to see me?" I hadn't come this far to sit in a library. It wasn't a romantic way to begin the weekend. That weekend set a precedent. With each visit to Chicago, I would bring a paper to work on or an article to read. Studying came first and after that came time to be together and get to know each other.

When we were apart, we wrote two or three times a week. We talked on the phone every second week because long-distance calls were expensive. I was often tongue-tied speaking to him because of the miles between us, and honestly, we didn't know each other very well.

Six months later, we were sitting in his car in the parking lot of the Museum of Science and Industry when he proposed. This was a favorite spot of ours. Not many others frequented this place and although it was dimly lit, it was reasonably safe. Tiger put his arms around me and kissed me.

"I love you. Will you marry me?"

I was at a loss for words. I thought that he would ask me, but not so soon. I wanted to marry him but deep in my heart, the thought of living in Alaska terrified me. I hesitated, but just for a minute. He was looking at me, waiting for my answer.

"Oh, my gosh! Yes, of course I'll marry you."

I was overjoyed and wanted to tell the world.

"Let's keep it a secret until I talk to your father," Tiger said.

Tiger came to Toronto three weeks after he proposed to attend my brother's wedding to Peggy Elliot. My grandmother was too old and frail to go to their wedding, but she was delighted to know that they were going to be married. From time to time, we noticed that she was having short-term memory loss. I hoped that she would be excited when she heard about my engagement. David and Peggy were married at the end of March, and the next day, after the wedding excitement had died down, Tiger asked my father for my hand in marriage. My parents were delighted, and my mother started making phone calls to everybody as soon as she could. I wasn't sure whether Goggy was happy with the prospect of me getting married. We never mentioned to her that we would be living in Alaska, but I often wondered if she knew.

Early May, Tiger presented me with a beautiful engagement ring. It was a large solitaire, elegant in its simplicity. Thrilled, I held it up to see it catch the sunlight and sparkle. Holding his hand, I said, "I can hardly wait until we're both wearing rings."

Tiger shuddered.

"I hate rings," Tiger said, shaking his head. "I don't need a wedding ring to be faithful to you."

I knew Tiger didn't like jewelry; he didn't even wear a watch. "That's okay," I told him. If you don't want a ring it's all right with me." In time, this decision would prove meaningful in ways we couldn't have imagined.

Mid May, my grandmother made another prediction. She said to my mother, "Ruth, I think it's mean to be moving to the mountain without me."

My mother looked at her and shook her head, saying, "We aren't moving to a mountain." Once again, I was standing in the doorway of the small kitchen and privy to every word. I knew that prediction would come true and wanted to tell my mom not to ignore it. After all, the prediction she had made for me was true, or it would be the next year. I shuddered every time I thought about it and wondered if I could really live with the Eskimos.

Two weeks later my father was transferred to Hamilton. My parents bought a home on the mountain there. Our lives changed after Mom and Dad moved to Hamilton. Goggy was put in a nursing home in Ottawa. My aunt and uncle lived there, and she would be well taken care of. Ottawa was close to 300 miles away from Toronto and there was little chance of seeing my grandmother before I was married. She would never share in the excitement of my wedding and I would miss her. She had been a major influence on my life.

This change meant that I wouldn't be living at home for the first time in my life. I was able to rent an apartment with a friend and complete my first year of social work in Toronto. I had graduated with a BA in liberal arts, but was now pursuing a BA in social work. Perhaps my MA in social work would never be completed since I was getting married in June of the following year.

My brother, Robert, would finish his last year of high school in Hamilton. The warmth and comfort of being with family was gone. Becoming independent was a new way of life for me and it was challenging. My parents didn't move until August of 1962, giving my mother and me a short amount of time to plan my wedding. Mom did most of the planning from Hamilton.

Tiger left in June for two months, on an archeological dig in Newfoundland. We spent very little time together before he left. It was a long-distance romance, with limited chances to get to know each other well. When we were together, we were on our best behavior, rarely disagreeing about anything. Later, when I did get to know him better, I learned that he had his, or rather *our*, whole life planned out. Chicago would be our home for nine months so he could take the classes needed to finish his degree. We would spend two years in Alaska in order for him to complete his research. After his research was finished, he planned for us to move to Wisconsin to write his dissertation.

Did I give any thought to the implications of a life away from everything I knew? Not at all, I was in love. What else mattered? I asked about children, and Tiger said, "We'll crank out two kids after we come home from Alaska."

Two children? For years, I thought I would have five kids. But having five children didn't fit into Tiger's plan. He believed in zero population growth. He told me we could have two of our own and adopt others if I wanted more. This was a first sign of how things would go with him: our life would be his way or the highway. He often said to me, half-jokingly, "You are entitled to your own erroneous opinion."

The day after Christmas, the winter before we were to get married, I flew down to visit Tiger. He surprised me with the news that he had to go to New York with his father on business. He wanted me to go with them. I could wander around New York by myself and meet them at one o'clock for lunch.

For the entire journey, after leaving at seven in the morning in Mr. Burch's private plane, I fantasized about what I would do alone in New York. We arrived in the middle of the city at around nine thirty, and by then, I was famished. The busy streets and the high buildings were overwhelming at first, but I knew what I wanted to do. I loved the song, "Moon River," almost felt it was "our song" as we used to listen to it together. I asked a stranger how to get to Tiffany's. He pointed me in the direction. It was only a few blocks away. I looked at the glittering jewelry on the first floor and then decided to go to the top floor, expecting to find the restaurant and have breakfast. At the top floor, however, there was no sign of a place to eat. I stopped at each floor on the way down—no restaurant. I didn't understand. What about *Breakfast at Tiffany's?* I thought that I could have breakfast there because I had never seen the movie. I felt immature and stupid and never told Tiger or his father my mistake. I met Tiger and his father for lunch at one and we flew back to Harrisburg late in the afternoon. The clouds were gathering, and snow was in the air.

The next evening the promise of snow turned into a blizzard. The wind shrieked around the Burch's house, and snow was piling up outside as we warmed ourselves in front of a blazing fire. I was lost in my own thoughts, remembering hesitating momentarily when Tiger asked me to marry him because of my fear of going to Alaska. When I said yes to his proposal, I was full of doubts. Could I really live in Alaska and immerse myself in a culture I knew nothing about? Still troubled over what lay ahead of me, I needed to voice my fears. Tears were streaming down my cheeks as I spoke. I had been afraid to discuss Alaska with him, but now, with the snow falling and the wind howling, I had to say something.

"I don't know if I can go to Alaska with you," I told Tiger. "Everyone says this will test our marriage, and they're right. I'm scared I won't be able to handle it. Maybe we shouldn't get married. Maybe I'm the wrong woman for you. I can't picture life there. I can't imagine being away from everything I know and love and don't want to be a burden to you."

Tiger laughed. He put his arm around me in a moment of affection. "The cold will be excruciating; the wind blows through the houses during most of the winter. Sometimes the wolves howl near the village, but never mind. I'll be there with you."

This was all I needed to hear.

III
BEGINNING OF A NEW LIFE TOGETHER

Wedding photo June 15, 1963

We married in June 1963, in a conventional wedding—four bridesmaids and a flower girl. Lynn was my maid of honor. It was the kind of wedding my mother had always dreamed of for me, and my new in-laws were happy with our plans. Tiger had wanted a simple wedding where we wrote our own vows, but as a child, imagining my wedding, I pictured myself in a beautiful white dress walking down the aisle with my father by my side. Our wedding fulfilled my fantasy, but leaving the church hand in hand with my new husband, I walked into a future I was totally unprepared for.

The day after we married, Tiger and I camped in Algonquin Park. We paddled to a beautiful island and set up camp there. It should have been magical, but we returned to Tiger's cottage earlier than planned. The weather was cold most of the time and Tiger slept a lot. He didn't really communicate with me either. Had I said or done something wrong? It was obvious that he wasn't happy and something was bothering him. He later told me the last weeks of his semester had been brutal. Then he added he was worried about getting married, had a case of cold feet, which he decided was common and that he was no different from any other young man embarking on a new life.

Before long, Tiger was back to his old self. It was time for our honeymoon, which would be in Europe. Tiger had been to Norway, Greenland, France, Germany, and twice to Labrador. He'd hitchhiked across the Swiss Alps and spent time in Italy and Spain. The farthest I had been away from home was visiting him in Chicago. He could travel on a shoestring and knew the least expensive hotels. I'd only stayed in a hotel twice in my life.

It came as a shock to me to discover that many of the hotels Tiger chose to stay in didn't have private bathrooms. He didn't think they were necessary.

"Tiger, walking down the hall to the bathroom embarrasses me. I hate waiting until someone has finished, and half the time it stinks. The bathrooms are dirty, and the bathtubs have black rings around them that have to be washed before I can take a bath," I complained.

"Living in a native village will be worse, believe me. You won't even have a toilet. All you'll have is some kind of a bucket. There won't be a bathtub to worry about, and if you do take a bath, it'll be in a washtub. You'd better get over this soon."

I had put Alaska out of my mind for a while but once again, I was worried. We would live in Alaska in an indigenous village without plumbing or electricity the next summer—just months from now. What on earth was I getting myself into?

Our honeymoon plans included going to the University of Bourgogne in Dijon for two weeks to learn French. Tiger wanted to stay in the dorms at the university so we could immerse ourselves in learning the language. I had no intention of doing this. "Tiger, it's our honeymoon, I want to spend it with you, not with a bunch of students. We don't even know if we can stay together."

Tiger reluctantly agreed and we rented a little apartment in a hill town called Talon, overlooking Dijon. The town itself was charming, with small cafés and restaurants, but our accommodations were less so. We had a small room, and others shared the same floor. Although the bathroom was communal, I was getting used to a lack of privacy by now. We weren't in the apartment much anyway.

I studied French in high school but was placed in a beginner's class. Tiger was in the advanced level. Our classes were held at different times of the day, so we went to classes separately, but met and walked back to our apartment together afterward.

I loved walking into Dijon by myself, passing street vendors hawking fresh raspberries and other tempting treats. The mornings were sunny and warm, and I felt confident our life was full of wonderful times to come. Each new day brought another adventure. My French never improved, but I learned to cook *coq au vin* and *beef bourguignon*. Weekends were spent roaming the French countryside, sipping wine in the local cafés, and enjoying escargots and *pommes frites*. I basked in the sunlight.

Appreciating my new experiences, I thanked Tiger one day as we sat in one of the cafés drinking a *kier framboise*. It had become one of our favorite afternoon drinks. Sitting there sipping the delightful concoction made me realize how lucky I was to be having this experience with the man I loved.

"Tiger, thank you. I'm sorry I've complained about the hotels. I love being here and love being with you. We have so much to look forward to." I smiled at him, happy to be sitting in this charming café.

Tiger beamed at me, but then he replied, "You're living in the lap of luxury here. You know, Alaska is a far cry from this. You certainly won't enjoy warmth like this, and you can forget about cafés and wine. I love Alaska, and I hope you will love it too."

He held his glass up and toasted, "Here's to our life in Alaska."

I couldn't tell him how frightened I was of living in Alaska. What I really wanted was a conventional life—a house with a white picket fence, a dog, and at least three children. I lifted my glass to his toast. "I hope so too."

Every country that we visited in Europe those first days of our marriage opened my eyes to a new culture and language. I looked forward to the life we would have together and all the dreams we would share in the future. By the time we reached Scotland, I was convinced I was pregnant. I had missed my period for three weeks and felt tired all the time. I complained to Tiger about how I was feeling one day.

"You can't be pregnant," Tiger said. "Haven't you been using the birth control you brought?"

"Birth control doesn't work all the time," I reminded him. "And what if I am? What'll we do?"

"Well, we'll just have to take the baby with us to Kivalina," he said.

I looked at him blankly, terrified by this prospect. Under any other circumstance I would have been thrilled to be pregnant, but a baby was not on my husband's agenda, and he certainly didn't want to alter his plans for one. Besides feeling listless and carrying these fears now about a pregnancy, I had asthmatic bronchitis and went to a local doctor who put me on an antibiotic that he assured me wouldn't hurt a baby. When I miscarried on our honeymoon, I mourned the little being growing inside me, but in retrospect, I thank God I lost the baby. We could never have taken a baby with us to Alaska and survived.

The days passed quickly as we traveled through England, Scotland, Switzerland, Norway, Denmark, and France. Soon, it was time for us to get back to the real world.

That autumn, we moved to Chicago, and Tiger immersed himself in his books. When he was home, and not in class, he worked all day. Often, he worked until eleven at night. I begged him to quit work, to talk to me or just come to bed when I did, but work constantly beckoned. There was little time left for us to socialize and have fun.

We lived in student housing in Hyde Park. Our apartment was tiny and full of grime. When the winds blew from Gary, Indiana, our windowsills were covered with dirt, and no matter how hard I tried, the apartment never seemed to be clean. Hyde Park wasn't a safe place to live, so going out at night by myself wasn't an option.

I hadn't anticipated marriage would be like this, never realized I could be homesick, miss my friends and family. And most of all, I missed Tiger. Were all marriages like this? I had no way of knowing and had no friends in Chicago to talk to. I couldn't tell my parents about my concerns because they would worry about me.

Around this time, Tiger was honored by a request to give a lecture at the university about his experiences in Alaska. He asked me to attend and critique his style of delivery. I noticed he used quite a few *ums,* and before I knew it, I was asleep. Tiger thought I was bored. Falling asleep in public was happening somewhat frequently. I started to fall asleep in banks when I sat on a bench waiting for Tiger who stood in line to do his banking. I craved naps, something that I had never done in my life. Then it dawned on me. I was pregnant—again. Three weeks later, I miscarried. Clearly, I needed a better form of contraception and though it was the early days of oral contraception, I was given a prescription for the pill. Neither of us was prepared to take a baby to Alaska. Still, I wondered if this would be a pattern with my pregnancies. Maybe I couldn't carry a baby.

Needing something tangible to do, I applied for a job at the Bruno Bettelheim School, which was well known for its work with autism. I had experience working with autistic children when I was doing my field work in my year in the school of social work at the University of Toronto. I loved the work and thought it would be a valuable challenge. Instead, The Bruno Bettelheim School encouraged me to finish my MA in social work at the University of Chicago. They told me that without an MA in social work, I wasn't qualified for a position there. Finishing my degree was not something I had thought about, and it never occurred to me to ask Tiger about finishing my MA. Perhaps we would have worked something out had I been determined to do this but Tiger had planned his two years in Alaska. I decided his plans were more important than my degree.

In the end, I prepared myself for Alaska by taking sewing lessons, sketching lessons, and graduate courses in general anthropology and psychological anthropology at the University of Chicago. Psychological anthropology intrigued me, and I looked forward to doing a study on the children when we lived in Alaska.

November of 1963 brought with it the assassination of President Kennedy. We glued ourselves to the radio the whole weekend listening to the latest developments in the shocking news. The country came to a standstill. From our open window in the apartment, we heard radios and television sets being turned on and off one by one. We knew without a doubt everyone was listening to or watching the same thing. Anxiety ripped the nation apart and destroyed its innocence and optimism. The golden age of Camelot, as it was called at the time, ended.

Meanwhile, Tiger's first semester at graduate school passed quickly. When Thanksgiving came, we spent the holiday in Kansas at a family reunion with Tiger's mother's side of the family. My family was small. I only had two cousins, and now was greeted by a new set of cousins to get to know. The families were vibrant and fun to be with. Their lifestyle was very different from anything familiar to me. Touch football was a tradition in this family, and I felt as though I were a part of the Kennedy clan. This was my first Thanksgiving in the States, and it fulfilled my expectations of a large family gathering, with good food and conversation.

Early December brought bitter cold and wind, a glimpse of our life ahead. I was shivering and trying to pull my coat closer around me to get warm whenever I was outside. It never was that cold in Toronto. The winter coat I had worn in Toronto wasn't adequate.

"Wait till Alaska," Tiger laughed when I grumbled about the cold. "This is nothing. We're going to buy you a better coat to wear here, and then I'm going to buy you a good parka for Alaska; one with a ruff on the hood that will protect your face."

I knew that I was in for an experience I didn't fully understand. How could I have been so innocent?

For Christmas, we drove home to Toronto in a blinding snowstorm, spent a whirlwind few days there with family and friends, and then drove to Harrisburg. Lynn came with us when we left for Chicago, and it was wonderful to have her along, if only for a few days. While she was with us, one morning when we took her out to breakfast, she fainted. She recuperated quickly, and later in the day we went to a movie. I worried about her, and realized she hadn't written to us that fall. Our communication, once so constant, had fallen apart. Maybe it was my fault. I was a new bride and busy learning new things. I had only written to her a few times, but she had never answered any of them. It was so unlike her and I wondered what could be wrong.

The days sped by and before I knew it, it was early March and time to leave Chicago. Leaving for Alaska wasn't a fantasy anymore, it was a chilling reality. Tiger had been talking about Alaska for months and I tried to stuff it into the back of my mind where I wouldn't have to think about it. Tiger intended to complete the research needed for his PhD by conducting a participant study of the inhabitants there. He would hunt and fish with the men and I was expected to participate in the daily activities of the women. I didn't really understand what this meant for me. I was young, naïve, and never questioned his decision. I was also terrified of the prospect of being so far from home in an unfamiliar place. A city girl at heart, having grown up there and loving everything the city had to offer, the thought of living on a small island, without modern conveniences, was not appealing.

Meanwhile, my friends were starting to settle down. My sister-in-law, Peggy was pregnant and having a baby in late May. She asked me to be a godmother. How could I accept the role? I wouldn't meet the child for two years! I couldn't even be a doting aunt. Reluctantly, I declined. Other friends were buying their first home; many were having their first child. I envied their lives and wanted a predictable existence like theirs. To say I was terrified to go to Alaska was an understatement, but I never told anyone how I felt, not even Tiger. I had made a commitment to him.

IV

ABOVE THE ARCTIC CIRCLE

We arrived in Harrisburg, where Tiger's home base was, in late March, preparing to leave for the Arctic in early May. On Good Friday, I learned there had been an earthquake with a magnitude of 9.2. Selfishly, I was relieved. Now, we wouldn't be going to Alaska, at least not for a while. But I was wrong. The earthquake had hit the southern part of Alaska and was nowhere near the tiny village of Kivalina. Despite my fear of living in Alaska, our journey was about to begin.

MAY 1964

Tiger planned for us to leave on Mother's Day weekend for his great adventure. And now the time to leave has arrived. I am filled with anxiety about what lies ahead but I keep it to myself. I don't want to upset Tiger with any of my misgivings. It feels strange to be saying goodbye the Friday of that weekend—a time meant for families to be together, but we are leaving our families to go to a little known part of the United States.

As our plane takes off from Harrisburg, I look out the window thinking of everything I'm leaving behind—our families, friends, and our life in a city. Glancing at Tiger, and seeing him smile, I know it's all worth my reservations. He's beaming, happy to at last be going on this expedition he has planned for so long. My friends often refer to him as a poster boy. His blue eyes, wonderful bone structure, and beautiful smile could melt any woman's heart. I gaze at him, happy to be married to this man and hoping I can live up to his expectations.

At home, the lilacs, bluebells, and daffodils are in bloom. This time of year, when everything is bursting with color, is my favorite. To my dismay, we arrive in Fairbanks to below-freezing temperatures and snow. There are no recognizable signs of spring. The city is piled with gray, dirty snow, and the streets are slushy. From time to time, there is a snow shower. Although it's said to be the thriving metropolis of the North, to me, this city feels like the end of civilization.

We spend time in the one modern store there, a Safeway, buying groceries for the summer. As we look for things I think we'll need, Tiger says that most of the time, we'll live off of the land. "We don't really need all of the stuff we're buying," he says. "We'll eat berries, seal liver and seal oil, caribou, and Arctic char."

Seal oil? This thought isn't appealing but Tiger explained it's a way to keep warm, because it is full of Omega-3 fatty acids. He says it has the consistency of olive oil and a slightly fishy taste. He also told me that when the native kids go away to school, they like cod liver oil because it reminds them a bit of seal oil. My mother used to give us a teaspoon of cod liver oil as it was said to boost the immune system and was full of vitamin D. I figure I can deal with seal oil, although I'm hoping not to try it for some time.

And live off the land? "Tiger, we need staples—flour, sugar, butter. And I want things like spaghetti and canned tomatoes. I can cook us good meals with some of these things." In the winter, I tell him, we can ship fresh meat up for ourselves. I'm not sure he agrees.

As we drive around Fairbanks, I grab Tiger's hand and squeeze it. To my surprise, he drops it as though he's been scalded. "You can't do that in Kivalina," he says. "Eskimos don't hold hands."

I'm hurt. Why is he saying this? Does being Tiger's wife mean I have to act like a native? I don't want to be an Eskimo. I want to be me and do the things I have always done. I turn to ask him, but stop, not wanting to make waves. I bury this inside me and plan to maintain my identity.

The people we meet in Fairbanks are warm and friendly. I hear a number of different American accents, which surprises me. Maybe they are looking for adventure on the last frontier. I wish I could give them mine.

We see a few natives in those first days in Alaska, many of them just sitting on the street, immobilized by an alcoholic haze. Tiger says they are the scum of the Eskimo population.

"There will probably be some drinking in the village," Tiger warns me.

"Why? I thought there was no liquor in Kivalina. I didn't know you can get it there."

"Someone will bring it to the village if they're here in Fairbanks. Kotzebue, the closest town to Kivalina, is dry, but there are lots of bootleggers there and it's easy to bring it back to the village."

"So what happens when there's drinking in Kivalina?" I ask.

"The men beat their wives when they're drunk. The women huddle together for support."

As if I need another thing to worry about.

"What am I supposed to do when you're not around?" I ask.

"Lock yourself in the house and don't answer the door under any circumstances," Tiger says.

I nod, praying I will never experience men drinking in Kivalina.

Snow greets us almost every day and I can hardly wait to tell my friends we had snow in the middle of May. Suddenly, I realize I can't talk to family or friends. Our only form of communication will be by the mail plane, which apparently arrives twice a week, weather permitting.

People here have told us spring is late, but I've also heard snow at this time of the year is not unusual. Despite the cold, the land is teeming with wildlife. We see robins, several species of ducks, and other assorted birds. We know there are moose wading in streams but we have yet to see one. During our stay in Fairbanks, the weather remains cold and dull.

I don't like Fairbanks much, and I'm worried about what it's going to be like further north. I am afraid to ask Tiger.

Finally, I speak up. "I feel as though Fairbanks is the end of the world. What is it going to be like in Kotzebue and Kivalina?"

"They're nothing like this. You'll just have to wait and see. Here you have all the modern conveniences: stores to shop in, one or two restaurants, and even a movie theater. I told you, we're going on an adventure."

I grit my teeth and prepare for the journey ahead.

We arrive in Kotzebue to find winter in full force. It is twenty-two degrees, with a wind blowing in from the ocean making it seem even colder. The ocean is frozen. We sent most of our clothing up to Kivalina, and neither of us is equipped to deal with the frigid weather. Each breath I take sears my lungs and my eyebrows feel as though they are freezing.

Kotzebue is a rundown town, and most of the inhabitants are Eskimo. At the far end is a hospital. There is one decent hotel, one rundown hotel, and a general store. The houses, clustered around the ocean, are little more than shacks. Tiger and I walk around town, objects of scrutiny by the natives. He assures me it will be different in Kivalina. He lived there the year before I met him and everyone knows and likes him. I worry. I hope they will come to know me and like me as well.

Our first night in Kotzebue, we visit Tiger's friend, Mamie Beaver. Mamie lives by the ocean in a one-room house cluttered with sealskins, a bed, several pots and pans, and a table with a couple of chairs. Mamie is petite, wizened by the sun and harsh weather. She could be thirty-five years old, or she could be sixty. She laughs a lot and is happy to see Tiger again. Mamie is accustomed to white people and makes us feel right at home. She is not shy, although Tiger has told me that most of the native women are. We accept her invitation to dinner and are served a bowl of sheefish soup. I don't know what sheefish is, but the soup is warm and filling. I like her and hope the women in Kivalina will be similar to her.

We visit a few more of Tiger's friends in Kotzebue. At the home of one of them, there are nine people living crowded together in one room, with no electricity or plumbing. The children are shoved closely together to sleep; a piece of paper wouldn't fit between them. Most of them have runny noses and coughs. The family shares one towel. It's filthy, covered with dirt from constant use. Perhaps this is the only towel in the house.

Even as a student social worker in the poorest part of Toronto, I have never seen conditions like these—Tiger tells me tuberculosis is rampant in the villages, and their way of living is partially to blame. In my naïveté, I think I can educate these people, help them live a better life. I have such different expectations than Tiger.

"Tiger, I know there's a hospital here. You pointed it out to me. Why don't the doctors educate these people about cleanliness and health?"

"I don't know the answer to that. You're experiencing culture shock. You'll get over it when we get to Kivalina. Besides, you're imposing the natives' standards of cleanliness with yours. You can't do that."

"Tiger, it's hard not to impose my standards of cleanliness on these people. I wish you had warned me." Tiger shrugs when I say this, not really interested in the way I am trying to defend myself.

There is no doubt in my mind I'm experiencing culture shock. Who wouldn't be? He never warned me about the conditions the natives live in. I hope he's right when he says I'll get over it in Kivalina. I also hope the people there will not be living in shacks like these with nine or ten children crowded together in one room. After all, Tiger is going to do a participant study. We will be living almost like the natives partaking in all their daily activities. And yes, I am imposing my standards of cleanliness onto the natives. I never thought about the lack of available water to wash clothes and towels. I need to gain more insight into the way these people have to live. Their life is far harder than mine will ever be. When I arrive in Kivalina, I'll have to adjust my standards of cleanliness.

We spend four days in Kotzebue because the weather prevents us from flying. It's windy, snowy, and cold. The land and sky are barely distinguishable from each other and everything looks as though it is bathed in a pale, yellow light. The glare from the sea ice makes it almost impossible to see. Right now, planes are not flying. We didn't bring sunglasses to prevent snow blindness and there are none in the store. Snow blindness is a painful condition, caused by the cornea being sunburned. When we get to Kivalina, we will have to order some from Fairbanks. The sun is high in the sky and appears as if it never sets. Tiger can hardly wait to get to Kivalina, but I want to stay in Kotzebue, where we are in a hotel with electricity and indoor plumbing. I'm afraid of what lies ahead and wish the fog and the glare from the ice would keep us here for several more days.

Tiger seems happier than I've seen him in a long time, and he's more comfortable with these people than he is with people back home. Even his voice and the way he talks seem to change. The timbre of his voice is altered, and his words flow differently. Is he trying to talk the way the natives do? I never hear him condemning the natives, but I often hear him criticizing white people, saying we are too caught up in an affluent way of life. He says the natives are satisfied with what they have and always seem to be happy. I'm starting to think he may like the natives more than he likes me.

At last it's time to leave Kotzebue. I gulp as the plane takes off. I'm leaving so much behind, friends and family, and the little things we take for granted every day—flushing toilets, lamps that turn off and on, the comfort of eating a hamburger and fries. Was it only three weeks ago that my mother was teaching me to bake bread? Her words that day are etched in my mind.

She was kneading the dough, almost pounding it as she spoke. "You know, dear, these two years in Alaska will either make or break your marriage."

"Yeah, Mom, I know. Don't worry. I know what I'm getting myself into," I said.

She was like a broken record, repeating the same things over and over again. She didn't have to say these things to me anymore because deep down, I knew that she was right. I was petrified of the prospect of going to Alaska. I'd been married for a year and had been told the first year of any marriage is always the hardest. Ours hadn't been easy. I learned my husband was focused on his life plan and nothing was going to stand in his way, especially me. A black cloud had descended on me and was holding me in its grip. If I voiced my fears to anyone, it would be like opening Pandora's Box. Everything would come flying out, including hope. It was better to keep my anxiety bottled up inside.

Mom finished kneading the dough. It looked as smooth as satin. She put a dishcloth over it to let it rise, and the yeasty smell permeated the room.

"Are you prepared to be his wife and lover, to wash his dirty underwear by hand, and to live in a place without plumbing or electricity for two years? You hate the cold, and you love being surrounded by friends and family. Do you want to spend your time there isolated this way?

Now Mom was really on a roll. In her own way, my mother was asking me to rethink my life. Maybe she wanted me to persuade Tiger not to take us to Alaska. I had no intention of doing so. I knew when I married him I was agreeing to live in Alaska for two years. Young women in the early 1960s didn't question whether or not they could live the life their husband wanted. They went ahead with his wishes and hoped for the best.

"Mom," I said, "you should have asked me these questions when Tiger and I were engaged. I was so in love with him it never occurred to me to think about what was ahead. It's too late now." I was not about to break my marriage vows and I was not about to tell Tiger at this late point I didn't want to go to Alaska with him.

It probably never occurred to my mother that in some way, I would give up my identity to live like the natives. It didn't occur to me either. My dad didn't say much to me about going to Alaska, but I knew he was uncomfortable with my decision.

All he said was, "Your Pappy is not happy you are going to live with the Eskimos." I wish they had talked to me more at the time about my future. They loved Tiger, and probably didn't realize how difficult life would be for me. Some of my friends did, however. One of them warned me. She said, "Don't lose yourself in your marriage." I was young, in love, and had no idea what she was talking about.

I assured my parents I would be all right but acknowledged my life would not be easy. It would be different from everything I had ever known, and I tried to emphasize our existence would be exciting, and we were lucky to be able to have this experience. Feeling more hopeful as I said these things, the darkness surrounding me for weeks started to lift. I thought of myself as *The Little Engine That Could*, and my mantra became, "I think I can, I think I can. *I know* that I will like living in Alaska."

As I sit on the airplane to Kivalina, I am so lost in thought I haven't even looked out the window.

Suddenly, Tiger pokes me with an elbow. "What were you daydreaming about? Look out the window. We're almost there."

Looking out the window I see a long, thin piece of land surrounded by ocean. Because of the snow, it's difficult to differentiate the land from the water. The plane is circling the village now, and I see tiny dots on the landscape.

"Tiger, what are those dots?"

"Those are the houses in the village."

"The houses must be really small. From this height, the houses back home never looked like dots."

As the plane gets closer to this snow-covered landscape, the houses clustered at one end of the island become more distinct. They look like dilapidated, wooden shacks, similar to the ones in Kotzebue. Zooming in, dogs can be seen tied up at stakes, some half buried with snow. The whole scene is bleak—desolate. This is where we're going to live for a year. Nothing prepares me for the sight I see from the airplane.

My hands are sweating and my heart is racing as the plane descends and begins to travel the runway. We're here.

Half the village meets the arriving plane to greet returning relatives. A sea of faces surrounds us as we step off the plane. Black eyes peer out from under hoods or caps. The crowd is predominantly women and children. Tiger tells me many of the men are out hunting or ice fishing. The women wear bright cloth coverings over warmer parkas. Some carry babies in their parkas, and I see one or two faces peeking out to see what is going on. Tiger is greeted enthusiastically. I hear, "Welcome back!" and "Good to see you again!" from many of them. He looks equally happy to see them; he's all smiles as he says hello. With my blonde hair, pale skin, and green eyes, I feel like a true outsider. We begin to walk to the village with the rest of the crowd. Some of the snow is packed hard and form paths where everybody walks. Even in mid-May, the snow is up to my waist, and everything's still in a deep freeze. This is Alaska, all right! We're north of the tree line and because of this, there are no trees. All I can see is a flat mass of land and ocean covered with snow.

Bobby and Sarah Hawley

The first house we come to belongs to a couple Tiger was friends with when he was here before, Bobby and Sarah Hawley. The house they live in is situated at the end of the village, close to the airstrip. As we enter through the storm shed, I see a bucket, which, Tiger explains, is used as a toilet, and is called a honey bucket. He tells me there is no odor because the waste inside it is frozen. I wonder if it will smell in the summer and shudder at the thought.

The house has one room, where they eat and sleep. There is one bed, a table, and several metal chairs. I sit on one of the chairs, although nobody suggested I sit down. I feel as though I am an inconvenience, but I can't just stand there feeling awkward. This would never have happened at home and right away, I notice the difference in our two cultures. Tiger turns to me and says, "Stay here. I'll be back in a while." With that, he's gone, out the door with his friend Bobby.

I'm surprised by this, and a little concerned about how Sarah will feel having me here. She carries on as though it's nothing, tending to her baby and going about her chores. She doesn't say much to me. In fact, she ignores me. I need to use the honey bucket, and hope I can hold on, as it's in the shed. People wander in and out of the shed without knocking. I would hate someone to see me sitting on it. There is no privacy there—it's the only entrance to the house.

The aroma of the coffee heating on the stove smells strong, and Sarah offers me a cup of it, which I happily accept. The taste is bitter and acidic, hard to swallow, but I don't say anything.

"What's in the pot?" I ask, pointing to a glass pot sitting on the table. It gives off a sour, yeasty smell, and bubbles are fizzing on the top.

"It's sourdough starter."

I've never heard of sourdough, and I ask Sarah what it is.

"Oh, there's flour and some sugar and water in it. Maybe some yeast from a long time ago. We use it for bread and pancakes. See those pancakes over there? They're sourdough pancakes. The men will probably take them hunting." She points to them. "You want some of my sourdough?"

I shake my head. "No thanks. Not now, but I'd like to learn how to use it." Sarah nods when I say this and seems to become friendlier. I hope she doesn't offer me any seal oil. I'm not prepared to try it right now.

Sarah has made duck soup, and anyone who arrives is offered a bowl. I'm hungry and happy when Sarah serves me some. The soup is delicious, a rich broth with small pieces of meat floating in it. Duck soup will become a staple later when I learn how to cook it. Sarah tells me how. She says that you just clean the duck, pluck off the feathers, and put it in a pot to boil. When the color is brown, it's done. Sounds simple enough, although cleaning the duck is not something I want to do and can't imagine myself doing this. I couldn't even cook when I was first married.

Sarah appears to be in her mid-thirties. She is tiny and quiet and has nine children. Looking at their living conditions and the difficult lives she and her husband lead, I am amazed they have managed to produce so many children. Some of the children are playing on the floor. Sarah carries the youngest one around in her parka.

As Sarah continues with her chores, one of her older daughters takes the baby from her and carts her around the same way. A couple of women drop by to visit. They probably came to meet me. Their presence makes me uncomfortable. Tiger is remembered by them as a carefree bachelor who lived the way they do. What do they think of me? Do they think I won't fit into life in the village? Maybe they're right. A wave of homesickness washes over me and I long for the familiarity of home and people I know. The conversation is limited, as the women sit quietly drinking soup or coffee. Sometimes they speak in their native language. I worry that they are talking about me.

Tiger returns after what seems to me like several hours. He has been at the house we will rent, a five-minute walk from the Hawley's. Apparently one can get everywhere in the village in ten minutes. He sits down for a quick cup of coffee and then we leave the Hawley's so I can see the house he has rented. Children from the village follow us. Some of them trickle into the house behind us; several press their flat noses against the windows.

Their dark eyes, golden skin, and black hair are a stark contrast to the children back home.

They are adorable, but at this point right now all I want is for them to leave. I've had to go to the toilet for several hours, and I long for privacy. I don't want them following me out to our honey bucket.

Finally, the children leave, and Tiger shows me our storm shed, where our honey bucket is located. We have two sheds, one attached to the front of the house and one attached to the side. The shed with our honey bucket is the more private one, not the one where the villagers have access to wander in and out.

More comfortable at last, I explore our new surroundings. Our house is huge by village standards. I feel lucky Tiger has been able to find a nice place for us. Still, compared to what I'm used to, the house is small. We don't have as much room as we had in student housing in Chicago. The bedroom is a cubicle. A twin bed, pressed against the wall under the window, dwarfs the rest of the room. There might be six feet of space beyond the bed leading to the living area. We are only there to sleep, but it would be nice to have a bed bigger than the twin—*if* it can fit into the room. I'm glad we are newlyweds and aren't older trying to adapt to this. Tiger plans to build a washstand so we can take sponge baths and brush our teeth. We decide to keep a chamber pot hidden under it for night time emergencies. There is a small dresser as well, but it's hardly big enough to hold the few things that we brought with us.

The living room is at most twelve feet long and seven feet wide. There is a large window that lets in a lot of light, as well as two other windows. I'm thankful for this because the less I have to light a kerosene lamp, the happier I will be. A tattered brown couch and a comfortable rocking chair are the only pieces of furniture, but we are fortunate to have these. Tiger plans to build a desk for his writing.

The kitchen is small, with no table. The oil stove will be used for both cooking and heating. There is no way to read the temperature in the oven, an added challenge. On the good side, the kitchen is well stocked with cookware.

"Hey, Tiger, we have a full set of Revere pots and pans here. We even have melamine dishes! It's all we will need for cooking."

We're pleased we don't have to order anything from the store in Fairbanks. An oil drum to store fresh water stands near the stove, in the corner of the room. When Tiger makes a table, it will serve as a counter to cook on, our kitchen table, and my desk.

The windows on the northern wall of the kitchen face the post office, the busiest place in the village. Mail is delivered by airplane twice a week. Tiger tells me the postmistress knows about everything and everybody. Soon she will know everything about us. We can watch the villagers going about their daily routine from all the windows. We have no curtains, so everyone knows what we are doing as well, especially during the season when the sun never sets. It is mid-May now and the sun is high in the sky. Life here will be like living in a fishbowl.

"I guess it's going to be difficult to keep everything clean, eh, Tiger? I suppose we won't take a bath very often."

He points to a wash tub, located against a wall in the kitchen, which will be used for washing clothes and taking the occasional bath. I can't see either of us fitting into it, but we'll make it work somehow.

Later in the day, Bobby takes Tiger upriver to get ice for drinking water and washing. The ice hasn't broken up. Because the land is still frozen, it is only possible to travel by plane or with a dog team and sled.

I start to unpack. We didn't bring many clothes, so it's an easy job. When Tiger returns, he's carrying huge chunks of ice in his arms. "It's great to be back here," he says with a contented sigh, as he puts the ice into the big oil drum. The ice will eventually melt, but it will stay cold. "I can't always depend on the people here. We're going to get a boat of our own and I'm going to build a sled in the fall for the dogs. You're going to love it!"

He is like a little boy now, anxious to do everything the natives do.

It's been a long day and a wintry one as well. I long for the spring, and hope the natives are right when they tell me spring is approaching. It's still light when we go to bed. There is nothing to block out the light from our bedroom window. We hear some of the villagers walking around, visiting neighbors, though it's well past midnight. Sleep doesn't come easily to me, but Tiger is snoring gently. I am crammed against the window in a hard, lumpy bed and as I lie there, unable to sleep, I remember the words that became my chant several weeks ago: *I know I will like living in Alaska.*

V

EXPLORING KIVALINA

Mid May 1964 Tommy Sage's house

We're awake early, and Tiger has made the coffee before I'm out of bed. I pull on my parka and go out to the shed to use the honey bucket. The chill of the air greets me with a force as I go outside, and I wonder how I will survive when winter arrives. Yesterday I found we actually had a toilet seat on our honey bucket and a deep hole was dug into the ground. The seat is cold to sit on, and I come back in as quickly as I can, knowing that I will learn the art of holding on. My trips to the honey bucket will be as few and far between as I can make them.

Tiger is eager to begin his day. He has made us bowls of hot oatmeal slathered with brown sugar and evaporated milk, which warms the stomach on this wintry day. These provisions from Fairbanks will be our breakfast every morning we're here. Right away I can see the stove is inadequate. It takes ages to heat up. I understand why Sarah keeps the pot of coffee on the stove all day. It may be strong, but at least it's warm.

"Ready to explore?" Tiger asks after we're finished with breakfast. "We'll wash the dishes later. I want to point out people's houses to you, so when you go visiting, you'll know which houses to go to."

"Okay. But let me make another pot of coffee first in case we have visitors when we get back here."

He is excited with the prospect of showing me the village. Through the window, I see people are walking around, though it's still early. Women are going to visit friends. Men are hitching up their dogs to go upriver for ice or to fish. These are the natives I hope to become friends with while I'm here. I want to love this place as much as Tiger does.

We set out to see Kivalina. The village is tiny, and the houses are clustered together randomly. There are no streets, but there are snow-covered paths throughout the village. At least I don't have to wade through snow up to my waist. Dogs are chained to stakes at almost every house and they bark when we pass. Sleds lean up against houses.

Kivalina consists of a store, a school, two churches, the National Guard armory, and twenty-four small houses. Some of the houses are made of sod placed over a wood frame, but most are wooden shacks. There is one log house. No electricity or plumbing exists in the village, except in the house where the teachers live. Because our goal is to participate in village life, we don't plan to spend much time with them. Nevertheless, they would become an integral part of our lives.

In Kivalina, there is a population of about 150 Eskimos, two white teachers, and 125 sled dogs. Everything is located at the south end of the island, and there isn't much distance between any of the houses. Tiger shows me where various people live. I've heard him talk about most of these people, and always in glowing terms. He points out eleven of the houses, and my head is spinning with all of the names.

Our house is ideally situated, as it is very close to the store. It's the perfect spot for visitors to drop in for a cup of coffee. I hope to have visitors. Even after one day, Tiger has picked up where he left off three years ago. I could be lonely if I don't make some of my own friends, and fast.

"Over there is Tommy Sage's house. And right behind our house is Mildred and Lawrence Sage's place. Clinton and Charlotte Swan live over there." He points his finger to the left. Mabel and Austin Thomas live in the sod house over there. Edith and Clarence Kennedy live there, in front of our house."

"The armory is just over there." He points to it. Visually, I trace a diagonal line across the blanket of white from our place. "The armory generates its own electricity, and sometimes they show movies there. The movies are usually pretty dumb, but it gives everybody something to do."

"If the school and the armory both have electricity, why doesn't the whole village have it?"

Tiger shrugs. "I heard talk yesterday about people getting generators for themselves."

"My God, that would be great. I'd love to have electricity. I'm nervous about lighting lanterns." For some reason, I had always been afraid of fire.

My stubborn husband doesn't seem to want to live better than the most poverty-stricken. "We're not getting electricity," he says, "even if some of the others do. We'll wait until the poorest families in the village get it."

The sod houses will never get electricity. It's not something that will be in our future here.

The one-room school is perhaps fifty yards from our house. The teachers live there as well. As we go over to the school, I notice that although the snow is still on the ground, there's nothing there, just the building. I don't see swings or slides or any type of play equipment for the children. What do they do at recess? Do they have a recess? This is a far cry from the schoolyards in cities and small towns in the lower forty-eight. There, all these things are taken for granted.

School house with barren playground

"Why aren't there swings and slides here?" I ask.

"I never thought about it. I've never seen the kids playing with balls or skipping ropes. I don't have a clue what they do when they're outside. I know the boys start to learn to drive a dog team when they're not at school, and the girls help their mothers with the chores."

"Do the girls ever drive dog teams?"

"I suppose it's possible but I've never heard of it. Only one woman here drives a team."

We walk to the beach from the school. It stretches the length of the island and although it's still snow-covered, Tiger tells me the sand is dark brown and a lot of it is gravel. There are piles of ice that sparkle like jewels along the edge of the beach. The ice on the sea hasn't started to break up, and reflects the colors of the sky. It's clear today, with a bright blue sky, a good introduction to the land I'm seeing for the first time.

We stroll up the beach and cross over the airstrip, and Tiger points out a lagoon. If we get a boat, we will land it south of here. Right now, our only transportation is by plane or dog team. Realizing these are the only ways I can get off the island gives me a sense of claustrophobia. The circuit tour of the village takes us about half an hour, and I am ready to go back to the house and warm up. Fifteen-degree weather isn't something I'm used to in the middle of May.

Back at the house, I take off my parka and stand near the stove, thankful for its heat. Friends of Tiger start to arrive. Although the day is clear, many of the men are not hunting until later today. I'm glad I remembered to make a pot of coffee before we left; everybody expects to be served a cup when they come over. I pour coffee for each of his friends in mugs that we found yesterday. The men sit in our small living room talking about the weather and whether or not they will go hunting today. I hope Tiger won't go with them if they do. I stay in the kitchen, happy to have an excuse to be there. I heat the water, wash our breakfast dishes, and then sit down and pour myself a cup of coffee. Like Sarah's coffee, it is bitter and acidic because it has been sitting on the stove so long. I hope to get used to it.

VI

VISITING

As the weeks go by, the weather starts to get warmer, and bit by bit, the snow melts. The surrounding hills and mountains, which are about fifty miles away, seem much closer. They are still snow-covered, but the blues and grays are starting to appear.

Meeting the women is a challenge for me. I am often met with a silence I'm not used to. Besides Sarah, I know the postmistress, Mildred Sage. Whenever the mail plane comes, I go over, hoping to receive letters from home. The post office is part of the Sages' house, which, like most of the other houses in the village, is only one room.

People have been welcoming us to the village for the last couple of weeks. Many have brought fish to cook. Usually it's Arctic char, which tastes a lot like salmon. The other night, someone brought us a crane. Shooting a crane is illegal, and there is no recipe for it in the cookbook I brought from home. Instead, I use a recipe that was originally meant to cook a chicken. It tastes good—it's certainly better than eating out of cans, which is what we do most of the time.

Getting used to the seal oil is a challenge. The consistency is similar to olive oil and tastes better than it smells, but not by much. I hope in time to become used to it because it's filled with nutrients and will keep us warm in the winter. In the late spring, Tiger will be hunting seals. As a woman, it will be my job to cut them up and remove the blubber from them. Already, I am dreading it. He must have told me this before we arrived in Alaska, but evidently, I had forgotten. Or rather, maybe I had ignored his warning, refusing to believe that this would actually be my reality. Either way, the day is coming, and I am not looking forward to it.

The Eskimo children are my main visitors, and they're adorable. They are always smiling and happy, despite the fact that they live in poverty. Sometimes they press their noses against our window and watch from the outside, curious to know what the white people are like. There's something very endearing about their look. Their faces tend to be wide, with high cheekbones. Black almond-shaped eyes seem to sparkle with mischief. Tiger says the word "urchin" must have been invented for them. The little boys don't visit as often as the girls, but they do come occasionally, with uncombed hair sticking up in little tufts. Most of the girls have long hair tied back in loose braids or ponytails. Their hair is black and usually straight. They wear faded dresses that are handed down from one girl to the next. Sometimes they wear skirts, which hang almost to their ankles and make them look like ragamuffins. I think of the little girls back home with their perfectly starched dresses, Mary Janes, and colorful bows in their hair; it's such a difference to the children here.

Girls who often visited

Although cute, the children can also be a nuisance. When they come into my house, they don't speak to me; they only whisper and giggle with their hands over their mouth as they watch. It's all they seem to want to do. Sometimes, I want to tell them to leave. Once, they came in and tracked mud all over the floor. Then, they stood and watched me trying to clean it up. Tiger finally got out his camera and took a picture of them, which they loved. They posed for the camera, pretending to be movie stars. When they aren't driving me crazy, I want to hug them.

Here in Kivalina, I'm not sure who I am anymore. My days are cut out for me. There are always the everyday chores of keeping the house clean, washing clothes, and baking bread. I have no friends here, and learning the ways of the village isn't easy. There's no one to share my thoughts with and I feel cut off from all that's familiar. Tiger is focused on his research. He has friends and goes hunting and fishing with them. This is, of course, part of doing a participant study. I feel totally alone because there is no one to bounce ideas off of. Tiger assures me that I'll be fine if I visit around and watch the women work. Why would this make me feel fine? It seems to me the Eskimo women believe white women aren't capable of doing their work. It's true, I have never cleaned fish or cut up a seal, but when it's time I'm going to show them I can do it. If the women here accept me, maybe I won't feel so lonely.

One day, I visit Sarah.

"Come in," she calls out at the sound of my knock.

I open the door to see Sarah's children playing on the floor, as she tries to scrub around them to clean it. Dishes are drying on the table.

"Have some coffee," she says, pouring me a cup. I sit in silence, drinking the bitter coffee as she continues with her chores. She's clearly busy, and I'm intruding, but I don't know how to leave without seeming impolite.

"You want something?" she asks, as she continues scrubbing the floor.

"No, I came to visit," I say.

At that, she stops cleaning and pours herself a cup of coffee, takes a seat with it, and lights a cigarette. I try to make conversation, asking questions such as, "How old are your children?" "What are their names?" It feels a bit awkward, but I don't know what else to say. Sarah answers my questions and seems a little more open than when I first came in. When I get up to leave, she says, "Come again."

"The next time I visit, I'd like to learn how to use sourdough in the bread I make," I tell her. Sarah smiles at this, but I don't feel the visit was terribly successful. At least she asked me to come again and that's a step in the right direction.

Back at the house, I tell Tiger about my visit with Sarah. "It's just so hard, Tiger. I don't know what to talk about, and I know how hard Sarah's working. She asked if I wanted something when I came in. Having me there is an inconvenience. It takes every ounce of courage I have to go knocking on those doors. These people are strangers. I don't feel welcome at all."

Tiger listens, but he doesn't seem to understand. "Keep trying," he says. "The women will get used to you and like you. Every person here will ask if you want something. I ask when they come here. Haven't you noticed?"

I have to admit I haven't heard him say this and probably haven't been paying attention.

For my next attempt at making friends, I summon up the nerve to visit a woman named Gladys Adams. To my surprise, she welcomes me into her place. Her house is just one room, with a bed, table, and a couple of chairs. I'm happy to be greeted so warmly, especially since Sarah seemed so uncomfortable with my visit. We sit quietly sipping coffee, and I try not to feel awkward in the silence. I thumb through a copy of *True Confessions* she has lying around, having read these magazines as a teenager.

"I like this magazine, all right," Gladys says. "Sometimes I think I'm like some of these women, but they're white, rich, and beautiful. They hide secrets too, just like me."

Many of the Eskimos end their sentences with "all right." It reminds me that I often end my sentences with "eh," like many other Canadians.

I want to know more about what she means by "hiding secrets," but don't ask. I should have. Perhaps she really wanted to confide in me, and I missed my chance. We talk about the magazine a bit, and I keep thinking I have missed a rare opportunity to find out what she meant. Gladys speaks English well and seems to enjoy my visit. Maybe we can become friends.

Sometimes visiting with the women is a success, and my presence is well received. Other times, there is a painful silence and I want to leave immediately. Used to the constant chatter of my friends back home, I'm uncomfortable with their reserve. These women all seem shy, and Tiger says they are especially shy around white women because they think we are better than they are. They probably don't realize that I'm shy around them too. I want to get to know them, but mostly want them to like me.

Every day, I try to call on someone different. I visit Lena, who lives in a house right behind us. She is petite, pretty, and younger than me. Lena is married to Mildred's son, Lowell Sage. She has two children, and she's expecting again. Her little girl has been very ill and isn't able to sit up yet, even though she is almost a year old.

One night, Lena and Lowell come to visit us. In keeping with the social style here, the men do most of the talking, while Lena and I sit listening. Lena carries her baby in her parka, and her little boy, Junior, has tagged along. He's afraid of us, cries a lot, and sits on his mother's lap much of the time. Then, he starts exploring and seems to enjoy having three small rooms to discover. His tears turn to smiles as he explores every corner of our house.

Ruth Adams always welcomes me and makes me feel comfortable. She's older than I am, but I feel relaxed around her. Ruth's house is like all the others, with one room where the entire family eats and sleeps. She has a couple of children underfoot—Roger and Rosalie. The rest are usually away from the house. Caleb, her husband, is frequently out hunting. She doesn't seem as hassled as

51

the other women, so I never feel as though I'm intruding when I visit. My relationship with Ruth is special because she shares my mother's name. Namesakes are important here, and I could call her "Ana," the Eskimo word for mother. She may be eighteen or twenty years older than I am and is certainly old enough to be my mother.

Ruth Adams

One day, when Ruth is visiting me, I show her a picture of my mom and Peggy, my sister-in-law. They both have dark hair, but Mom has an olive complexion and hazel eyes. Peggy is fair, with blue eyes. Ruth says, "Oh, they look just like us, like Eskimos." I imagine she equates white women with having blonde hair and blue eyes. Now, she knows that we don't all look alike.

When Gladys and I visit, she shares a lot about herself. But there's also a lot that she doesn't tell me. Gladys is Mildred's daughter. Two other girls, Gladys's sisters, live at Mildred's place. These girls are about nine and eleven, much younger than Gladys. The younger girl looks so much like Gladys that I wonder if she is really Gladys's daughter. I want to ask but don't. This could be one of her secrets. Is Mildred raising her grandchild? Adoption is common in Kivalina and in the small villages around Kivalina. It's possible that Lucille, the eldest of the two daughters, is adopted. She looks different from the rest of the girls in the village.

I tell Gladys bits and pieces about my family, enough to share some of my life with her. "Everybody asks me why you don't have babies," Gladys says one day.

"I take a pill so I won't have a baby," I tell her.

"A pill? I never heard of a pill like that. Why do you take it? How come you don't want a baby? We all love our kids."

"I want children, but not now—maybe in a year or so. Then, I'll stop taking the pill." I couldn't tell her I would love to have one right now but Tiger doesn't want me to.

Gladys stares at me. She doesn't understand. Apparently, the doctors in Kotzebue, the nearest place with a hospital, can't talk about any sort of birth control, as it could seem they were promoting the extinction of the race. This would never happen because the Eskimo women love their big families, even though life is more difficult with seven or eight children.

Lying on the couch one day, while nursing a migraine, there is a knock at the door. I don't want to ask anyone in, but it would be rude not to. Tiger is home, and he asks the two women in. Then, he stays in the kitchen with his papers because he can't work at his desk in the living room. He should probably leave the house because he knows Eskimo women clam up in the presence of men.

Neither of the women who visit that day has visited before, and I'm happy that they've made the effort. One is seventeen and married with a baby. The other is just a little younger than me and has three children. The younger of the two is looking after her sister-in-law's five children. A parade of kids follows them through the door, which means there are eleven little ones running around my house. The place is a zoo. The women are used to this kind of chaos and they sit quietly, watching.

My training in social work comes in handy because I can ask questions and know that they will answer. I put it to work, asking the women questions about their lives. But it's not a two-way street; the silence is awkward. I wish that they would leave. My head is still pounding and with all the children running around, it's getting worse by the minute. The women just sit and chew gum, occasionally popping a bubble or two. I will have to return the visit; this is expected. They'll be more comfortable in their own homes, so visiting them there may be easier.

As I visit more and have more women call on me, the pattern repeats itself. The women never initiate conversation. Perhaps "visiting" means being in the presence of others and conversation isn't necessary. Maybe I'm trying too hard to chat, while the women just want to have a cup of coffee and sit quietly. It's an outing, a way for them to leave their daily chores behind. When they do talk, I gather a lot of information for the study and feel guilty doing this. The women think the reason for my visit is to gossip, but I'm getting information for Tiger. After they leave, I write up notes and hand them to him. I want to be friends with the women in the village, but sometimes I feel as though I'm visiting under false pretenses.

VII

THE RHYTHM OF LIFE IN KIVALINA

Our days have developed a certain rhythm to them. The mail plane arrives twice a week, weather permitting, and keeps me from being totally isolated. Cards and letters arrive, with gossip and news. Sometimes our parents will send us "care packages"—boxes with candy or potato chips or even something new for me to wear. These packages are fun to open, and they lift my mood. My parents and my in-laws are getting ready to go to the lake. The letters they write are full of the beautiful weather. I envy the warmth and sunshine they are experiencing. The weather is still cold here, with temperatures hovering in the low thirties. How different it is from the late spring at home.

My niece, Judy, was born three weeks ago, and Mom is ecstatic. Sometimes, it's all that she talks about in her letters. This is the first grandchild, and it's exciting for her. I hope she will send photos soon. Loneliness is a constant companion. I miss my family and the myriad of friends that are easy to talk to.

I haven't heard from Lynn and worry about her. The last time I saw her was in Chicago, and she seemed stressed or unhappy. Mom Burch has said nothing about what Lynn is doing or how she is. In fact, when I ask about Lynn in my letters, she avoids the subject. Lynn should be getting letters from me about every two weeks. It's a curiosity that she hasn't answered one of them.

I bake two loaves of bread every day. It's something that I like to do because the house is filled with a wonderful aroma, and watching it rise, I know we'll have something good to eat. As my mother once told me, it feels good to pound away my frustrations. The bread disappears quickly because we eat it while it's still warm from the oven.

Washing is another story. Fortunately, I only do the wash once a week. The water is too cold to put my hands into and has to be warmed before I can even begin. This means all of the pots that we have in the house are heated on the stove, and it takes an eternity. I have a scrub board and a large tub—the same tub that we'll use to bathe in, if we ever do. I scour all the clothes, leave them in the bottom of the pail, dump the water, and then rinse them in clean water. Even though it's cold, I work outside, bundled up in several layers. When the clothes are rinsed, they are hung on the line outside in the sun and the wind. Everything smells fresh because of this, but I wonder if the clothes are totally clean.

Sheets are harder to wash. It's early June, and they have yet to be done. I have to admit when we arrived here, the bed was already made. Tiger and I were so tired we didn't even think about it. We since found out there was only one pair of sheets and had to have some sent up from Fairbanks. Mom always used to say, "Cleanliness is next to Godliness." Already my values have changed. I don't know who slept in the sheets before we did and frankly, I don't care.

The process will be more complicated in the winter. In the winter, the wash will be done inside, and everything will freeze on the line. I will have to wash the clothes, carry the water outside in the tub, and dump it. The water will probably spill all over the floor when I carry the tub outside. Even though I want everything to be dirt-free, including our house, my standards have changed because water is scarce. At first, I was shocked by the natives' lack of cleanliness, but as I live here longer, I am beginning to understand.

Last week, Tiger borrowed someone else's dog team to go upriver for water. Soon, the land will no longer be frozen, and we'll have to borrow a boat to get water. Tiger tells me we'll take an oil drum, which is stored in our shed, with us and use buckets to fill it with water. When we arrive back in the village, we'll both have a bucket and will carry the water from the oil drum in the boat to the drum in the house.

Sponge baths are taken using a small basin in our bedroom. We heat up water and carry it to the basin in the bedroom. This is how we bathe each night and how Tiger shaves. We've been here for weeks now, and have yet to take a bath. I hate feeling dirty and often wonder if I smell. Maybe after hunting season, we'll use the tub. Right now, we need most of our water for drinking and washing clothes.

Days go by, and Tiger decides to get our radio in working order. A functioning radio is a link to the outside. We probably won't get many stations or even much news, but it's better than nothing. I had mentioned to him that we don't know what is going on in the outside world; we only know what's going on with our families. I told Tiger that it worried me. All sorts of terrible things could be happening in the world and we wouldn't even know it. News of what is happening beyond this tiny village is essential.

Magazines arrive with the mail deliveries, but by the time that they arrive, they are already out of date. We subscribe to *Time* and *Life Magazine*, as well as a few scholastic journals. It doesn't matter if the scholastic journals are dated, because we can read them any time and learn from them. We know the crisis in Vietnam is escalating, and it's frightening to read about. *Life Magazine* is full of devastating images—photos of helicopters flying low to the ground, and of soldiers walking through mud and water. Most of the magazine covers feature a color photograph of the war. The thought of war and all the men who may be drafted into a war that they don't believe in is terrifying. From time to time, we have visitors who thumb through these magazines, but they don't ask questions. They isolate themselves from the outside world. Perhaps, they don't care.

June arrives, bringing with it a flooded lagoon. Spring is here at last, the sea ice has started to break up, and the fishing and hunting seasons are upon us. Bunches of pussy willows grow by the airstrip. It's tempting to go out and cut some, but I don't have the right sort of container to put them in. I'd love to have something in the house to brighten it up. As I am thinking this, Dolly Hawley appears at the door with a bouquet of wildflowers almost as big as she is.

"Here, these are for you, Deenie," she says shyly. All of the kids in the village call me Deenie. They probably can't pronounce Deanne. It's comforting to be called Deenie. Many of my friends at university called me this, and my father-in-law does as well. Sometimes Tiger refers to me as Deenie Bird.

"Thanks, Dolly," I say, taking the flowers from her. "They're beautiful. Where did you find them? I haven't seen any in the village."

She smiles timidly. "Out past the airstrip."

She walked all of the way out there just to pick those flowers for me. I'm touched and want to give her a big hug, but I'm not sure if this is appropriate. I put the bouquet of yellow, pink, and white flowers in a glass with water and thank her again.

Because we have perpetual daylight, people visit at all hours of the day or night. Often, we see people walking around the village at midnight and we join them. We stay up late and sleep late if we want. Living like this is an amazing experience. I can survive on little sleep and never feel tired. I wish these long, light days would never end.

Kivalina is lovely in June. The weather is beautiful, and the land comes alive with wildflowers. I'm beginning to understand why Tiger loves this place so much. When we first arrived here, the sun used to slip below the horizon for a few minutes and tinge the sky with a soft peach color. Now, we have no darkness, and the sun is with us all the time. No wonder Alaska is called the land of the midnight sun.

On the other side of the island, the sea ice hasn't melted, and in the sunshine, the ice is turquoise. Colors of teal, azure, and blue-green sparkle like multicolored diamonds. It's strange to see a sunny sky that is reminiscent of summer when the land is still covered with snow. Now that June has arrived, we have settled into the rhythm of life here—the daily chores, the excitement when the mail plane arrives bringing letters from home, and the people who drop by to visit. One day blends into the next in an unchanging pattern, and I'm slowly getting used to life here.

The water in the lagoon reflects the deep blue of the sky, and in the distance, the hills are losing their cover of snow. When the lagoon fills with water, the fish will start jumping and my work will be cut out for me. It's the women's job to clean and dry the fish. I'll be learning to do this soon, yet another task I'm not looking forward to. When the hunting and fishing season arrive, the natives will repeat the same rhythm of life they have always known. I guess it will become mine as well.

VIII
HUNTING SEASON

Beyond the airstrip, the Arctic grass is growing, reminding me of the smell of sweet grass at home. Tiger and I love to walk along the beach in the half-spring, half-winter atmosphere. Wildlife pours into the region, with flocks of geese and ducks and other birds. Tiger goes duck hunting with the men in the village, and I clean the birds and pluck their feathers for duck soup. The feathers go into a big bag in the storage shed.

Spring and summer are the seasons when the natives prepare for the long winter ahead. The men spend their days and nights hunting and fishing. The women prepare the fish and meat to store and use over the winter. Both are usually dried to preserve them. Tiger joins the men whenever he can. When Tiger's home, I'm often getting up just as he's going to bed. We have very little time together, but he's learning a lot and seems happy.

Tiger's clothes are filthy after a long night of hunting. I soak the animal blood and grime out of the clothes in cold water. Mom always told me that hot water would set the stains and so I don't heat the water. I let the clothes sit for about two hours to get the blood off and then rinse them and hang them on the line, hoping they will dry in time for Tiger's next hunting expedition. All of the men wear white anoraks over their parkas when they hunt because they act as a camouflage. I made the anorak very crudely without a pattern to go from, but it works for him. I wish I had made two.

* * *

Since we arrived, Tiger has been looking for puppies to raise for a dog team. Recently, he bought two adorable two-month-old puppies. I'm going to have trouble not spoiling them. We plan to get more dogs for our team, but don't know where to get them yet.

The puppies are endearing and loveable. I want them in the house to keep me company when Tiger is away, but Tiger tells me that they have to stay outside. Here, dogs are raised only for work, not for pleasure. When the dogs outgrow the pen, Tiger will tie them up to a stake like the rest of the dogs in the village. They will remain tied up for the majority of the time.

Tiger has named the pups Hans and Blitzen, names he's always wanted for his sled dogs, names I don't particularly like. I imagine him shouting commands in a Germanic sort of way. "Halt, Hans! Come, Blitzen!" I think the dogs are too cute for these names. Soon, we settle on new names, Pepper and Coco.

I enjoy the dogs and their antics, barking and jumping when they're happy, and they're happy most of the time. One day, we take them upriver in a friend's boat. Both dogs are itching to get out, and finally, Coco jumps overboard. Laughing at this fearless puppy we have, we pull him back in the boat, but he's one bedraggled, shivering dog.

At night, we take the dogs for a walk past the airstrip. True scavengers, they manage to pick up things on our walks and drag them back to their pen. Their favorite finds are tin cans, probably because of residual food smells. The dogs use the cans at night like pillows, not too comfortable, I'm sure, but it's an engaging sight to see.

Tiger hasn't had time to start disciplining them. The dogs hate being trapped in their pens, and Coco tries to dig his way out sometimes. I'd like to let them run loose, but every time I try, they take off on a run. They bark at the little kids and scare them half to death. If we let them run loose, they'll follow anyone who is friendly to them. I take the dogs for walks on the beach frequently, delighting in their antics as they jump at the waves and bite at the foam. I have to be careful that they don't drink too much of the seawater, because too much salt can kill them. When we get home, they run and hide under the house, putting up a fuss about going back into their pen. Sometimes, when Tiger isn't around, I secretly bring them into the house for company. He's afraid I'll spoil them. I plan on spoiling them but just a little.

Spoiling the dogs

IX

OUR FIRST ANNIVERSARY

Many evenings, Tiger and I go fishing. Most of the time, we come home empty-handed because the water is muddy, and the fish aren't running yet. On June thirteenth, we sit on the beach for a while, relishing the beautiful evening light. It's warm for this part of the world, and a slight breeze is blowing. We watch the clouds skitter across the deep blue hills, enjoying the quiet time together.

"It's hard to believe our first anniversary is just two days away. How would you like to celebrate?" I ask, leaning towards him to give him a kiss.

"We'll figure it out tomorrow. Let's see what the weather is like," Tiger answers. I'm not sure that he was aware our anniversary was so soon.

June fourteenth, a Sunday, brings the bustling village to a halt. Everyone is at church. It's not warm today, but the sky is full of the promise of summer.

"Let's celebrate our anniversary today," Tiger suggests. "I'm sure the water will be clear and the fish will be jumping tomorrow. I want to take advantage of the day if the fishing is good."

I'd prefer to celebrate our first wedding anniversary on the actual day. My parents always made sure to make their anniversary special. My father called my mother every year, at two o'clock in the afternoon, the time of their ceremony, in order to say how happy he was that they were married and that he loved her. My father was such a romantic. But Tiger isn't my dad, and he has a different way of looking at things. I decide not to say anything.

Tiger's favorite meal is steak. Here, spaghetti will have to do. We have it with homemade bread and a chocolate cake with buttercream frosting for dessert. I'm always hesitant to cook because of the inconsistency of the oven temperature, but the cake is delicious, better tasting than our wedding cake, which was a fruitcake. To my surprise, Tiger has a bottle of champagne stashed away, and we drink a toast to the past year and to all the years ahead of us. It's a quiet but festive celebration.

After dinner, Gladys comes by to visit. People often drop in during the evening. I don't know whether this is due to the long days, or if people visit like this during the winter as well. Her company is enjoyable, but I would have preferred to have tonight alone with Tiger. Gladys leaves after a short visit and we have the evening to ourselves. Ultimately, however, before the night is over, Tiger takes off to go duck hunting, leaving me to spend the night alone in Kivalina. Is this his way of celebrating our first anniversary, or is he trying to avoid it? Maybe he's simply not as sentimental or romantic as I am. I thought since we were supposedly celebrating today instead of tomorrow, he was planning on spending the night with me.

Tiger is still asleep after his night of duck hunting, but I am sitting in the kitchen with a cup of coffee remembering our wedding. Last year, I went to the beauty salon and had my hair done. I felt beautiful as I walked down the aisle beside my father. Our wedding was a wonderful gathering of good friends and family. It was exciting celebrating the day with everybody, and most of all, with my new husband.

Today it's different. Now, I've resorted to sponge baths and dry shampoo. Every day is a bad hair day, and I never feel clean. My nails are ragged because of all the work I do with my hands. Washing the clothes, I scrape my knuckles along the scrub board, leaving me with raw, red hands. I break my nails doing this and sometimes, when I'm nervous, I bite them down to the quick.

The girl I was last year, with the manicured hands and the perfect hairdo, is gone. I long to be that girl again.

I'm grateful our mirror is small and I don't have to see what I look like. Sometimes, I set my hair in bobby pins at night so it's not stick-straight. Jeans are my dress code, but at times, nice slacks take their place. My mother made me several Viyella shirts to wear when the weather is warm, and Tiger's mom has sent up blouses as well. I doubt if Tiger even notices what I wear. It would be easy for me to never pay attention to how I look.

Tiger spends the morning in bed. Duck hunting was fruitless for him. I bake bread and do the laundry, two chores that take a long time to complete. What a way to celebrate our anniversary, but the day still lies ahead of us and it is bright with possibilities.

Taking a long walk away from the village and spending time by ourselves would be an indulgence for both of us. Maybe we can take a picnic supper and spend the evening quietly together. Like a bubble floating in the air, my fantasy of our day quickly dissolves. When Tiger wakes up, he says, "I heard Amos is home now. Let's go visit him. I have so much to ask him." Amos was Tiger's best friend when he was here before.

"I thought that you wanted to go fishing today. And even though you wanted to celebrate it yesterday, you left me alone at night. It wasn't much of a celebration."

Tiger sits there as I talk and just shakes his head. He doesn't answer me. And so, despite my disappointment, we go to visit Amos, who has been in the hospital for several months with tuberculosis. Like most of the other people here, he lives with his wife and children in a one-room house. Amos played a big role in Tiger's life three years ago, and Tiger says they will help each other out in any way possible.

I watch Tiger and Amos interacting. They are so in tune with each other and seem like they have known each other forever. They could be brothers. Sometimes I think Tiger had another life before this one. His mother used to tell me that at the age of eight, he would draw pictures of what he thought Eskimo houses looked like. He was always fascinated by their culture.

When he arrived in Kivalina, before we were married, he melted into the community as though he had always lived there and he became an Eskimo in every sort of way. No wonder I have had a hard time fitting in. If I had a past life, it certainly wasn't this one!

After we visit him, Tiger tells me Amos is known as The Artist because he has fathered so many children. Apparently, all his children and grandchildren bear a striking resemblance to him. After meeting him, I realize that the little girl who lives behind us looks like him, and I wonder if he is her father or grandfather. I wish Tiger hadn't told me this. Now, I'll be on the lookout for his resemblance everywhere.

I take Tiger's hand when we leave Amos' place and say, "I can see why you like Amos so much. You seem to understand each other so well. I really wanted to do something else today, but I'm glad we went to visit Amos instead. It was something you have been looking forward to all summer."

Tiger looks at me and smiles. I know he told me the natives don't hold hands or show public displays of affection, but I am going to do it anyway because I don't want to lose my identity

Amos Hawley: The Artist

Tomorrow is another day. Maybe tomorrow, we can make an effort to take the picnic and walk to the end of the island by ourselves.

X

THE ORDINATION OF MILTON SWAN

Milton Swan is the first native to be ordained as an Episcopalian priest, and it is a landmark event. The quiet village of Kivalina has been taken over by preachers who have come in from all over Alaska for the ceremony. Tiger has been seining (fishing with a big net) with Lowell, but he arrives home in time to go with me.

To my surprise, Tiger tells me that he's not interested in going to the ordination, and he has decided to go fishing again. Tiger is not a believer, but he likes Milton and will probably use him to gather information. It's insulting not to attend. I understand his concerns. He's told me he doesn't like what Christianity has done to these people. The Friends Church, which is the other church in Kivalina, has banned dancing and storytelling because it is considered a sin. Tiger is incensed by this. How can drumming, dancing, and storytelling be evil? Storytelling is a way of telling about the past and the beliefs the natives held for hundreds of years. How would the native culture be passed from one generation to the next? What if it dies altogether? Tiger wants to preserve the native culture, and I agree with him. I would love to see all of the traditions brought back. I don't understand why the missionaries thought that dancing and storytelling were sins.

Gladys comes over and asks me to go with her and her family. Perhaps Gladys saw Tiger go back out to fish and knew if I went, I would be going alone. I put on a pair of good slacks and a sweater, and hope I'll fit in. Gladys doesn't ask why Tiger isn't going; she accepts it when I tell her we had an argument. How could I possibly tell her that he didn't want to go to Milton's ordination?

We enter the small Episcopalian church to find it filled with people. The whole village is here; even a few white people from Anchorage and Kotzebue have come to share this occasion. The native women wear their best parka covers; decorative shells made of flowered calico with colorful rickrack. Women in Kivalina spend time poring over the Sears catalog, their wish book. The catalog is full of dreams of things that they would buy if they lived beyond their restricted world: beautiful dresses, stoves, washers, and dryers. It's a gateway to a whole other world. Yet no one complains about the life they have, a refreshing change from the lower forty-eight.

The choir is dressed in spotless red and white gowns. The hymns they sing are ones I have sung all my life, but their rendition sounds more like gospel music. This is a joyous occasion, and one the villagers take great pride in seeing one of their own as the first Eskimo ordained. I am happy to be a part of this. Tiger has definitely missed out.

Looking around the church, I notice a white woman seated a couple of rows ahead of me. She looks a few years older than I am, and I ask Gladys about her. She tells me the woman is from Kotzebue and is married to the priest of the Episcopalian church there. Gladys relates a heartbreaking story about her. The woman had been married before and lived in Tanana, Alaska. Her first husband and three children were killed in a fire. This tragedy overwhelms me, but I'm impressed she has made a new life for herself and returned to another small village to be with another preacher. Some people have so much strength of character and spirituality. If something happened to Tiger, I could never be as brave as she is. I would love to talk to her and find out how she adapted to life in Alaska, but I don't have the courage.

The sermon is delivered in the native tongue and the ordination ceremony is over quickly. After, the churchwomen serve coffee and cake: a white cake and a spice cake. Spice is my favorite, and I reach for a piece.

"Oh no, this other cake is for you," Mildred Sage says to me.

I'm embarrassed when I learn the white cake is for the white people in attendance. A piece of it is served on a saucer to me, with a paper napkin. The spice cake is handed out to the natives. There is no plate for them and no napkin. I don't understand the reason for this differentiation and can only guess they want to treat us better than they treat themselves. Maybe they think we expect that of them.

When the reception is over, I go to Gladys's house for coffee. Visiting with her is the next best thing to being with a girl-friend back home. Sadly, she and her husband will be moving to Kotzebue in a few weeks. I will miss her when she's gone. I am finding as I get to know the women a little better that they are like the women at home, barring the extreme cultural differences. There are hypochondriacs, gossips, and ones I hope to be friends with. It doesn't matter to me if they are hypochondriacs as long as I can relate to them. As for gossips? I love to gossip myself on occasion and the gossips contribute to Tiger's study.

Tiger comes back at nine o'clock and then disappears again until midnight, which means I'll have fish to clean and put out to dry on racks when I get up in the morning.

At breakfast, I tell Tiger about the ordination. "I still don't know why you wouldn't go. It was one of the most important things to happen in the village. A lot of nonnatives came to celebrate." Tiger just nods his head and listens. "You were the only person in the village who wasn't there. Everybody asked where you were. It was sort of embarrassing."

"You're right. I wish I had gone. I just wanted to be by myself. You know I'm not a Christian. And I don't like what Christianity did to these people."

I tell him about the white woman sitting in front of me, the one whose first husband and three children were killed in a fire. "God, Tiger, I don't know what I'd do if something happened to you. I don't think I could stand it."

"You worry too much," he says. "Nothing will happen to me. But you're stronger than you think you are." He is the optimistic one, thinking that nothing will happen to either of us.

XI

LIFE IN THE VILLAGE

The day is bright and sunny, and Austin Thomas, a neighbor who lives close by, is sitting on the ground, watching me clean the fish Tiger has brought home. He doesn't speak much English, and he is crippled. Language is a barrier. His vantage point from the ground doesn't help either.

I begin the job. First, the scales are removed by scraping the fish with a sharp-edged wood chip. Then, the head is removed, and lengthwise slits are cut through the body on both sides of the backbone, beginning at the tail and ending where the head had been. This leaves the meat intact and attached to the skin. Transverse cuts are made in the meat to provide better air-drying. The fish are then hung on a rack to dry. It may be two or three days before the fish are dry enough to store in seal oil.

Fortunately, it's a warm day and it feels good to be outside. The fish will dry quickly. The job isn't finished, but I don't have to spend all day cleaning the fish. A woman from Nome is giving a talk about how to can salmon, and all the women in the village are going. I join them at the armory where there is electricity for the demonstration.

The demonstration is good and although the process takes a long time, it doesn't look too difficult. I can't help but think that it would be so much easier to can the salmon if families had electricity and could afford pressure cookers. Many of the families here are on welfare.

Tiger goes seining with the men almost every day now and arrives back with fish for me to clean and dry. When he is away, I visit women in the village. I feel the most relaxed with Sarah, Gladys, Ruth, and Mildred. Mildred is a wonderful neighbor, but much of her time is taken up with her duties as postmistress. Tiger and I often visit Sarah and Bobby, the couple we are the fondest of.

One day, after we leave, Sarah comes running out. I can tell she's agitated.

"Did Gladys say something to you about Tiger and me? When he was here last time, she teased me about being his girlfriend. Don't worry. It's not true. She's a real troublemaker." Tiger looks surprised by this.

"No, Sarah," I tell her, "Gladys never said anything, and I know it's not true anyway. Why do you ask?"

Gladys never said anything to me about Tiger and Sarah. She likes to gossip, but I don't see her as a troublemaker. Does Sarah have a guilty conscience? Honestly, I don't want to know if she does. It could be that Sarah knows Gladys and I have become friends and it threatens her. Life here is rife with gossip.

After we leave, I give Sarah's words more thought. Tiger once told me if he ever saw a blue-eyed child in Kotzebue or Kivalina, it might be his. I wonder who he was with when he was here before. Could it have been Sarah? I don't think so because Bobby is one of his best friends. I don't care about what he did in the past, but now, I think I had better be more observant. Tiger said he'd want to adopt the child. I'm not sure I could be so generous.

* * *

Tiger is away most of the time hunting with the men, and I'm lonely. Often, he's gone overnight, and I worry about him. I never know when he'll be back, and I hate the uncertainty. There is no way of communicating, and I sit on pins and needles awaiting his return.

Letters from home make me homesick. I miss being there. Mom has sent me pictures of my new baby niece, Judy, and I'm dying to see her. Friends are having babies, and two or three are planning their weddings. I try to confide in Tiger, telling him about the things that I miss from back home and how lonely I can get. Two months here has felt like an eternity. He brushes it off at first, but later, he tells me it's my fault.

"You're not making enough effort to visit in the village," he says, looking annoyed with me.

"But Tiger," I protest, "I'm trying."

"Well, if you're so lonely, go home." He starts to put his parka on, so he won't have to listen to me, even though I'm not finished with what I have to say to him.

I can't believe he's saying this to me. I can't go home. Home is where Tiger is. If I go back to my family and friends and the creature comforts, I'll never come back.

"I'm homesick, Tiger," I tell him. "But I'm not saying that I want to leave here, I'm not giving up. The trouble is, you're never here. I have no friends to bounce ideas off of. Don't you understand?"

Tiger shakes his head. I know he's disappointed in me. We don't discuss it anymore, and he can't understand how I feel. How can he? He's in the village he loves, and with people he loves.

Despite being lonely, I love the land around here and often walk by myself enjoying a quiet time communing with nature. Most of the island is barren and desolate, yet there is beauty in its desolation. Suddenly the land around here has erupted into bloom. Though the soil is sandy, flowers are bursting with life everywhere. There are clusters of flowers that look like tiny orchids and bushes with flowers resembling lilacs. Daisies, buttercups, and wild roses pop their heads up. And past the village lies a carpet of wildflowers.

* * *

Today is the Fourth of July. There will be some festivities this afternoon, maybe some games and races. I look out the window to see if flags are flying, but none are in sight. Two old ladies wandering around the village are dressed in red, white, and blue. When I ask Tiger what's planned, he says he doesn't think there will be food since I haven't been asked to bring anything. He tells me not to expect any fireworks. "There would be no point," he says. "It's light all the time. And one little spark could ignite one of these houses." He doubts that anyone here has ever seen fireworks. They are missing out on an incredible experience, one I know they would enjoy. At three o'clock, the church bells start to ring. I look out the window to see everybody heading out to the end of the village.

"Tiger, let's go see what's going on!" I say, getting up and heading for the door. He joins me in following the villagers to the place where the games and races will take place.

The races start out with the little ones, some of them trying the three-legged race, others just running to see who is the fastest. There is a wheelbarrow race where one child holds another child's ankles and pushes him along. I enjoy every minute watching them. Then I hear a voice saying, "All ladies line up here for a race."

Tiger nudges me and whispers in my ear, "Deanne, you need to go up there and join in."

"I'll feel stupid," I tell him. But I know that I have to join the women. There is a large group of us running—old women, fat women, a few pregnant women, and teenagers. I don't feel stupid at all, joining in. I'm just one of the herd. The younger women cut me off a couple of times, but I am far from the last in the race.

The day ends with a ball game for the men, while the women stand around chatting. Most of them speak English and I listen to their conversations, from time to time trying to add to their discussions. Slowly, I am getting to know some of the women and starting to enjoy being with them.

When we walk home the sun is high in the sky, and the warmth feels good on my face. I grab Tiger's hand. "This has been a great day."

"I'm happy you're beginning to enjoy yourself here," Tiger says with a smile. He leans over and gives me a kiss on the cheek. "I'm glad you didn't listen to me when I suggested that you should go home. I'm sorry."

XII

SEAL HUNTING

Cutting the blubber from the seal with Austin Thomas watching

Seal hunting takes place just after the sea ice breaks up, in June or early July. Tiger will be seal hunting and I'm dreading the time when I have to butcher one. Cleaning and drying the fish hasn't been great, but I've managed. But cutting into a seal and getting all the insides out? It makes me squeamish. I could hardly dissect a frog in high school.

Today, Tiger caught three small seals. He was excited telling me about his success but I shudder, realizing I will have to clean them.

"Let's take them out to the area near Tommy Sage's house. There's plenty of room to work there. I'll help you with these. Then you're on your own," he says, as he starts to drag one of them over. Reluctantly I follow behind him, wishing he would do all the work.

I'm lucky; he could have caught a huge one, a bearded seal. Bearded seals are known to the natives as *oogruks* and are usually close to seven feet long and can weigh as much as 700 pounds. A seal's average weight is 400 to 500 pounds. The females are larger than the males.

Tiger does most of the bloody work on the three seals he's caught, since this is my first time working on them. He splits the seal down the middle and removes the innards, takes out the bladder and the intestines, and discards them in the ocean. "Watch me because you're doing this the next time," he tells me, as I observe him, feeling sick to my stomach. I hate seeing blood and feel faint at the sight of it.

The blubber under the skin on a seal is about two inches thick. Most of the weight of a seal is blubber, which is a dirty yellow color. Blubber is used to create seal oil, an important food that is full of nutrients. Seal oil has a myriad of uses. It's used to preserve food, as heating in some of the homes, and is taken on camping trips as a staple to keep the campers warm.

Sealskin is used to make light parkas and *mukluks*, which are often lined with fur for added warmth. The skins are sewn together with waterproof thread made from sinew and tendons from the seals or caribou to stretch over wooden boat frames. These boats, known as *umiaqs,* are very seaworthy and can get into places other boats can't. Kayaks have sealskins stretched over wood frames as well. I think of Jackie Kennedy, who appeared in a sealskin coat once, putting sealskin into high demand ever since. I'd like to learn to make a sealskin jacket. Maybe one day, one of the women will teach me how to sew the skins together; it's fun to imagine what I might be able to do, given the chance.

Listening to Tiger explain the importance of seals, I can see cleaning them is an essential job and one I'm determined to learn. Tiger shows me how to scrape the blubber away from the skin. It's a difficult, long, and slow process because the skin needs to be completely clean and free of blubber. Once the blubber is removed, it will be cut into small strips and put in a bucket to render for the oil. It's easy to cut the sealskin when working on it and takes care to avoid doing this. If the skin is cut, it will be essentially useless.

"Do the women here expect me to do this?" I ask.

Tiger nods. "Of course they do, but it's okay. You'll learn fast. It isn't as bad as you think it's going to be."

"That's easy for you to say," I tell him. "I hated taking a fish off the hook when my dad and I used to go fishing. I've never even seen a seal until today. I'm not sure I can cut up an animal this big. Won't I be working on the seals with another woman?"

"Probably, because I will be hunting with someone else. Certainly if we catch an *oogruk*, you will have another woman to work with."

Removing the blubber from the skin takes over three hours. Tiger has given me a large knife to cut the blubber off and it's awkward to handle. I hate every minute of this work. I wish I had a mentor in the ways of Eskimo women's work, someone to help me be more efficient. Mabel Thomas is working nearby, and at one point offers to help me. She doesn't speak much English and I can't understand what she's saying when I've done something wrong. At least she's trying to help me and I'm thankful for her attempt.

Now and then, some of the women come over to watch me work—the anomaly, a white woman cutting up seals. I get more nervous by the minute, with them watching me. I can't get the blubber away from the skin, and I'm terrified I'm going to nick it. I wish they would offer some kind of direction, but they don't, they just watch.

When the wind comes in from the west, the men don't hunt, and so for several days after the first seal hunt, I'm released from this onerous task. Eventually, however, the day arrives: hunting conditions are perfect. Bobby Hawley knocks at our door at 7:30 a.m. to ask Tiger to go hunting, but he takes off without waiting for an answer.

Tiger wakes when Bobby knocks and he's upset. He thinks a friend has let him down.

"Tiger, Bobby thought we were asleep," I say, trying to console him. I know he was looking forward to hunting with Bobby.

"He's a friend. He should have knocked again. I need food for the dogs. Now what am I going to do?"

"Maybe you can go with someone else. Lots of men in the village are going out today. Why don't you ask Clarence?"

I hope I don't regret making this suggestion. Clarence lives with his mother, Edith, one of the oldest women in the village. She walks around with her hands behind her back. Edith intimidates me, never speaks to me, and probably resents my presence here. If Tiger asks Clarence and they have luck hunting, I'll be cutting up the catch with her.

Edith Kennedy

78

Conditions continue to be good and, much to my chagrin, Tiger takes my suggestion and goes out hunting with Clarence. I'm being selfish, but I hope they come back empty-handed so I won't have to work with Edith.

While Tiger is hunting, I walk around the village a bit and watch some of the women cutting up seals, wanting to get tips from them. Unfortunately, I don't. The day passes, and by 11:30 p.m., there's still no sign of Tiger. It's light outside and I have buried myself in a book, *The Wapshot Chronicle*. It's fun and fast paced and takes me out of my doldrums.

Tiger comes in after midnight. He and Clarence have caught one small *oogruk*, maybe 450 or 500 pounds. Damn. I'll be working all day tomorrow with the old lady.

The next day, Edith and I work in between her house and ours. Tiger and Clarence have dragged the *oogruk* to this area because Edith likes to be close to home. That's okay because I am beside my house too. I dreaded cutting up seals with her. Now I know why. She rushes ahead with her work, instructing me to watch her. Do the young women here learn by observation? It certainly is not helping me.

There isn't too much blubber on this *oogruk*. When the blubber is thicker, it's easier to remove from the skin. It's just my luck to have to work on a seal without much blubber. Edith works on one end of the seal and I work on the other. I'm not only afraid of Edith, I'm afraid of cutting the skin. I know she'll be furious with me.

In the few hours I work with Edith, she never points out what I'm doing wrong or offers any advice. She's probably disgusted with me because I don't know what I'm doing. While we work, our pups run around loose and their antics bother her. Finally, I put them in the storm shed so I can get on with my work. As soon as I do it, I regret not tying them up in their pens or putting them in the house. The storm shed houses all of our supplies. Heaven only knows the kind of damage that they'll do in there. But it's already done.

At long last, Edith suggests a break and I go to the storm shed to let the pups out. Chaos greets me. Rolls of toilet paper barely within the dogs' reach have been shredded. Feathers are scattered all over. The dogs broke into the bags of duck feathers that I had put away to be used to make a comforter. Instantly, any thought of making one disappears. They run out of the shed covered in feathers and seem to be smiling despite the fact there are feathers up their noses and covering their eyes. They sneeze and start rolling around, happy to be released from their prison. When they start to sniff at the sealskin we have been working on, I drag them away and put them in the house. Edith is cleaning up the tools when I return to our work area.

"Time to stop, Edith?" I ask, trying not to sound too hopeful.

She glares at me and continues to clean up. Clearly, she isn't impressed with me.

Tiger has been hunting all afternoon while I cut up the *oogruk* with Edith, and he comes home to tell me about it. "We were successful this afternoon. We caught three small seals and one huge *oogruk*." He is taking off his anorak as he tells me this and then adds, "You know I would love a shower or even a bath."

"Well, so would I," I mutter under my breath.

He's excited, but I'm hardly that. "So tomorrow I'm going to have to work with Edith again? Damn it, Tiger. I can't do this." I plunk myself on our couch. "Do you really expect me to work with her after I spent all day today with her? It wasn't fun." Now I feel my face getting red and I can hardly speak.

"You're going to have to. What would I tell Clarence if you decided not to help? Anyway, tomorrow will be better."

"I hope so." I go off to bed, disappointed he was successful with his hunting trip. I lie in bed apprehensive about the following day and what it's going to bring.

Working on the *oogruk* today isn't any better than yesterday. In fact, it's worse. I can't keep pace with Edith, and she makes it clear she doesn't want me working alongside her. At one point, she hands me the bladder of the *oogruk*. "Here. Take it to the ocean and dump it." By the expression on her face, she knows what's going to happen and she delights in giving me this task. The bladder is not only huge, it's full. Tiger would say it's a good learning experience, but I don't need a learning experience like this one.

Slowly, I stagger to the ocean, carefully carrying my disgusting load, hoping nothing happens with it on the way. When I reach the ocean and dump the bladder, it bursts, and urine splatters up in my face. Great, now I smell of saltwater and *oogruk* urine. I feel like puking and I can't even take a bath. It hasn't been an option since our arrival here.

Edith and I work on the *oogruk* for several more hours. When Tiger comes home, he helps me by working on the smaller seals for the rest of the afternoon. Thank goodness he is helping me now. It was torture working with Edith. Mabel, the old lady who speaks very little English, stops by to see how we're getting along. Since she offered to help me the other day, we invite her in for a cup of tea. She's happy in our house, listening to the radio and singing along with the hymns being played. She's content, full of the joy of life. We ask her to stay for dinner and attempt to tell her that we're having noodles served with corn oil. Tiger tries to explain that corn oil is like seal only it's made from corn. She's probably never eaten corn and perhaps doesn't even know what it is. I haven't seen corn sold in cans or had it served at anyone's house.

Around nine o'clock, Edith comes over to return a pair of socks Tiger lent to Clarence. When she sees our neighbor, she sits down and makes herself comfortable. I'm knitting, and Edith watches me like a hawk. She knits too, she says, and this surprises me. I've never seen anyone here knitting.

"I'd love to learn how to make mukluks," I tell her.

Edith says, "Oh, I'm afraid you'll never be able to make mukluks. You can't even skin a seal."

I don't understand. What does skinning a seal have to do with making mukluks? My confidence is shattered, but I don't speak up.

Tiger and I are working again on the smaller seals together. It's early morning and we hope nobody comes to watch. Who should show up, but Edith? I wish she'd leave. She's making me nervous.

"I think you should hire someone to work on the seals for you," Edith says. "Neither of you know how to do this properly. You're ruining the skins."

Frankly, I would be happy to hire someone to do this work for us, but I know it would never fly with Tiger.

"We're just practicing." Tiger says calmly. "How else can we learn? We have to try."

Good for him, I think. Now what is she going to say?

Edith seems impressed with Tiger's reply. After that, she gives us both some hints and even lends me her ulu, a tool shaped like a half-moon. It's easier to use than the large knife I've been using. Tiger should have found an ulu for me to work with. Surely he had seen women working with them. The last time that Tiger was here, he went hunting with the men and probably gave whatever he caught to the women to work on. I wish he would give the seals to one of the women and not make me do it. If I had more confidence, I might even tell him to cut up the seals himself. I certainly didn't bargain for this when I married him.

I notice that Edith bends from the waist when she's working. I work on my knees. I decide to try it her way next time. Bending at the waist may give me a better grip on the skin to remove the blubber. Tiger has washed the skins we've been working on and they look nice and clean on the furry side, but there are still patches of blubber clinging to the underside. They may not be perfect, but we both feel we have done a good job.

The house, by now, is a wreck. There hasn't been time to clean it all week, and there's been no time to bake bread. What on earth can we eat tonight? Then, inspiration hits. I can fry a seal liver with onions I've stored in the shed to keep them fresh. Even without bacon to add, I'm happily surprised with what I've prepared, and not only that, the seal liver with onions tastes good. It's like calf's liver, only better. Tonight, I feel happy. Slowly but surely, we're learning to live off the land. It is a challenge, and a good one.

XIII
MID-JULY HUNTING

Belugas hauled to shore

In early July, seal hunting has come to an end, and the village is waiting for the belugas to appear. The beluga, or white whale, is an Arctic and sub-Arctic marine mammal important to the natives here in order to keep the dogs fed through the winter. The natives don't typically care much for beluga meat besides the stomach, tongue, heart, and liver.

Today, after breakfast, I hear Tiger yell, "Belugas!" He's been watching for them, and it sounds like he's spotted activity in the ocean. This is the first beluga sighting since we arrived. Tiger has waited eagerly for this and rushes to get ready to hunt with the men; there's no time to lose.

What an experience this is for him! The natives have hunted belugas using harpoons and boats for hundreds of years. Now, they use an outboard motor with their skin boats. They still use harpoons, but they have rifles as well. The traditional way of hunting is combined with the new.

I hurry to the beach to watch the activity but find that there is very little to see. The hunt is taking place on the ocean side of the island, out of sight. I hear the drone of the outboard motors and the occasional shot. Finally, I leave for home to wait.

Tiger comes home after about three hours of hunting, and he's excited.

"We drove the boats close to the belugas and killed four with harpoons," he tells me, his eyes sparkling with enthusiasm. "We tried with our rifles too, but only caught the four. Come watch us haul them up on the beach."

I follow him, running to the beach to watch the action. The entire village has arrived to celebrate.

The belugas' appearance surprises me. I thought they would look like small whales, but they look more like white porpoises. A beluga weighs two to three thousand pounds. Forty or fifty percent of its body weight is fat. Other species of whale weigh two to nine tons.

The men heave the catch up on the shore, and as soon as they do, the women and children rush forward with their knives to cut off pieces of the flippers. In minutes, they're eating the meat raw, their faces filled with delight over this delicacy. I'm witnessing an ancient custom, repeated thousands of times over the centuries, and think how lucky I am to be able to do this.

Children Enjoying Beluga flipper

Tiger comes over to offer me a piece of a flipper. "Try some, Deanne," he says.

"No, thanks, I don't really want any," I say, forgetting for a moment that we're doing a participant study and I need to try some. I've never eaten anything raw before, it's not appealing to me.

When you're offered native food, it's rude to turn it down. I change my mind and try some. Tiger hands me a piece and everybody around us watches for my reaction. I take a taste of the raw meat and find it tough, tasteless really. I imagine this is what shoe leather would taste like if salt was sprinkled on it. I smile to let the villagers know the raw beluga flipper is okay with me. So far, I can stomach almost everything I've tried. Like it or not, I'm learning to be a part of the life here.

The men do most of the work on the belugas, cutting them up to share with the whole village. The men who caught them are given the most amount. Tiger helps me with our portion, which is large since he was one of the hunters. We cut off the blubber and prepare the meat for drying. The work isn't as hard as the work with the seals was, and it's much cleaner, because the innards are taken out as soon as the belugas are lugged to the shore. The meat is cut into strips, rinsed, and dried on racks Tiger laid out on the grass.

We now have an impressive amount of beluga hanging up to dry. Tiger is relieved to have enough food for the dogs. We don't have to worry about having enough food for ourselves; we can always order food from the Safeway in Fairbanks. Having enough food for the dogs is always a concern. Couldn't we get dog food from the Safeway as well? Probably, but the dogs thrive on the dried fish and meat they are served here. Besides, buying food would cost a fortune.

Mildred visits the day after the beluga hunt and invites us to lunch. "We'll be having real Eskimo food," she tells me.

I'm surprised by this invitation. Until now, I thought people just dropped in and stayed if lunch was ready. I tell her we'd love to come, though in truth, I'm squeamish about it. This will be the first Eskimo meal I have eaten.

At the lunch that day, Mildred's son Lowell and his wife join us. We have something called *muktuk,* fresh beluga skin with the blubber on it. *Muktuk* is most often eaten raw, and this is how I experience it for the first time. I taste it and am surprised to find I like it, although it is rich and fatty. As a result, I can't eat much of it. Along with this, Mildred serves partially dried, partially cooked oogruk meat and the seal oil that is traditionally served with it.

After eating lunch, Tiger and the men talk about hunting, while the women and I relax. Mildred tells me that *muktuk* is stored in seal oil or beluga oil for the winter. It's considered a treat when it's stored in beluga oil. We'll probably have this a lot during the winter ahead.

I'm happy listening to the chatter going on around me. Lunch has been an eye-opening experience. Their food is so different from ours, but their diet is healthier, or at least it was before they learned to love sugar and bake pies and cakes. It's hard to imagine they've never eaten fresh fruit or vegetables. Would they like cantaloupe or other melons, carrots, or peas? I have never seen these things in the store. Maybe someday, I'll invite them over to experience white people's food. I could make spaghetti with tuna fish and tomato sauce. This would certainly be a new experience for them.

After lunch, Tiger and I go back to work on our share of the beluga. When we're finished, Tiger leaves to go and get another dog for us at the Wesley's place. He needs more dogs to complete his team. Tiger expected that he would be able to buy dogs from one of the other men in the village, but the dogs drank too much saltwater and died. We're going to have to make do with three until we can find another opportunity to get more dogs.

When Tiger comes back that day, he introduces me to the mangiest looking white dog I have ever seen. The dog's name is Star. He is shedding but Tiger tells me he'll look better when his new fur comes in. Star is skinny with wild-looking eyes, and he howls incessantly. He probably misses the rest of his team. I'm definitely not tempted to bring him into the house for company.

* * *

In the evenings, we often have a chance to be together as a couple, and sometimes we visit with other couples. Tiger plays his accordion while another man plays guitar. The women have a good time, tapping their feet in time to the music. For other sources of entertainment, we go to the armory for an occasional movie. The whole village turns out to watch, so we go too. We think that the movies are somewhat senseless, but it's something to do. Most of the movies are old, but the occasional one is educational and we learn a lot from these.

The weather is beautiful and clear, but hardly like summer; it's only thirty-eight degrees and there is a stiff wind blowing. One day, I am sitting on our couch, reading, when Tiger comes into the house. He's not happy to see me relaxing. "You seem to do an awful lot of reading. If you have time to read, you should have time go out to visit more."

"I'm taking a break, Tiger. I just finished scrubbing the floor, and there's bread rising in the kitchen." I am hurt by his words. "What more do you want from me? You know I hate doing the work the women do up here, but I'm doing it anyway. I've baked bread, cut up seals, kept the house clean, done the wash, cut up and dried the fish, and tried to cook you a good meal every night. Did you really think I would enjoy all these things?" Maybe he's projecting his own frustrations onto me here and with his own daily chores because he rarely has time to read his professional journals. "Seal hunting is over. Beluga hunting was successful," I say. "Why don't you catch up on letters and notes?"

As I say this, I hear the sound of an airplane overhead and know it's going to land. The mail has already been here for the week, and we rarely get any other planes. What could this be? I put my book down and go outside with Tiger to join everybody heading out to the airstrip to greet the plane. It's a small plane, a two-passenger. We watch it come to a stop on the ground.

"Hey, everyone, I just spotted some fifty thousand caribou," the pilot says, climbing out of the plane. Lowell, Mildred's son, asks Tiger to go with him and his dad to hunt with them.

"Let me get my stuff, I'll be right over," Tiger says, and he's off, hurrying back to our house. I go with him and watch as he rushes around packing his hunting gear. Tiger was given the Eskimo name of Tuktu, which means caribou. He's fascinated by them and has been waiting for a caribou spotting for a long time.

From the window, which looks out to the post office, I see Tiger, Lowell, and his father, Lawrence, dash to the boat. I've sent them off with the bread I made earlier. While they're gone, I'll stay home and wait for their return; they have no idea when they'll be home and there's no way to communicate. The village women are used to this, but it's a new experience for me. I worry about something happening to Tiger when he's gone and don't relax until he returns home safely.

Reading has lost its interest to me for now. To occupy myself, I get to work in the kitchen baking more bread. When Tiger gets home tomorrow, he will want some. Mom is right, baking bread does release tension. I knead it over and over again, practically pounding it. I seem to get frustrated over so many things—the work I wasn't prepared to do, my loneliness, and the limited time that Tiger and I spend together because he's so focused on his work.

Since Tiger is hunting, I visit a few women in the village and get home around eleven. The bread has risen, and I put it into a hot oven. When it's finished baking, it will be time for bed. I can't imagine doing this at home at this time. Here the sun is high and it feels like morning instead of evening.

The next morning, Tiger arrives home at 7:30, exhausted and freezing. Relieved to see him, I sit and listen to the story he has to tell. "The noise of the plane drove most of the caribou away, but we landed and walked four miles into the flats and managed to get seven. This is the first caribou caught this season, all the village gets a share."

"Seven! How did you get them back here?"

"We hauled them to the boat. Lawrence warned us not to shoot too many because we'd have to do that. Of course, we didn't listen. But the old man was right. It was a lot of work carrying them back."

I tiptoe around the house, trying not to disturb Tiger while he sleeps. When he wakes, he'll have fresh bread to eat, and I know that he'll eat the whole loaf. I heat up some water and soak and wash Tiger's bloody hunting clothes—by hand, of course. I hate washing these gory clothes. Tiger will have to go upriver where the water is fresh to get water today because we only have a bit left for drinking and cooking.

After Tiger gets up, we go upriver together in a borrowed boat to get water. It's a lot of work, but the trip upriver is always worth it—the water is clear, and sometimes we have a chance to fish. The time away from the village is our alone time. We hope to get our own boat soon, because we don't like being dependent on the villagers.

Getting water takes over an hour, as we fill our oil drum by dipping a large pot into the water and transferring it to the drum. Back home, we transfer the water bucket by bucket to the water drum in the kitchen.

As soon as we're back from upriver, we start to work on our share of the caribou meat, cutting it into long strips for dog food. We keep some of it for ourselves to eat as well. I haven't tasted caribou yet, but I'm looking forward to having fresh meat, a nice break from fish. I love Arctic char, but when it's not available, I often cook tuna. I've become an expert at cooking canned tuna fish a hundred different ways. Tiger says caribou tastes a lot like gamey roast beef or moose, but it's not as tender. I had moose when we were in Norway. It was from a moose preserve and tasted better than roast beef.

Tonight, we have a visitor and Tiger is up until midnight with him. They sit in the next room laughing and talking. I can smell the cigarette smoke drifting into the bedroom. Tiger doesn't smoke, but most of the men and many of the women in the village do. I know my husband is about ready for bed, but of course he doesn't ask our guest to leave or even drop a hint that he's exhausted. Meanwhile, I can't sleep with their talk and laughter.

When his guest leaves, Tiger says to me, "Hey, Deanne, I want to sleep in tomorrow. Don't wake me up, okay? And try to be quiet."

I point out to Tiger that he and Chester have kept me awake with their laughing and talking. I feel my anger at the whole situation boiling up inside, ready to choke me. I'd love to sleep in too, but I have to get the chores done.

In the morning, I wake in a foul mood, not prepared to let him sleep in. I make a lot of noise, and he wakes up angry. He gives me the silent treatment, something I hate. My mother always gave me the silent treatment when she was annoyed. It drove me nuts. Now, Tiger is driving me nuts.

I cook our partially dried *oogruk* meat to keep it from rotting, and then I scrounge around in the kitchen, considering what I can do with the caribou meat. I know that we will have a large piece of caribou to roast, but right now, we have small portions. Perhaps if I cook something nice, Tiger will get out of his funk. In the fifties, when I was growing up, Mom always told me one way to a man's heart is through his stomach. I decide to make beef stroganoff. We don't have sour cream for it, but I think I can make some by adding vinegar to our evaporated milk. We have canned mushrooms and noodles.

The stroganoff is cooking and the aroma wafts throughout our tiny house. When Tiger comes in, his face lights up and I know I've scored. He is out of the doldrums.

XIV

CHANGES

One day, in July, Tiger and I are sitting at the table having lunch, listening to the latest news about Vietnam. Each time we listen, we can tell the war is escalating.

Tiger says, "You know, Deanne, I might get drafted."

"But you're married. I thought if you're married, there is less of a chance for you to be drafted."

"You're right, but I also heard that most of the men being drafted are from poor families. I don't feel right about this. Just because I have money doesn't mean I should be exempt from serving in the military. If the war gets much worse, I'll feel it's my duty to enlist."

I'm aghast. Does he believe in this war? Why would he volunteer when he knows he might never return? What about me? Doesn't he care?

I'm fidgeting as I say to him, "If you volunteer, I'd like to try and have a baby. You know how much I've always wanted one."

Tiger shakes his head. "Don't even think about it. I wouldn't want to leave you with a child unless I knew I wouldn't die there."

Since that conversation, I attempt to shut out the news. What is happening in the outside world is atrocious, but there is nothing that we can do about it. We carry on with life up here and I try not to think about it. I can't even imagine that Tiger would actually volunteer for this war, but then I remember he cares about the inequalities in life.

Meanwhile, we need a boat. When we borrow a boat to get water upriver Tiger usually rows, and it's tiring for him. Then we have the job of filling our oil drum with water and transporting it back to the house. Sometimes one of the villagers takes us upriver in an outboard. If we have our own boat, we'll have the freedom to come and go whenever we want and to explore areas farther up the coast.

One of the men in the village, a good carpenter, is building a boat, and Tiger decides to ask him if he can buy it.

"You can buy it all right," the man says. "You can give me your accordion or five hundred dollars."

This isn't a good trade. A boat would never cost this much, and he would have to buy a motor for the boat, as well. Asking for Tiger's accordion for payment is out of the question. He gets so much joy out of playing it. Sometimes he plays when we're alone in the house, which isn't often, but he loves playing with the other men whenever he can. I can't believe this man would ask such a high price, but Tiger says that's the way people operate around here.

Tiger decides to go to Kotzebue to buy a boat and find more dogs to round out the team. He leaves on the mail plane toward the end of July and says he'll be back when he finds a boat and some dogs. I hope he is not gone too long. I hate being by myself.

When Tiger is away in Kotzebue, some of the teenage boys come to visit me. I don't feel threatened by them; I find it amusing that they come around when Tiger is not here. "Do you want to go swimming with us in the lagoon?" one asks.

"The lagoon?" I miss swimming, but I know the lagoon will be cold. "I wish I could, but I don't have a bathing suit," I say. "Anyway, it will be too cold."

"It won't be cold, and you don't need a suit. Just swim in your clothes."

"No, thanks," I tell them. I find it flattering they wanted to get to know me. Maybe they were even attracted to me, but it was obvious they were curious about the white woman.

The days slip by, and it's early August. With no means of communicating, I begin to worry. At last, Tiger comes home with five dogs and a small wooden boat with an eighteen-horsepower motor. The boat cost seventy-five dollars with the motor, a far cry from the asking price here. Now we have eight dogs to feed through the winter, and Tiger is relieved to be able to round out his team.

Tiger is back from Kotzebue, and the teenaged boys don't come over. I tell Tiger about their visit.

"A lot of the natives think that you're their age," he says.

"They just think I'm young because I don't have children. So many of the girls here have babies at sixteen or seventeen. They don't understand why we haven't had one by now." I sigh. "Sometimes I really want a baby."

Tiger shakes his head. "Well, that's not going to happen any time soon." I have always wanted a child and wish Tiger had responded differently. He could have said to me, "I want one too, but we'll have to wait until the study is finished." But he didn't. I'm not even sure he wants a baby.

Having a boat of our own is a Godsend. We are no longer dependent on someone to lend us their boat. This has given us a great sense of freedom. We take river trips, which we love. The water is clean and sparkling, and we can see all the way to the bottom no matter how deep it is. We fish for dinner and bring water home for our daily use.

Since we have a boat of our own, water is more plentiful. One night, we heat water and take our first bath in the tub. I let Tiger go first and laugh when he lowers himself into the tub. Water overflows all over the floor. My bath is heavenly. It feels good, even if I can't add more water from a tap when the temperature cools off. At long last, I feel clean again.

The weather is warm, which surprises me, since the days are already getting shorter. Work is finished for the morning and I am sitting on the beach in the sun, savoring its warmth and watching the ocean. I feel nostalgic about the summer I'm missing at home, but the gorgeous weather here almost makes up for it. I like to be in the sun whenever work is done.

Tiger arrives, surprising me when he takes a seat beside me on the warm sand. "Do you want to take a trip up the coastline?" he asks. "We'll head for Cape Thompson, about forty miles north along the coast. You'll love it, and the weather's perfect right now."

I lean toward him and give him a kiss. "I'd love to." I'm excited to get away by ourselves for a couple of days and leave everything behind.

Back at the house, we pack our camping gear, seal oil, and dried fish. We take the two pups and ask Amos to feed the other dogs. The seal oil will keep us warm and the dried fish is easy to transport. It's not exactly the sort of food I want to eat, but I'm getting used to it.

And like that, we're off on an adventure together. Tiger sits in the back of the boat, steering the outboard, while I sit in the middle seat. The scenery along the coast is similar to that around Kivalina, with flatlands and rolling hills, though the hills are closer to the coastline. As we continue up the coast, the hills are steeper and more impressive. High, rocky cliffs replace the hills as we near the Cape, with sheer drops to the ocean. Jagged rocks rise out of the land. The ocean has cut a natural archway into the rocks. I'm in awe of the magnificent beauty surrounding us.

"I drove my sled under this archway," Tiger says, remembering the winter he was here. "It was one of the most beautiful sights I have ever seen." I imagine a fairyland of ice crystals and soft white snow. Tiger tells me that we'll go snow camping at Cape Thompson when the season turns. I look forward to this sort of adventure with him, although I am somewhat intimidated by camping in the snow. I don't tell him this, of course. He doesn't need to know.

"What are those black lines along the edges of the cliffs?" I ask, pointing to them. I've never seen anything like it.

"Those are birds," Tiger says. "Watch." He shoots his rifle into the water and the birds lift en masse and fly away from the cliffs. Thousands and thousands of them dart and swoop around us.

They squawk and fly low, angry with us for disturbing their peace. There are colonies of breeding birds here, the most common of them the murre. We've eaten murre eggs before. They're bigger than chicken eggs and taste just like them. They're good, but sometimes there is a tiny chicken when we crack the egg open.

I try to shout over the noise of the boat engine. "I never dreamed that we'd see anything like this!"

Tiger cuts the engine and we sit quietly and watch the birds soaring overhead. I hope none of them decides to deposit a prize on us. Bird poop is thought to bring good luck, but it's very hard to wash out of clothes. We didn't bring anything extra with us to wear.

We decide to camp that night near the Cape so we can wander around the cliffs exploring tomorrow. Unfortunately, however, as soon as we start to unload the boat, we realize the ocean swells are so high that our anchor can't hold. "Change of plans!" Tiger calls out, and we retreat to find a place to set up camp further south.

We are cold and tired, but the seal oil and dried fish help us warm up. Tiger doesn't sleep well because he knows the anchor isn't strong and he's troubled by visions of the boat drifting away. What would happen if the boat did drift away? No one knows where we are. Worse than that, we probably wouldn't be missed here. We could even die.

Somehow, exhaustion wins. We fall asleep, and the next day wake to find the temperature is in the seventies. It's heavenly. Warmth like this is rare so far north, Tiger says.

On our way up to the Cape that day, we pass a building that Tiger says is the Arctic Research Laboratory. Someone is outside the building, a white man, who calls us in to shore.

"Hello, there," the man says, beaming as we dock and climb out of the boat to meet him. He's in charge of the lab, he says, and he likes to get every boat coming by to come in for a visit. Two natives are here too, and the group of men asks us to stay for coffee and lunch, an offer we happily accept. We sit down to a meal of fresh ham sandwiches and chocolate icebox pie with them, and they give us apples and oranges to take with us when we leave. After all of the months up here, ham sandwiches and fresh fruit are quite the treat. It sure beats the seal oil and dried fish that we brought. This is the first fresh fruit we have had since we arrived in Kivalina four months ago.

After lunch we continue up to the Cape, but the swells are still too big to land. We abandon our idea of walking around the cliffs, choosing instead to be content gazing at the scenery. I want to capture this beauty on film, wish I had learned how to use a camera before I left the lower states so I could capture scenes like this, and village life, as well.

Heading home, we're beckoned into the lab again and dock the boat to get out and say hello. To our surprise, we're treated to a meal of spareribs with sauerkraut, potatoes, lettuce, and zucchini. Wow! I didn't realize how much I missed these foods until now. We leave with three steaks, more fresh lettuce, and a bagful of canned goods. The lab closes in September, we're told, and whoever was in charge ordered too much food. How lucky we are!

"I feel like we're charity cases," I whisper to Tiger.

I can tell by his smile that he's looking forward to one of those steaks. Before we pull up anchor, the Eskimos tell us the man who heads the lab is lonely, he loves having visitors. I understand. "I wish we could visit here again," I say, and just then I notice our anchor, which is a sack full of stones, has broken. "Oh dear, Tiger, look!" I cry, just as the boat starts to drift away from the shore. Our short holiday has come to an end.

* * *

The new teachers, Jim and Dorothy Keating, arrived when we were at Cape Thompson. On our way to the store to get food, Tiger and I meet Jim. He is a very fast talker and anxious to make a good impression. He'll teach adult education, he tells us, and his wife, Dorothy, will teach at the school. They have two children, a girl, fifteen, and a boy, seventeen. Their children are in higher grades than the Kivalina School offers. Here, they will have to be home-schooled, or leave Kivalina for school outside of the village.

Jim Keating asks us to his house to meet his wife. The Keatings are congenial, and their living quarters are nice. Dorothy is a bleached blonde who looks tough. Perhaps being tough makes it easier to teach in this little village, which is so remote from everything.

Dorothy takes me to see their bedroom, where paintings of nudes she painted hang on the wall. The paintings are fairly abstract, but they're sensual. I feel embarrassed by the sight of them and can't help but wonder if the Keatings' sex life is as erotic as the paintings. We don't know quite what to make of the Keatings. But it's okay, we didn't come here to socialize with another white couple, we came to be part of the natives' lives.

The next morning, we wake up to find it's a beautiful day. Tiger decides to ask the Keatings to go with us up the coast in our boat. This is interesting to me because Tiger says he doesn't want us socializing with the teachers. Apparently, the remnants of old houses are there, part of the old village of Kivalina. Tiger and Jim stake out old houses while Dorothy and I sit on the beach, enjoying the sun and a nice picnic lunch. She made tuna sandwiches to take along and I brought peanut butter sandwiches. We leave earlier than we'd planned because once again, the anchor wouldn't hold.

At the Keating's place for dinner, we learn about Shungnak, another small Arctic village, from the teacher the Keatings are replacing. She is so enthusiastic about the village that she convinces us to spend our second year in Alaska there. She and her husband taught there and loved it.

I like Dorothy. She's easy to talk to and probably happy to have another woman living in the village, someone she can relate to. She may be one tough cookie, but I enjoy her company. I'm going to spend time with her, even though Tiger reminds me we are here to participate with the natives and not with the teachers.

Behind the Keating's back, we refer to them as Dorothy and Jim. To their face we don't call them anything. It's awkward, but because they are twenty years older than we are, we don't know what to call them out of respect, but we will probably call them Dorothy and Jim. Alaska is so informal.

Out on the flats with dogs (Photo probably taken by Jim Keating)
last photo of Tiger before his accident

XV

A TRIP TO KOTZEBUE

By mid-August, the summer's warmth has disappeared. One day, Tiger announces that he's going to Kotzebue to buy lumber to build a sled and put shelves in the kitchen. "Come with me," Tiger says. "Let's get away from the village for a couple of days."

I'm excited. The idea of getting off this island for a couple of days is a welcome one. It will be a good getaway, too, before the cold sets in.

There's one decent hotel in Kotzebue, and I'm hoping we'll stay there. I dream of having a long, hot bath and a few creature comforts. But before I can go too far with this fantasy, Tiger has news for me. "Our boat is too small to haul all the lumber that I want to buy," he says. "We're going with Lawrence in his skin boat. Some other men from the village are going with us, too. There is safety in numbers, and the men know the signs of the winds and bad weather."

I'm disappointed because I wanted to go with Tiger by myself and not with other men. It doesn't last long though. I've never been in a skin boat, known as an *umiaq*, before. The boat is very sturdy and holds several tons. A whole new experience is waiting for me.

"Sounds exciting," I say, and I mean it. This is going to be an adventure.

We leave on a cold, windy day, and head south along the coast. We won't stop until we reach our destination and realizing this, I have to pee. It's difficult for a woman, especially one bundled up against the cold. Finally, I tell Tiger I need to make a pit stop, and he tells the men, who are not happy. Finding a stopping place and landing will take time, and they're anxious to reach their destination. I can see having a woman along hampers their travel, and having a white woman along may do so more. They beckon me to the side of the boat and, reluctantly, I summon my courage, take down my slacks and long underwear, and with great difficulty, manage the situation. The boat is being tossed around by the waves and I sit away from the side of the boat while Tiger is right there making sure I don't fall in. The rest of the men sit inside the boat and avert their eyes. Maybe by the time I've lived here for a couple of years, this sort of thing won't be an issue.

For seven and a half hours we hug the shoreline. The trip is cold and wet, and the waves are high, but we make it to our destination in what the men say is almost record time. As we land on the beach, several natives come to the boat to greet us and they invite us into their house for hot soup and coffee. I'm more than ready to be inside and warm up with a cup of hot soup. Most of these people are friends of Lawrence's, and since we're with him, it's assumed that we'll come along. Gladys Adams, Lawrence Sage's daughter, lives here. We spent time together when she lived in Kivalina, and I hope to visit with her so that I can hear how she is doing. She left a gap in my life when she went to live in Kotzebue.

At this point, we don't know where we're going to stay. I'm still hoping for a room at the hotel, but Tiger hasn't made a move to book a room there. Gladys stops in while we're having coffee and says hello to everyone. When she sees us, she invites us to stay with her and the rest of her family. Lawrence will be staying there, and others probably will be as well. I'm not interested. I'm sure her house has only one room and we all will be sleeping together in it.

"Thanks, Gladys," I hear Tiger say, much to my chagrin. "That's a big help to us. We'll get our things and come over." He hasn't even asked if it's alright with me. I'm dismayed, as she tells him where to find her house.

"I thought we'd stay in a hotel. I wanted to have a bath and feel clean for a couple of days," I complain to Tiger, as we leave to get our things from the boat.

"Whatever gave you that idea?" he says. "I never planned on staying in a hotel, and I certainly didn't say anything to you about staying in one."

"Well I'm not a mind reader you know. I just assumed we'd stay in a hotel."

I should have asked what our accommodations would be before we left. It never occurred to me we would be staying in someone else's house. I see now that Tiger has brought a mattress, towels, and our sleeping bags. Why hadn't I noticed what he brought along? I resolve to look at it as another learning experience and hope for the best.

The first night, there are eleven people sleeping in the same room. The room is at most twelve feet by twelve feet. It feels as though we are sleeping on top of one another. The family of five sleeps in two beds pushed together. Three other mattresses besides ours are crowded together on the floor. One other person sleeps on the only couch in the room. I'm nervous sleeping like this, and I know sleep will not be easy for me. In the best of times, I don't sleep well.

After lights out, I hear snoring and coughing for most of the night as I toss and turn in my sleeping bag. I can't get comfortable, and the noise doesn't help. By morning, I have to wonder if I slept at all. Tiger is oblivious to the fact that I couldn't sleep.

As if the sleeping arrangements aren't bad enough, things are even worse when it comes to the bathroom facilities. The toilet consists of a bucket with a tiny seat on it, and it gets fuller and fuller during the night. There is no privacy. All of the people, except for Tiger and me, share the same dirty towel, and everyone uses the same water. By the time they finish washing, the basin is full of gray, scummy water. I understand why they use the same water to wash with; water is hard to get, and they are all comfortable with one another. I notice people only wash their hands after eating, not before, most likely because of the short supply of clean water. We were always told to wash our hands before dinner, not after.

Gladys, the woman of the house, is awake at six. I want to get up with her, but she's busy serving everybody coffee in bed, and I can't refuse. We have our coffee before getting up. I've never had room service, and having coffee in bed would be a treat if it were not for the fact that drinking coffee in a sleeping bag is quite difficult. We drink the coffee in a half-sitting, half-lying position. It's embarrassing to have Gladys wait on me, but I accept this. I don't know if I am supposed to offer to help, but fear I'd be intruding if I offer.

The day starts at seven o'clock, when the four-year-old wakes up with an upset stomach. He is sick and vomits several times. Great. We've been sleeping in close proximity to everyone, and whatever illnesses are going around are sure to affect all of us. Poor little guy—when he was sick, he would cry, and instead of getting a hug, he was given a spanking. Later, when he felt better, he threw a temper tantrum and was hugged until he calmed down. This is hard to watch. I know he needed affection when he was sick. Thankfully, we spend most of the day shopping and aren't around to see what else happens.

Later, we go to Homer Russell's place. Homer owns a taxi service and has one of the only phones in Kotzebue. I can call home and can hardly wait. This will be the first time I've heard their voices since I left for Alaska. When I reach Mom and Dad, I'm at a loss for words. There seems to be so much to say, but the miles between us don't help, and the reception is poor. I hear an echo every time I speak. When we start to have a meaningful conversation, a call comes through for the taxi and we are cut off. I suppose it's just as well. I might have cried if I'd been on the phone longer. I don't want them to know how homesick I am. They would worry, and they worry about me enough already.

Tiger and I spend the rest of the day shopping at the small general store. Canned goods line the shelves. It's difficult to find what we want, because the store is very small and filled with a mishmash of things. There are the usual staples—bread, eggs, coffee, and cigarettes. The prices shock me. Bread is $2.50 a loaf. Bread at home is thirty cents. Prices are inflated, probably because of the cost of shipping to Alaska. A pack of cigarettes is an exorbitant price, and I imagine my mother would probably quit smoking if she lived here. I wonder how the natives can afford bread and cigarettes.

I look through bolts of fabric, in search of something for curtains for the house. I want different material for a curtain to cover the shelving where we'll store our food when the cargo ship arrives. There's not much to choose from because most are calicos intended for parka covers. Nothing appeals to me. Finally, I find a blue and green floral pattern that will bring a little sunshine to the rooms during the dark winter days ahead. I find something plain for the shelving. It's the color of dry grass in summer, and though it doesn't match the curtains, I think it will work. I leave the store feeling happy to know I'll have a project to work on when we get home.

Back at Gladys's house, there is pandemonium.

"I smell smoke," I shout.

"You must be imagining things," Tiger says.

"I'm not. I know I smell smoke," I insist.

Just then, the church bells start to ring, and we leave Gladys's house to find out what's going on. It's a house fire. We rush out of the house and see flames rising from the roof of the house where the fire is. Probably, the fire can't be put out before the house is destroyed altogether.

Fighting fires is difficult in this part of Alaska because of the lack of available water. There is no way to pump ocean water up to the houses, most of which are made of wood and burn fast. I'm nervous thinking about all the wood houses in Kivalina and what could happen if a house fire happened there.

Tiger tries to help by holding the hose as men fight the fire, but it just rips through the building, and there is no way to stop it. Fortunately, no one was home when the fire occurred, but now the residents are homeless and will have to live with another family. Although conditions will be crowded, someone will take them in. The natives open their hearts and homes to those who are less fortunate. I'd like to think this would happen back home.

When we get back from the fire, I don't feel well. My stomach is in a turmoil. I must have the same thing as the four-year-old. I need to keep running to the makeshift toilet to be sick. I am sick from both ends. I feel miserable, and all I want to do is go back to Kivalina.

The wind is howling when we wake up the next morning, and I know we'll be here another day. Tiger and I leave the house to preserve our sanity, even though my stomach is still upset. I think he's as dismayed with the whole situation as I am, but he takes it in stride.

At one point when we were in the house, the three-year-old girl, Millie, peed all over the floor. She doesn't wear a diaper, and I suspect that this is the way the natives toilet train their children. Later, when I have children, my pediatrician tells me to let my child go outside without diapers, and I realize that this was the same method the natives used. At Gladys's, little Millie had a friend in the house with her and they tracked in the urine, so most of the house was wet with it. Gladys didn't even bother to clean up the floor. I know that we will probably put our mattresses on the floor that night and it would still not be washed. More than ever, I want a room at the hotel, but I know we can't. We'd risk losing the rapport we've established with the family, and Tiger is getting valuable information for his study.

On our third night in Kotzebue, we go to see a movie at the naval base, which isn't far from town. We both need to get away from the house. Just as we're getting back, Gladys and Russell are preparing to go to town. Gladys has the baby wrapped up tight inside her parka, and I know he'll be fast asleep. There's no sign of an adult around. Perhaps Gladys is expecting Lawrence to appear, or maybe she's hoping Tiger and I will look after the other two.

I hate seeing a parent putting their child at risk. The Eskimos seem to have a different outlook on child-rearing than Tiger and I do. We would never leave our kids alone or let them do some of the things these children are allowed to do. I watched the baby get put down on the edge of the bed. If he rolls, he could roll right off. A couple of times, Tiger and I adjusted the baby's position to keep him from falling. This morning, I saw Millie playing with a lighter and I was petrified she'd burn herself. I reached over to take the lighter away, but her father said, "It's okay. Just let her do what she wants." To top it off, Millie played with some of the things I had in my parka. Gladys knew what was happening but didn't stop her. Millie smashed my lipstick over my parka and over our mattress. I don't know how she managed to get my parka because it was out of reach of the children. There was a pen gun full of tear gas in my pocket, and I shudder to think what would have happened if it had gone off. Tiger wants me to have one ready for safety, but after staying at Gladys's house, it doesn't seem to be a good idea.

Privately, I say to Tiger, "I can live among these people and study their lives, but I can't live with them." Tiger calls me ethnocentric.

Finally, we leave. It's a cold trip home, but we're happy to be inside our own house again. It's warm, it's quiet, and it's clean. As I look back on the trip we just made, I understand why I had such a difficult time there. Gladys was my closest friend when she lived in the village. She seemed to be the most like me. I was disappointed to see the way she lives, but I can't impose my standards of cleanliness on the people here. We come from two very different worlds and I just have to accept it.

XVI

AFTER KOTZEBUE

For a couple of days after the trip to Kotzebue, I am sick. Tiger calls it the Kotzebue Crud, but it's more than that. It's my reaction to all the things that bother me. I have been swallowing my angst and pretending everything is all right. Does Tiger not even realize it's stress that's giving me headaches and making me sick?

I take it easy, and as I do, the work piles up. The drizzle and gray skies match my mood. The laundry can't be put off any longer. We didn't bring a lot of clothes with us, and if I don't do the laundry soon, we'll run out of clothes.

Tiger is off duck hunting with Amos. While he's gone, I do the laundry, scrub the floors, and sit down to make the curtains for the shelves. I'm excited to do this. It's something I've been looking forward to. I work the better part of the day to make them because everything is done by hand. When I finish, I hang the curtains over the shelves Tiger built and I step back to take a good look. I have a sinking feeling I don't really like the fabric.

When Tiger gets back from duck hunting, I watch for his reaction. He sees the curtains right away.

"Hmm, I see you made the curtains. Good job, but—"

"Yeah, I know. The color, the green is god-awful. It's almost snot green, isn't it? Do you think the lighting was bad in the store?"

I decide to ask Tiger's mom to send some new fabric up, sure she can find something we'll love. Anything would be an improvement over this. In the meantime, we make do with what we have.

Life here has changed me so much since our arrival. It seems strange to not care how I look anymore. When I first arrived, this seemed so important and in a way somewhat conceited. Here, baths are a precious commodity and I rarely wash my hair, using dry shampoo instead. The other night I tried to give myself a Toni home permanent because I suddenly grew tired of not caring and looking like the Wicked Witch of the North. Mom made it look so easy, but for me it was a bit of a disaster. My hair is long and now I have partially curly hair. I love the length though and won't let anyone cut it. When we go upriver, the wind blows through it and the windblown look almost gives me a sense of freedom—free to be me and not have to worry about what others think. So many things back home now seem superficial to me—the clothes I wore there, manicured nails, and lipstick. It's only occasionally that I do pay attention to my appearance, and besides that, Tiger never seems to notice. Toward the end of August, he tells me I have lost weight and says I look thin. This to me is quite a compliment.

Tiger is tanned from all the hunting and fishing he has done. He looks so contented and healthy. To see him this way, makes me happy to be in Kivalina because he was never relaxed when we lived in Chicago. I cut Tiger's hair for him all the time. He thinks it's fun to have his wife cut his hair. It's an easy task because he has a crew cut and it's one I enjoy doing for him. I may end up a permanent barber.

As the summer goes on, sometimes, we can feel the heat streaming through our windows. Other days are like the cold, windy ones we had in Kotzebue. One early morning, the thermometer hit seventy-five degrees. What a gift this was to me. I enjoy the warm weather and take every opportunity to relax outside. Sometimes I take a book and sit near the beach enjoying the sun. It's almost as good as being at the lake for the summer.

The warm weather motivates us to take Sarah Hawley and her children upriver to pick berries. It will be a few more days until they are ripe, but we manage to pick enough ripe berries to take home for dinner. Suddenly Sarah yells, "Come on! Let's get to the boat. I see a bear!" When we're safely on board, we look and see that Sarah has mistaken a crane for a bear.

It's beautiful upriver and the heat of the day is still with us. I'm annoyed and don't want to leave, but Sarah is nervous. The air is warm and the water is clear and suddenly, I have a mad desire to go for a swim. Weather permitting, we may go back by ourselves another day to swim.

Unfortunately, the warm weather doesn't last and instead of swimming upriver in my underwear, I go berry picking with Mildred Sage and a group of women from the village traveling in one of the skin boats. One man always comes along to drive the boat. A whole slew of kids come as well.

"Lots of berries to pick," Mildred says. We both see an abundance of blueberry bushes growing by the lagoon.

"We're going to have to work fast to pick them all," I tell her.

I love watching the older children scampering around and picking the berries. Their lips get blue as they pop berries into their mouths. They are adorable, and I decide to ask Tiger to give me a camera for Christmas. I am ready to learn, and I think he could teach me.

We work most of the afternoon, taking only a couple of breaks, and head home at sunset. The days are getting noticeably shorter and our time to work is limited. Occasionally, Tiger and I go berry picking by ourselves, but usually, I go in a skin boat with the women from the village and several of the children. It's a treat going on these expeditions with the women. With them, I feel as though I am a part of the village life. We take a thermos of coffee along for our breaks, chat for a while, and then go back to picking. Often, the women carry a baby in their parkas, and during the break, they might nurse the child and change its diaper. The infants are content in the parka and sleep most of the time. The women carry toddlers this way also, and sometimes, I see the child peeking out of the hood. I seldom hear a child crying.

The berries we pick on these outings taste just like the wild berries we get back home, although they are larger and plumper. It reminds me of my childhood summers at the lake picking berries. Back then, I could hardly wait until the berries were ripe enough to pick and was always proud when I had a pail full enough for my mother to make a pie. I feel a pang of homesickness as I think about those days. Right now, the berries growing at the end of the point would be ripe and the raspberries that grew near our cottage would be over for the season. Looking around, I realize that here, there are enough berries to last a winter for all of us. At home, we usually only picked enough for a couple of pies.

As I fill my bucket, I look forward to pies and oatmeal covered with the ripe fruit. The women will preserve the berries in seal oil for the winter. Tiger wants me to preserve them in seal oil too, but the thought of mixing oil and berries is not palatable to me. I figure that it won't be long before the first frost and tell him the berries will keep when it freezes. It will be so much nicer to have frozen berries than ones that are preserved in oil. I decide instead to put them in water and wait until they freeze.

Two weeks later, I'm sorry I didn't listen to Tiger. We have yet to see frost, and the berries have fermented in the water. If I had put them in the shed where it's cold, they would have been all right, but I didn't and now they're ruined. We have to dump them in the ocean.

Fortunately, there is more berry picking to do before the season is over and I intend to go on as many expeditions as possible to make up for the berries I ruined. Berry picking doesn't last as long as I hoped it would, but now we have enough berries to freeze and put away.

Taking a break during berry picking

There's a chill in the air, and upriver, the banks are covered with touches of crimson and yellow. Autumn comes quickly here, as it's only early September. Back home, when fall arrives in mid-October, the trees would be a kaleidoscope of colors—red, yellow, burgundy, and orange. There would be the smell of smoke from burning leaves and children would jump in the leaf piles left at the side of the road. Usually, the air would feel crisp; as the leaves fell, we could tell that winter was not far away.

It's beautiful here. The light still seems to shimmer with tiny crystals when we take these trips and, coming back in the boat, we enjoy the sunsets. I've never seen sunsets as vivid as these. The clouds dance across the sky in a rainbow of colors, and then the sky turns a blue velvet with thousands and thousands of stars—far more than we see even on the clearest of nights back home. We are waiting for the first frost, heralding the true beginning of fall. Tiger tells me that after the first frost, winter will make its appearance quickly. I'm not prepared. Already the days are getting shorter and the time when there is no daylight is something I'm dreading.

XVII
MY GIFT

Sarah seems to welcome my visits unlike the first time I tried to visit. Sitting with me at her kitchen table, she watches the children and usually lights a cigarette as we chat about our lives together. I sip her acidic coffee, which I am now used to and have even started to like. One day while visiting, Bobby is there. I comment on the beautiful puppy that they have. The puppy is about six weeks old—a gray ball of fluff with silver tipping at the ends of her coat. Bobby says she's part wolf. As I play with her, Bobby surprises me by offering me the dog as a gift from him.

I can't believe that he would give me this puppy as a present! "Bobby," I say, "you're not joking, are you? I would love to have her. I'll ask Tiger."

I hurry back to our place and tell Tiger that Bobby offered me a puppy. "Do you think he's joking?"

"If Bobby told me you could have the dog as a gift, his offer is genuine," he assures me. Tiger doesn't encourage me to take the pup, but he doesn't say I shouldn't take it, either.

I'm excited. This dog will be mine. I'll have her for company when Tiger is away. We pick up the dog the next day and I carry her back to the house and bury my face in her soft coat. I love her already.

"You know the dog can't stay in the house with us, don't you?" Tiger asks when we get back home with the dog.

"Why? She's mine, and I want her in the house to keep me company."

Tiger has other ideas, however. He has noticed what a sturdy pup she is, and now that he has seen her, his eyes are on her for another dog on the team. I think he may even have designs on her for a leader. She will sleep with the other dogs, but I can take her on walks with me the way I used to take Pepper and Coco. I decide that if he wants my puppy to lead the team, she'll need a sexy name. I think of showgirls and champagne, and so we name her Bubbles. Bubbles howls for a while after we bring her home, and I take her into the house with me. Once she settles down, I take her outside and she tries to play with the other dogs, but they ignore her. Even though she is going to be a sled dog, I'm going to spoil her just a little. After all, she's a gift to me.

Deanne with Bubbles

XVIII

DRINKING IN THE VILLAGE

Today, we take the dogs when we go upriver to get water and do some fishing. We bundle up against the chill, and despite the cold, it's lovely. With every day, the light is noticeably shorter. Darkness will descend upon us too soon. I loved the days when the sun never set, but the beauty of the sunsets makes up for the shorter days. The skies are painted with deep pink and lavender, and the vivid colors are reflected in the water.

Of the three dogs we have with us, Coco is still the most adventurous. Tiger points out that because of Coco's fearlessness, he'll make a good sled dog. Bubbles is growing fast, but I doubt she will be part of the team this winter. How I wish she could be a pet for me and not part of the team.

This day, alone together, is one to treasure. The air is pristine and the water, as always, sparkles in the sun. We have a lunch of homemade bread and peanut butter. The peanut butter is shipped up to us from the Safeway in Fairbanks and is a staple for us. Sitting on the riverbank, we talk about the days ahead.

"We're so lucky to have this boat," I say. "We've been able to do so much and there's still so much I want to see before it freezes."

"Speaking of doing things, fish camp is only a couple of weeks away. I'm going to take the boat upriver to the place where we will camp and fish with the Hawley crew. You can come along to help Sarah cook if you want. It'll get you away from the village."

Tiger has told me a little about fish camp. The river is full of fish now, and the men use this time to prepare for the winter ahead. They will go out during the day with long nets to catch the fish. Each man will make a cache of fish for dog food and will be able to go upriver to get it, when needed.

"I'd love to see how fish camp operates. You sure it'll be alright?" I say. "I'll go if it's okay with the Hawleys."

When I say yes to something, I'm always a bit apprehensive about what I will be getting myself into, but I don't like staying alone either. Lately, the natives have been talking about the wild people, known in this part of the Arctic as Enuchen. Nobody sees them, but they are said to steal things and create a lot of mischief. Some of the villagers believe that they are wild Indians, and others think they are some sort of supernatural being. Whatever they are, everybody is afraid of them. The natives talk about them frequently and say they are more apt to play their tricks at this time of the year. Having been partially raised by a psychic and superstitious grandmother, I believe these spirits, or whatever they are, exist. Usually, Tiger believes everything that the Eskimos talk about. For some reason he doesn't believe in the Enuchen, and tells me not to worry.

Tiger and I drop our lines and both of us catch a fish. Tiger misses the challenge. "It's boring fishing here," he says. "All we have to do is drop our line in."

With that, we decide to go. We dip the fresh water into our oil drum and head back to the village. The peaceful mood that we found upriver remains with us as we walk from the beach to our house. It's late afternoon, and we don't see anybody walking around, which is unusual. The village is eerily quiet.

At home, we fill our drum with the fresh water we brought back with us. I'll clean and fry the fish we caught and open a can of green beans for dinner. Before dinner, Tiger will light the kerosene lamp. We need to use the lamps by about four p.m. these days. I long for the summer days when the sun never set and the lanterns never had to be lit. Tiger will work on his notes, and

I'll read or work on the sweater I'm knitting. It will be a quiet ending to a happy day. I hope no one comes to visit tonight.

Looking out the window, I see several men staggering past. Tiger warned me about this, and I prayed we would never witness drinking in the village. I shudder at the sight. Thank heaven Tiger is home right now. I call Tiger to the window and it's obvious he wants to go out immediately. We wonder how long the drinking has been going on and how many men are drunk. Maybe it was going on in all the houses, and the reason why it was so quiet when we pulled our boat up on shore.

Just then, there's a knock at the door. I'm afraid to answer it, but do, to find Emmaline, a woman who lives a few houses away. She looks frantic, and I ask her in for tea.

"The men are drinking," she says. "There's been a fight in the village. The men who aren't drunk have hidden all the guns. After the guns were taken, it was quiet for a while, but the drinking has started again, and it's not going to be quiet much longer." Emmaline doesn't stay long. She only came to warn us of the situation.

Now Tiger is more than ready to go out and observe. He's interested in seeing the social control when there's a fight because it's an important part of his study.

"Please don't go, Tiger," I say, reaching out to hold his arm. I know I'm being selfish, but I don't want to stay in the house by myself. "I'm terrified of being alone with so many drunks around."

Tiger stays, but I know he's itching to be out where the action is. Soon, we hear dogs barking and he leaves to locate the disturbance. Tiger runs back to tell me what he learned. Jimmy Hawley, Bobby Hawley's nephew, arrived from Kotzebue, bringing liquor with him. He went to our boat, untied it, and before anyone could stop him, he jumped in it and started to drive around in a frenzy.

Tiger leaves with the men who are sober, hoping to stop Jimmy. I stay home with my doors locked, wondering what's going on. I'm scared to death and hope none of the drunks come here. When a knock comes on the door, I'm terrified to answer it.

"Let me in. Let me in." It's Sarah Hawley. I open the door and quickly close and lock it.

"Is Bobby here?" Sarah asks. She tells me that there was a fight in the village and Jimmy had a knife. He said he might kill someone with it, and the men got it away from him. "I hope one of them other drunks don't have it now," she says.

I tell her Bobby isn't here and explain what Tiger is doing.

Sarah's concerned. "I hoped Bobby wasn't out there drinking, but I guess he is. I wish he was with Tiger. I'm afraid of Bobby when he drinks. He's mean, and he beats and kicks me."

"Do you want to stay here?" I ask Sarah, seeing the look of fear on her face.

"No, I want to know where Bobby is so I can hide from him."

She doesn't stay long. She's heading someplace she thinks will be safe. She would have been fine here, but maybe she thought our place was one of the first places Bobby would go. Bobby easily could have come here thinking that we would offer his wife refuge, and all hell would have broken loose. On second thought, she might not have been safe here and I might not have been either.

My nerves are on edge. I didn't know Jimmy had a knife, and I am afraid some of the other men might have knives on them as well. I hear the wind rising as Sarah leaves, and I worry about the men in the boats. It's pitch black and the boats don't have lights. I say a quiet prayer for them all to return in one piece.

The teachers will be home, and I run the short distance to the Keatings' place. Tonight, it feels like miles. Nobody will go there, except perhaps some of the other women who want a safe place. I don't leave a note for Tiger but assume that he'll know I've gone to the only house where I'll feel protected.

After a couple of hours, Tiger comes to get me. He's boiling mad. "Jimmy managed to pull up the anchor on our boat. He raced around in it, crashing into the boat I was in. Now, our boat has a big hole in it and will be out of commission until next spring."

The Keatings are listening to Tiger as well, and Jim says, "You should report him. Maybe punishment will stop this type of thing from happening again."

"I can't," Tiger tells him. "Jimmy is related to the most important families in the village. I don't want to ruin our relationship with them."

Back at our house, Tiger and I lie awake talking, afraid Jimmy might come to our place. Every time we hear a sound, we pray it's not him.

"The whole village knows Jimmy's broken the law. If I weren't so afraid of ruining my friendship with Bobby, I would report him. Bobby knows Jimmy has broken the law too, but families stick together in this sort of thing," Tiger says.

"I still think you should report him, but it's your decision. Regardless, the whole village will soon know what he's done."

I toss and turn, thinking about the drinking here. It's terrible to see the native people drink. When they do, they seem to release all of their pent-up rage and anxiety, and the wives take the brunt of it. The children are the innocent victims because they all know what's going on and aren't sheltered from anything. It's a normal part of their lives, handed down from generation to generation. I pray the liquor is gone. If it happens again, I'm afraid there may be a serious accident, or even a death. Knives were wielded, guns were taken away, and women lived in fear of being beaten. Thank goodness the worst thing that happened, so far anyway, was the hole in our boat. It could have been so much more devastating. I pass the night without much sleep and although Tiger is quiet, I doubt that he is sleeping either.

Walking around the village this morning, I hear via the grapevine there is a council meeting tonight. I think that Jimmy should be punished but doubt this will happen. Most of the council is related to him. Tiger's relationship with the Hawleys is still intact, and we'll be going to fish camp with them sometime next week.

Finally, after the council meeting, Tiger lodges a complaint because nothing was mentioned at the meeting about the hole in our boat. They tell Tiger a warning will be issued to Jimmy, since this was his first offense. Tiger says that this is okay, but I wonder if we issue a complaint not directed toward anyone, whether the council would pay any attention to it. Jimmy has broken the law, wrecked a boat, and brought liquor into the village, creating havoc for the weekend. I don't think it's enough. He is only given a warning and doesn't have to fix our boat or pay for the damages.

"Tiger, I can't believe you are going to sit back and accept this. Relative or not, he broke the law. He should never have gotten off with only a warning. If he was punished in some concrete way, an example would have been set for the rest of the village. I don't even want to go to fish camp with the Hawleys. Bobby is on the council, and he's just as guilty as the rest because he was drinking too."

"You don't have to go."

"Well, I don't want to stay here. The men might start drinking again and I would be alone. What else has to happen before they learn their lesson?"

XIX

FISH CAMP

Without the use of our own boat anymore, we are once again dependent on others. There are thirteen in our party as we head upriver to a place where the men go fishing. We share two small tents. Bobby, Sarah, their two children, and Tiger and I sleep in one tent. The rest of the crew—all men—sleep in the other.

Most of my time at fishing camp is spent cooking and cleaning for thirteen people, no easy task, though Sarah prefers to do the cooking herself. She thinks white people cook differently and I have to agree. I would never cook Arctic char for over an hour. Arctic char is a lot like salmon in taste, and overcooking makes it lose its flavor. After the men fish all day and bring home part of their catch for us to cook, Sarah puts it into the wood stove they brought and bakes it for at least an hour with no way to gauge the oven temperature. The fish is dry and crusty, but can be moistened with seal oil. There is no seasoning, not even salt or pepper, to improve the taste.

When I'm not helping Sarah, I try to knit without much light in the tent. I'm working with a difficult pattern and decide my attempts to do this are futile. There's not enough light to read either, so I spend most of the time watching the family dynamics.

Lizzie Anne who accompanied us to fish camp

Sarah spends a lot of time with the children. I'd be happy to help, but Sarah doesn't seem to want my assistance. She probably feels that she shouldn't ask me, and I'm too shy and inexperienced in raising children to ask. Lizzie Anne is still being nursed and cries whenever she is put down. When she has finished nursing Lizzie, Sarah chews dried fish or fish left over from the day before and feeds it to her little girl directly from her mouth, like a mother bird feeding her baby. Baby food is not sold in the store and there is no way to puree any of the food here. It's fascinating to watch. I'm learning more and more about ways of survival among the natives and continue to gain respect for them.

We don't leave the tent except when it is necessary. Sarah is nervous about bears and the Enuchen. I stay in the tent with her, as her fears have become some of my own as well. When I do leave the tent, I am on the lookout for a bear or for the wild people and have no idea what the landscape looks like around here.

The men come home hungry and tired. They eat in the other tent, away from Sarah and me. They usually talk and laugh as they fill their bellies with the food that Sarah prepared for them. Tonight the men are silent as they eat, unlike the other nights. I ask Sarah why the men are so quiet and she puts a finger to her mouth, warning me not to say anything.

When Bobby and Sarah are asleep and Tiger and I are in our sleeping bags, he whispers to me. "The men sat with their backs against the tent tonight because they thought they heard the Enuchen outside and hoped they could ward off the enemy by doing this. I didn't believe in these people or whatever they are, but I sure do now. Do you hear that rustling outside?"

I didn't. But I don't sleep well that night, or any other. Sometimes, I fall asleep and wake up to find Sarah's four-year-old lying on top of me, practically suffocating me. Another night, I wake up to diapers on my pillow and all I can say is, I'm relieved they are clean. The baby wakes in the night to be nursed, and the two men snore, ignoring the night music.

In turn, we haven't been the best roommates for Bobby and Sarah. Bubbles is with us, as she is too young to leave at home with the other dogs. She sleeps all day and wanders into the tent at night, wanting to play with us. This probably hasn't gone over well, but we think it's funny. We have managed to get her to sleep at our feet or in between the two of us. So much for not spoiling our dog.

We spend four days at camp because the cargo ship *North Star* is about to arrive, and the entire village has to be there for that. The ship will be delivering food and other things to the village and there is always great excitement when it comes.

The men have been successful with their fishing, although they have to spend a few more days like this in about two weeks to make sure there will be enough fish for the dogs over the winter. Tiger will go with them, a thought I dread, because I have decided not to go with them and will be alone. I am glad I went to fish camp. I learned a lot there, and Tiger is thankful to have fish for the months ahead.

XX

THE VILLAGE CLOSES IN

Suddenly, the village has closed in on me. I never thought that living here would cause me so much anguish. Every time I do something that makes me uncomfortable, I get sick to my stomach. Fish camp is no exception. Although I never thought in any detail about living here, I am beginning to believe that I am too emotionally immature to be living this way. I think about this and wonder if our married life is headed for disaster. Although from time to time the study is going well, Tiger has been disappointed with its progress. In many ways I have helped the research. Visiting with the women, and participating in their activities, has enabled me to give Tiger a lot of information about what it feels like to be a woman in Kivalina. Still, I find myself worrying that I'm holding him back because I can't seem to adapt to village life. I have one foot in city life, in the life I left behind in the lower forty-eight.

After our return from fish camp, the pressure takes its toll on me. I'm swallowing the stress and getting sick from it. Two or three times I have been violently ill and in excruciating pain. Tiger sits up with me all night. Lately, I've been plagued by headaches, which I know are from anxiety as well. Tiger thinks I should go home for a while and reluctantly, I agree.

Jim Keating makes a reservation for me to go as far as Chicago. I don't know where I'll go from there. I don't know if either set of parents are home—mine or Tiger's. I can't go crashing in on my brother David and his wife, with their new baby, and I doubt if I would be welcome at a friend's. I worry that if I leave, I will lose my marriage. My mother's words ring in my ears. "Alaska will either make or break your life together." I may never come back if I leave, and Tiger will be too proud to come and get me. Do I want it to end this way?

As I throw my stuff into my suitcase, I realize leaving isn't the right thing to do. Running away doesn't solve anything, and I would never forgive myself if something happened to Tiger without me here. He wants, and he needs, me to stay here. Besides, I love him, and maybe that's the only thing that counts. The *North Star* is due any day now and I should be here to help Tiger with the things we ordered. I know that I'm doing the right thing.

XXI

THE *NORTH STAR* ARRIVES

Before we left for Alaska, Tiger told me the natives only eat what they have prepared and stored. After hearing this, I wondered if we should be ordering food from the *North Star*, the cargo ship that brings food to the village, or if we should go totally native and live off native food all winter. Thankfully, Tiger is a bit of a foodie, and he wanted to eat things besides the native diet, and so together we came up with this list.

The *North Star* arrives in September, which meant I had to order food for an entire winter practically six months ahead of time. I did this the best I could, though shopping for an entire winter is a monumental task. Sugar, salt, yeast, butter, and canned goods were certain items on the list, and so was toilet paper. But how much toilet paper would be enough? The list of items seemed endless, and as the arrival date grew closer, I wondered if what I had ordered was adequate.

I am excited about the cargo ship's arrival. Duck soup, caribou stew and stroganoff, seal liver, and fish have been our main diet since we arrived here four months ago. Cooking canned tuna fish a different way each time we eat it has tested my culinary skills. Now, those challenges will be gone and we'll have a house full of food.

The worst thing about this would be hiding what we had bought from the rest of the village. Tiger didn't want anyone to know that we could afford to buy and store all of this food. He built the shelves so our food could be hidden behind the curtain I made. He's naïve to think that they won't find out.

The arrival of the cargo ship, the *North Star*, is a special occasion. The whole village goes out to meet the ship, excited to know the store will soon be well stocked. The women dress in their prettiest and brightest parka covers. They're smiling and chattering amongst themselves while the children play and watch the ship unload the cargo.

It's been hard to connect with the women in the village, and yet, after seeing them dressed up for the arrival of the *North Star*, I realize we're not as different as I once thought. Tiger says the Eskimo women are used to white women coming into their homes and telling them they live in filth and squalor. No wonder they hesitate to invite me into their homes. They're also self-conscious about their inability to speak English well. They should be proud of their language and of the fact they can speak English at all. Their language is entirely foreign to me.

The women here seem to have the impression that all white women do is sit around, look beautiful, and have a good time. They feel we are snobs and wouldn't stoop to do the kind of work they do. Several have said to me, "White women don't do this type of work. Let me scrub the floor for you." I was embarrassed to hear them say that to me and of course rejected their offer. In truth, when it was time to cut up seals, I wish someone had said, "White women don't cut up seals. Let me do this for you." I think they were so astonished it never occurred to them.

Where do these notions come from? Many of the women here don't read. The only magazine I've seen in any house is *True Confessions*, which is full of photos of beautiful women who have time to have a secret life. The women here barely have time to finish their own chores.

I am becoming aware of the many ways that the missionaries who brought Christianity to the north have forced their beliefs on the natives here. The missionaries came in 1910, Christianizing the natives all over Northwest Alaska. Who are they to say that the way they live is better than the way the natives here once lived? The missionaries have taken much of their culture away from them.

Unhealthy aspects of our culture have influenced life here as well. The native diet and lifestyle, for example, was healthy until sugar, cigarettes, and alcohol were introduced to them by white people. Now, alcohol is rampant in the villages. For thousands of years, the Eskimos survived in the harshest of climates imaginable, depending on their hunting prowess to live. Not many non-natives could have done this. I am beginning to understand why Tiger wants to study these people and learn more about life as it used to be here. There is so much to learn.

* * *

Children enjoying swings (probably spring of 1965)
By the time North Star arrived, it was already cold and days were getting shorter

The *North Star* left early this morning. Now, it's damp and chilly and as I look out to the schoolyard, to see a crowd of children. To my surprise, the children are playing on swings and slides.

"Tiger look what just arrived! I'm going over to see what's going on."

The *North Star* has been like a fairy godmother, transforming the barren earth into a fantasy land. I watch the children as they try to pump their legs so the swings soar high into the air. The looks of delight on their faces as they try out the slide for the first time is something that I'll remember forever. There is even a teeter-totter, and it's fun to watch the little ones learn to balance on it.

Dorothy Keating comes out to chat as I watch the children playing. She tells me paint and soap bubbles have arrived as well, and the children will be using them for the first time. Blowing bubbles was one of my favorite pastimes as a child. What joy it will be to see the kids enjoy some of the simple pleasures of life we take for granted.

As I talk to Dorothy, I understand how difficult teaching here must be. The school has one room and goes from kindergarten to eighth grade. Some children leave the village to attend more school, but for the majority, eighth grade is the end of any formal education. The readers used in school here discuss aspects of privileged life that most of the economically deprived in the lower forty-eight are aware of. The first grade reader is the one I used: Dick and Jane. I still remember the words. "See Spot run. Run Spot, run." Pets don't exist. Dogs work. I've never seen a cat wandering around the village. A milkman, for example, is mentioned in the first-grade reader. Up here, milk doesn't come in bottles. It's not delivered and comes only in cans. I can't imagine how the children can relate to the readers they are given but maybe they are the only readers available. Their world is totally different from the world they read about.

Education in a one-room schoolhouse

Two days after the *North Star* arrives with all of its goodies to distribute, the excitement has died down. For the children, the novelty of the playground hasn't worn off; they play there from sunrise to sunset. It's wonderful to see their enjoyment. The store is stocked and we have put our food away. It's time to get back to reality.

Tiger announces he's going to fish camp soon. He'll be gone four days. "I hate to leave you alone," he says, "but we don't have enough fish for the winter." He tells me I can come along, but as much as I don't want to stay in the house alone, I don't want to go to fish camp. It was too stressful last time, with the diapers on top of my sleeping bag, and cooking with Sarah. Her fear of the Enuchen also infiltrated into my thinking.

With Tiger away at fish camp, I find that my four days alone are not as bad as I thought they would be. The Keatings invite me over for a delicious meal and good conversation. Mildred Sage comes over to check on me every day. She's a good neighbor, one I can count on. She loves to gossip, too, and I get all sorts of tidbits about village life.

When I don't have a visitor, or don't go visiting myself, I spend my time reading, writing letters to home, and knitting. The days drag, but I have time to reflect. I decide not to let things bother me as much as I have been. If I'm happier, Tiger will be too. I make a promise to myself to try to be a better person and a better wife to Tiger. I resolve to get over my fear of lighting a Coleman lantern. With the days getting shorter, the lamps are on most of the time and my fear of lighting them has become an issue.

Tiger returns, glad to see that my morale has improved. He looks as though a burden has been lifted from his shoulders.

* * *

October arrives, and the air is bitterly cold. The sky is clear and blue, and the limited sunlight casts an array of colors on the ice, making it sparkle like an opal. The lagoon is frozen. People walk across it from the village. I love the idea of having a pair of ice skates and skating across this clear swath of ice. Of course, there are no skates here in the village. I can't help but think what fun it would be to be able to ski across this flat land, but there are no cross-country skis here either.

It's a sunny day, and Tiger suggests we cross the ice. We wear mukluks and heavy clothing to ward off the chill. The ice is slippery, and I feel apprehensive as I slip and slide across it. It's work trying to keep up with Tiger and I'm sweating with the effort. He is more used to this than I am, and he is heavier. The wind starts to whip across the ice, and I am practically blown across to the other side.

Tiger sees the weather as an opportunity to take the pups out for the first time. Bubbles is still young, and she refuses to go on the ice. Tiger doesn't force her. Pepper and Coco are frightened. We drag Pepper across the ice by his collar and he yelps with fear all the way. Coco is characteristically more adventurous than the other dogs, and he falls into a hole someone has made to get water. He clutches the side of the ice with his paws and Tiger pulls him out to find his coat is frozen and his paws have big clumps of ice clinging to them. We have to get the ice off his paws before we cross the lagoon again, or he'll have trouble walking. In time, Coco's fearlessness will teach him many lessons. Tiger thinks Coco's boldness will make him a good sled dog, possibly even a team leader.

The wind changes as we make our way back across the ice. It is blowing from the northeast, and Tiger tells me that our house will be cold because of this. At home, the stove is chugging away, but it doesn't warm the house at all. Tiger tacks a blanket over the door to act as a wind barrier, but even this doesn't help much. It doesn't bode well for the winter. When the temperatures drop to well below zero, it will be difficult to keep warm.

XXII

NEW EXPERIENCES

Before we came here, I imagined the two of us forging a new life together. Five months later, I have to wonder if I really know Tiger, and if he really knows me. Sometimes I think that if we talked together more, I wouldn't get sick or have the headaches that plague me from time to time. These days, we never seem to talk about anything but his study.

Except for early in the morning and late at night, we always have company. The men who visit completely ignore me. I'm left out of conversations, even when I'm in the room with them. This is a cultural thing, and I doubt that I ever will adapt to it. If I do, it will mean that I have lost my identity and become like a native woman. For now, this mght be a good thing because I still seem to have one foot planted in my life at home, and because of this, I am not fully immersed in village life.

It's mid-October, and the time has come for Tiger to make the sled he's talked about since we moved here. He hires an experienced carpenter to do all the difficult work while he saws and planes the wood. He spends most of his time working on his sled—in the living room. The sled takes up most of the space there, as it will be at least six feet long, and our living room is only twice that length. Men from the village drop in often to see how Tiger's doing. They love seeing a white man work like an Eskimo. Occasionally, they offer welcome advice.

For three weeks, Tiger does virtually nothing besides work on the sled and the dog harnesses. He's discouraged; he thought it would only take two weeks of work. Still, he's confident the sled will be sturdy once it's done.

Edith arrives at the house from time to time and these visits come as a surprise. I didn't think she liked me. Over the last few weeks, she has visited several times, bringing her knitting along (she's making a pair of socks). She sits on the couch, appearing to seem quite at home here now. Her English is good—she was raised by schoolteachers who spoke English fluently—and she keeps up with current affairs by listening to her transistor radio.

Edith is a private, crusty old lady, but she is more knowledgeable than most. "What do you think is going to happen in Vietnam?" she asks one day.

I'm amazed she's interested in this. I tell her I think that what's happening in Vietnam is scary. I listen to the news as much as I can. Tiger and I haven't discussed the war for some time. I worry that he's still considering enlisting. I'm afraid to ask, but it weighs heavily on my mind.

Edith's knitting needles click away. "I heard from Mr. Keating that Goldwater is a better man than Johnson. I wonder who is going to win the election. We natives usually vote Democrat. I'm going to." She doesn't ask me how I am going to vote and I'm glad. I would have to explain to her that I am a Canadian and can't vote right now.

I look forward to Edith's visits. She is so intelligent and aware of things outside the village. I want to talk with her about her childhood and her upbringing, but I need to gain her trust first, I know that. From everything I've heard about her, she's led a fascinating life and I'd like to know more, not only for Tiger's study but simply because I like her. She's an inspiration to me.

"You know, Edith isn't in good shape financially," Tiger tells me one day after Edith has visited. "She wanders from house to house, trying to keep warm. I'm sure that's why she's here a lot."

"I don't care why she visits me so much. I like her. I admire her stubbornness. She's a survivor." I tell Tiger, too, that I think Edith gained respect for me when I cut up the seals with her.

"I never really thought about that," Tiger says. "You probably did."

I want to feel a part of the community, and a great way to do it is to volunteer to cook at the school lunches on Wednesdays. The first week I was supposed to cook, I was sick. Tiger went over and explained to the woman I was cooking with why I couldn't be there. He even tried to get a sub for me.

I went the following week and apologized again for my absence. The woman shrugged and didn't try to engage me in conversation. In fact, she totally ignored me. For three of the four weeks I have been at the school cooking, I do it without help. No one seems interested in preparing the food with me. It's frustrating and depressing. No matter how hard I try, most of the women want to avoid me. Tiger suggests I quit if it's bothering me so much. Finally, I decide to speak to Dorothy Keating about it.

"You know, I don't mind doing the work alone," I tell her. "It's not even that difficult. I just think the woman who is supposed to be working with me is shirking her responsibilities. It seems as though she is taking advantage of me."

"This is a constant problem around here. It's magnified because you're white, and you're looked on as a free handout. She knows that you'll be responsible enough to show up, so she doesn't feel she has to."

"That may be true, but I also think she's intimidated by me. I don't think she wants to work with me," I say. "I'm not sure any of the women want to. It's discouraging because it's important to me to be a part of village life. Anyway, I'm quitting."

Dorothy nods her head in agreement. "I don't blame you at all, but if you want to help out again, I would be glad to have you back. I hope that I can get someone to take your place."

As the days go on, I feel lonelier than ever. I'm not doing anything to help the community. Maybe I should have ignored the situation and kept helping instead of taking it to heart. I'm grateful there are women here like Ruth, Sarah, and Mildred, women who are willing to be my friend. I miss Gladys and despite our differences, wish she lived here still. It's strange that so many of the women my age seem to avoid me.

Adult education classes start in early November, held in the school room on Monday nights. Jim Keating is teaching. I decide to sit in on his class on government and voting. The 1964 presidential election is just weeks away.

At one of the class meetings, Jim says that no one can influence people in how to vote, and he instructs the students to stop him if he sounds biased in any way. He tells us that if he had voted in the last election he would have voted for Kennedy, but he has no use for Johnson. I consider speaking up—his comment could influence the people who are attending—but I don't think it's my place. After all, I'm not enrolled as a student, I'm only an observer. He almost sounds as though he is trying to persuade them to vote for Goldwater. Isn't he biased and don't the natives understand this?

Besides the adult education classes, there are also first aid and sewing classes offered and a curriculum that gives older villagers an opportunity to get an eighth-grade education. I want to help with the sewing classes, but Jim Keating prefers trying to get a woman in from Nome to help. If he can't get her, he says he'll teach the class himself. If I help teach, he believes my presence will hinder his program. How ridiculous! He probably realizes that I know far more about sewing than he does.

Whether or not they're aware of it, sewing is one of the ways women here express their creativity. They make beautiful fur parkas and mukluks. With encouragement, they could start a business. Jim looks at their work as purely mechanical.

He is not like anyone I have ever known. He mentioned the other day he has no use for anyone living east of the Mississippi. This statement seemed to be pointed right at Tiger and me, although Tiger was not present. We both grew up east of the Mississippi. Not only did I grow up east of the Mississippi, I grew up in Canada and I bet he doesn't a lot about it. Possibly he is threatened by our presence because we know as much as he does; he is not the only one with all the knowledge. I hate these remarks but ignore them. What good would it do?

The first-aid course promises to be interesting. The midwives here will do a presentation on childbirth, which I'll record and have it translated into English. The presentation will be beneficial to the study because it will demonstrate the way that birthing takes place here. I want to learn about the birthing experience here so that I can help if I ever have to.

XXIII

OUT WITH OUR DOG TEAM

The days are getting shorter as we near the end of October. We now have more twilight than daylight, and it seems as though each day is getting shorter. When the weather is nice, the surroundings are beautiful. There is ice in the lagoon now, but the wind has swept away the snow. It reflects the blues, peaches, and lavenders of the evening sky. The ocean is not frozen and the ice piles on the beach are the color of dusk. Bubbles and I often walk along the beach, and I enjoy the breathtaking beauty of this untamed wilderness. It's another world to explore and enjoy. I've never experienced this kind of magnificence in the city. I may be lonely, but I am lucky to be here.

At the house, the sound of hammering and sawing has become a constant part of our life. The sled still isn't finished, and Tiger says he needs another week on it. Boxes are strewn all over the place, and the floor is thick with sawdust. The mess that it's making in the house will all be worth it when the sled is finally finished. We're planning a getaway upriver right after Thanksgiving.

Meanwhile, men in the village have taken their teams out several times already. Tiger is itching to go out. Finally, he borrows a sled so he can see how the dogs work together. I can hardly wait to go as it will be my first dog sled ride.

We have eight dogs, a mangy looking group, all of them mutts. This is common here, as it turns out; working dogs are typically mixed breeds. I had imagined that we'd have a handsome team of Siberian huskies or malamutes; photos I've seen of the North Country have always shown beautiful teams of dogs pulling the sleds. But they're strong dogs; they can pull a sled with hundreds of pounds of weight on it. Some of our dogs have German shepherd in them, some are part malamute, and most are mixed with Siberian husky.

As Tiger is hitching up the dogs, Bubbles prances around in her excited state and is caught under the runner of the sled. It's a wonder she isn't killed. If the snow hadn't been so soft, she would have died immediately. We leave her at home, worried we'll find her seriously hurt or dead when we come back, although she seemed fine when we left.

We take off, but we aren't moving at a high speed. Tiger chose Chipper as his leader and it's obvious that this was the wrong decision. Suddenly the dogs become tangled up in their harnesses. I'm thrown off the sled and stand in the snow watching the dogs fighting with each other. It's frightening to see how fierce they are. One of the dogs, Star, has a bloody muzzle. I'm afraid one of them will get killed. This is dreadful to watch, and I'm grateful we left Bubbles at home.

Tiger is swearing like a trooper, whipping the dogs. I've never heard some of the words he uses and I'm so nervous now I'm on the verge of hysterical laughter. "Cocksucker!" he yells. "Goddamn mother fucking dogs!" All of this is so out of character.

It's horrible to see Tiger beating the dogs. He hates doing it too, he loves animals. As minutes pass, Tiger's shouting gets louder and louder, and I am getting more frightened, and then, suddenly, the whole thing is over. The dogs seem to have calmed down, but Tiger is exhausted from his ordeal. He looks like he might pass out, so he rests for a while before he climbs back on the sled to try again. This time, Chipper is more focused on being a leader, and the trip is successful. Despite the difficult beginning, the feeling of being on a trail alone with the dogs and the countryside is exhilarating.

Later, when we get home, Tiger ties the dogs up to the stakes. There is a furor as he gives them their food of dried fish. They get their water from the snow. Bubbles comes running up to us and we are relieved to see that she isn't hurt.

We go inside to get warm and sit down on the couch together in our small living room. I take his hand. "I probably should have waited to go along with you, let you have a chance to take the team out the first time by yourself. It was frightening to see you whip and scream at the dogs."

"I didn't like it any better than you did. But the team was fighting and I was sure that Star was going to be killed. If I hadn't stopped the fighting, he might be dead."

"But whipping them? Did you have to do that?"

"Whipping's the only way to control these animals. Hopefully, they learned a lesson and I won't have to do it again."

Tiger is training Coco to be a leader, and he thinks in time, Bubbles will make a good leader too. Somehow, my puppy has turned into his dog. Tiger is anxious to take the dogs out as soon as possible, and two days later, he borrows a sled for our second ride. We're dressed for the excursion, both of us wearing long underwear, jeans, an extra pair of socks under our mukluks, and down parkas with a woolen hat under our fur hoods.

It's beautiful today; the sky is tinged with pinks and purples with the remnants of daylight. The air shimmers with tiny ice crystals. The cold is biting and it's difficult to take in air through my nose. My lungs hurt with each breath, but it's magical being out again on a trail with the dogs.

Tiger was right to show the dogs who was boss the last time we were out. The dogs are working more as a unit now. He borrowed a good leader from one of the men here, and it's much better. This dog knows what "gee" (turn right) and "haw" (turn left) mean. He is old, obstinate, and not happy with his new master, but we're told this is natural.

We climb onto the sled. I take a seat and Tiger stands on the back on the runners. We're the only people on the trail—if we're on the trail at all. I can't even tell if we are still on the island; I have lost all sense of direction. There are vast stretches of white and the only sound is the runners of the sled and the panting of the dogs. I feel like we're on a roller coaster as the sled twists and turns through the high snow. I could be thrown off the sled any minute. Despite the frigid weather, I love it. I understand Tiger's fascination with the sport. There's only one woman here who drives a dog team. Perhaps, I'll be another, though I couldn't be as forceful as Tiger.

At home again after the ride, we tend to the dogs and change clothes. After we warm up, Tiger starts to paint the sled. I realize the date suddenly—it's Halloween. How could I have forgotten? At home, the children will be out in their costumes running from door to door to get their bags filled with candies. They will all have costumes on—some princesses, some black cats and witches, some pirates, or dragons. Fortunately, we have candy and popcorn put away in case we get trick-or-treaters.

A knock comes on the door and we open it to find four of the older boys in the village standing there, their faces painted black. They are the same boys who visited me in the summer.

Tiger says, "You want something?"

Sheepishly, they mutter, "It's Halloween."

It's obvious they don't know how to trick or treat, but they know we will have something to give them. We hand out the candies and popcorn, and they happily go on their way to their next stop—undoubtedly the teachers' house. As it turns out, those boys are our only Halloween visitors. I imagine no one has taught the kids here about Halloween and the tradition of costumes. There's no party at the school, nothing to mark the day. Did the missionaries teach the Eskimos that Halloween is a pagan holiday and shouldn't be celebrated?

* * *

Before Halloween, Tiger asked Mildred to make a parka for me from muskrat skins. The parka is very warm, and it's beautiful. I feel like a queen walking around in the parka, but everyone stares at me. Most likely, they know we paid a lot of money for it. Probably Mildred told them. I plan to reserve it for special occasions and am touched that Tiger did this for me.

* * *

On Election Day, November 3, 1964, Alaska voted overwhelmingly Democrat. Most of the natives voted a straight ticket. Johnson would have been my choice. He's taken over in a time when the country is in turmoil and he seems to be opposed to war, unlike Goldwater. Election Day is over, and our next big day will be Thanksgiving.

Each day in November, our hours of light diminish quickly. I don't have the energy I had when the sun never set. Now, I feel like a bear, hibernating, staying asleep in the cave I made out of our warm bed. Twilight lasts for about six hours, followed by total darkness. Snow covers the lagoon and the ocean; it's a white world everywhere I look. Drifts are starting to pile up around the houses as winter howls in.

XXIV

THANKSGIVING

Thanksgiving approaches and the entire village prepares for the feast. The Keatings invite us for dinner, and I want to go. Tiger shakes his head when I tell him about the invitation because of the village feast.

"But why can't we do both?" I ask. "I want a real Thanksgiving dinner, not just seal oil and muktuk."

"There will be more than seal oil and muktuk," he assures me. In the end, after much coaxing on my part, we agree to do both.

Now, I have a dilemma. We were told to dress up. What will I wear? I don't have good enough slacks for this occasion. If I wear a skirt or a dress, I'll have to wear nylons, but my legs will be cold with nylons, and then there's the garter belt I'll need to hold them up. Why can't they invent pull-on hose made of something warmer? I decide to wear a Norwegian dress Tiger bought me. It's a pretty wool dress, so it's warm, and the hemline reaches past my knees. I'll wear the stockings too, with the darn garter belt, and my mukluks will come almost as high as my dress. With my muskrat parka, I'll be warm and dressed for the occasion.

Our first stop is the teachers' place. We are greeted with the aroma of turkey cooking. The table is set with a white tablecloth. I haven't seen such an elegant display since we left Harrisburg. Tiger contributed a bottle of wine for dinner to add to the festivities. We seldom drink, and it surprises me when he hauls out his gift. I don't know and don't want to know where he keeps his

142

stash, because the thought of having a native come to our place looking for liquor is a frightening one.

Dinner is delicious. The turkey is roasted to perfection and the stuffing, my favorite part of the meal, is outstanding. There is fresh lettuce and coleslaw. The cranberries didn't arrive by the plane, so cranberry sauce is all that's missing.

Tiger asked me not to eat too much at the Keatings' dinner because he wants me to have an appetite for the afternoon feast. How on earth can he ask me not to eat too much? This is the best food I've tasted since we arrived here. Tiger's plate is heaped, and he goes back for seconds. So much for not eating a lot.

After a healthy slice of delicious pumpkin pie, we leave the Keatings' house and its warmth for our second meal of the day: the Kivalina Thanksgiving feast. It's been a wonderful afternoon, full of good food and interesting conversation. The Keatings are at the feast, but sit off to the side by themselves not eating the food—something I understand after a meal like the one they just served. I'm going to have to make an effort to eat because I'm not hungry either.

The feast is held in the armory. Every household contributes food to the event. I had planned to make sticky buns but decided to make five hundred chocolate chip cookies instead when I heard there would be 150 people there. It takes a lot of time to prepare and bake so many cookies. Without a Mixmaster, like I had at home, I mix the dough by hand. Heaven knows what the oven temperature is! But the stove chugs along, heating the house, and after a burned first batch, I'm off and running. Tiger samples a cookie hot out of the oven, then I take one, and before I know it, we've demolished a handful each. I'll have to make these more often.

The Eskimos have gone all out for Thanksgiving. The offerings crowding the tables include caribou soup, dried fish, stewed fruit, and crackers. I pass on the greens, which look a bit like spinach and taste bitter despite being preserved in seal oil. Tiger takes a bite and says that he loves them. Is he just playing along to fit better into village life and should I do this too? For dessert, there are cakes, my chocolate chip cookies, different kinds of Jell-O, and Eskimo ice cream, which is called *aakutuq*. *Aakutuq* is considered a delicacy and it is made with caribou fat beaten to the consistency of whipped butter. Meat and berries are often added. *Aakutuq* is too rich for me to eat much of, though I do like the taste of it. I think about how it is made from caribou fat, which means there is no doubt the odd hair in it, and that thought makes me a bit nauseous. I tell myself to get over it—it's not that much different from finding a strand of hair in a meal.

Thanksgiving is a time for thanks and celebration. Three of the young boys celebrate a rite of passage tonight because they caught their first seal or caribou this year. Sometimes, the fat of the first caribou shot by one of the boys is used to make the ice cream for the Thanksgiving feast and this year is no exception. I don't know who hunted down the first caribou, but we were told that the aakutuq was made from a caribou one of the boys had shot. Tiger has learned from some of the elders that this special occasion would traditionally have included storytelling, drumming, and dancing.

After everyone has eaten, there is general chaos in the armory. Tiger plays his accordion, and some of the other men play guitars. I love watching Tiger play. He smiles as his fingers dance over the keys and I'm impressed with their dexterity. He is so much happier here than he was in Chicago, more relaxed. The women tap their feet in time to the music, with big smiles on their faces. After cooking for hours, they're enjoying an evening of fun. I notice they have made new parka covers for themselves and all their children. While the adults enjoy the music, the kids run around like whirlwinds. They are overtired and the excitement is mounting, not winding down. Some of them have a nosebleed, a scraped knee, or have gotten into a fight.

Despite the hardships they face by living here, these people are happy. I am starting to love life in the village and all the people who live here. It's been wonderful to have been able to share Thanksgiving with two cultures. Last year, I had my first American Thanksgiving. Having read about these celebrations, it was everything I anticipated. This year, I've shared both a traditional-style meal and one that is entirely unlike anything I could have imagined.

Christmas is around the corner, just weeks away. It will be interesting to be here during the darkest days of the year. I'm told that the Christmas feast will be much like the Thanksgiving feast, but for the boys and men, there are games of strength, such as arm wrestling. We'll see if the women participate in these games in any way.

The turkey for the special meal that I'll make for us is in our storage shed, and soon I'll start baking. I want to have cookies in the house so we can offer visitors something along with coffee. I also want to bake cookies for us—the kind we both remember from our childhoods. I'll be homesick, and the smell of cookies baking will bring Christmas into the house. I'm determined to make the holidays happy.

Tiger's aunt Sallie has sent bourbon balls. Because they're full of booze, we could never put them on a plate to offer to the natives. We keep them hidden. My favorite kind of fudge and other goodies arrive. Everybody has sent things to help make our Christmas a merry one. In all of the many letters and cards, there has been no mention of snow. At least here in Alaska, we'll have a white Christmas.

XXV

FROZEN FEAR

Travelling in the thirty below

It's two days after Thanksgiving and we are about to go on another trip with our dog team. Tiger has been planning a trip for us to get away from the village and be by ourselves for a few days. I am not sure if I am nervous or excited about our winter camping trip—our time away from the village by ourselves.

Tiger is outside hitching up the dogs to our sled while I've been inside, looking for clothes to keep me warm on this expedition—long underwear, two pair of socks, and two sweaters for under my parka.

I can hear the dogs barking with excitement as he hitches them up. It's been nine months since we left Chicago and began to prepare for living in Kivalina. Now, seven months after our arrival, we are ready for another of Tiger's big adventures.

"Okay, time to get moving. It's a long trip up there. You warm enough?" Tiger asks.

"I hope so," I say, climbing onto the sled. Already, I feel the cold searing my lungs and wonder if I will be able to stand the chill in the air. What am I thinking? Camping in this frigid weather is going to be a challenge and not fun the way Tiger is making it out to be.

We're headed thirty miles upriver, to a place where we'll pitch our tent and enjoy some time together. We haven't had a chance to relax and talk since we went to Cape Thompson in the summer. Tiger is so focused on the study that we don't have much time together for pleasure, but really it's all right. He came here to learn and participate in the lives of the natives.

I'm not a big camper; in fact, I've only camped twice in my life and both of those times were in the summer with Tiger, when it was warm. But Tiger has me convinced that midwinter camping is fun. As I gathered my warm clothes, I wondered for a moment why we aren't going somewhere to enjoy a bit of civilization for the first time since we arrived here. The answer came to me quickly. Maybe I wouldn't want to return to Kivalina.

There's a Coleman lamp to read by, but I'm not planning to read. I do so much of that at home on a regular basis. I'm anticipating spending time talking and maybe snuggling together in the sleeping bag. It's a good way to keep warm. The stove will be used for cooking and for heating the tent. Because heat rises, the ground where we'll be sleeping will be cold. I shudder, thinking about how cold it will be. The thermometer tells us it is in the negative twenties as we get ready, and I know it will be colder where Tiger has stored the fish. His fish cache is upriver several miles inland, and this is where he decided we should camp.

It's ten a.m. when we set out on the dog sled with our team of eight dogs. The cold is excruciating. It bleeds into my bones like a festering wound. Despite the severe cold, it's spectacular out here. The only sound is the panting of the dogs and the sound of the runners gliding across the terrain. There is a glow in the sky, and for the next few hours, we will have a period of twilight before total darkness sets in. Everywhere I look, I see vast stretches of white and little Arctic willows blanketed with snow. There is nothing and no one else in sight.

Tiger is driving the sled and is in constant motion. He stands on the back of the runners, and occasionally yells at the dogs to gee and haw as we travel. There is no type of lead, and everything the dogs do is by command. Sitting on the sled, I watch the dogs. Their tails wag and they sniff the air, as happy to be out on the trail as Tiger is. I am getting colder by the minute and am reluctant to tell Tiger.

He has a lot of experience with winter camping, with many stories of trips that he took the last time he was in the Arctic, when he traveled from village to village. Once, he even killed a rabid wolf with his bare hands on March 10. To us, that day is no longer known as my birthday, but rather as Wolf Day. If Tiger could kill a rabid wolf with his bare hands, I believe he is capable of doing anything.

But it's different now that we're on the sled in temperatures under twenty below. I must be crazy to have agreed to go camping in these conditions and doubt that any sane Eskimo woman would do it if she didn't have to. I'm wearing mukluks—high, padded sealskin boots—with two pair of socks, but they don't help. My feet are icy and beginning to hurt. Very little of my face is exposed, but my eyebrows have frost on them and when my nose runs, it freezes. Damn, it's cold, but I can't disappoint Tiger. Finally, as my feet start to lose feeling, I say to him, "Tiger, I can hardly feel my feet."

"You have to keep moving," he says. He has been alternately standing on the runners and running. "You can't just sit still and expect to keep warm." I should have known this, but it would have been nice if Tiger had told me beforehand. I know nothing about travelling with the dogs because I have only been on two short rides before this. I get off the sled and run and walk a little behind it, but I'm so bundled up it's hard to move. I am panting harder than the dogs.

Twilight is slipping away into the endless night when we reach our destination. It's about two in the afternoon, but it feels like midnight. Here in the Arctic I am faced with perpetual darkness. When we lived in Chicago, the sun didn't set until four thirty or five. And even then, I hated the shorter days.

"I'm going to set up the tent as quickly as I can," Tiger says, as we pull up. "I don't want you to get colder than you already are."

I watch Tiger pitch the tent and set up camp at the top of a steep riverbank. He stakes out the dogs and tethers each to a wooden pole. Huskies love to run given the opportunity, and we can't take that chance. We'd be left on our own here with no way of getting home unless we were lucky enough to have another camper find us. I wish I knew how to help, but all I can do is stand and watch, feeling totally useless. Am I really going to find that winter camping is fun or is this just fulfilling a dream of Tiger's?

Around us, the landscape is carpeted with snow. Here and there are Arctic willows and looking around, I see footprints of other animals. Bears and wolves are probably lurking near our campsite. There is no sign of any other dog team or any other person. I feel as though we are totally alone and hope we will make it home safely from the adventure.

Pitching the tent took longer than I thought it would, and soon, it will be time for dinner. The fresh air and the cold make us hungry and tired. The tent is warm and comfortable, thanks to Tiger, and I'm happy to be inside it. The tent is about eight feet by ten feet and we can stand up in it, although barely. Tiger says it's made of canvas and will be a good buffer against the wind. I plunk myself on a sleeping bag on the ground, removing my mukluks, and rubbing my feet to warm them up. They have pins and needles in them, and I must have narrowly escaped frostbite. Tiger lights the Coleman stove for heat. I had been concerned about using a Coleman stove to keep our tent warm, but Tiger had said I worry too much. "It'll be fun. Winter camping's an adventure."

He didn't like my idea of using a wood stove, like we did when we went to fish camp with the Hawleys in late September. If we had a wood stove, he said, we would have to find wood and twigs to feed it, and there would only be Arctic willows where we would be camping. He says using a Coleman stove is more reliable. I hope he's right. The wood stove we had at fish camp chugged along and was easy to cook with. Tiger makes us a cup of hot tea and after our tea, suggests that we take a walk. My feet have warmed up now, so I put on my mukluks again and we venture out into the freezing weather.

It's peaceful here, ten feet from the edge of the riverbank— rugged and lonely. The moon and stars light up the snow, and we can see clearly despite the early night. Our walk is brief, but we enjoy it, glad to have this time together. Tiger loves the village and all of the people there. I knew when I married him last year what this place meant to him. I didn't know, however, that he would be participating in every activity that came along and I would be left alone much of the time. I have been lonely, and living without plumbing or electricity is difficult. Sometimes I long for the comforts of home, but I'm slowly adapting to the native ways. Tiger will be happier if I adjust, and I'm determined to try.

Tiger brought a steak along for a special treat, along with canned food and dried fish. There is also seal oil, rendered from the blubber I removed when I skinned seals in spring. Last year I had never heard of seal oil and now it's a staple in our diet. Back at the tent after our walk, Tiger suggests we cook the steak tonight to celebrate being away from the village.

"That sounds fantastic!" I exclaim. It's the first steak we've had since we camped near Cape Thompson. In fact, this steak is one of the ones we were given when we were there. My mouth waters just thinking about it.

Tiger is ready to put the meat on the stove when we hear our dogs barking and know someone is near. Soon, from out of the darkness, we hear a voice.

"Tiger! I knew you guys were here."

It's Bobby Hawley, and even though he's a friend, we hadn't planned on anybody coming to our campsite.

"I don't know where the other men are camping," Bobby says, as Tiger steps out of the tent to greet him, "so I thought I'd visit you. I don't have my camping gear. Is it okay if I stay with you for the night?"

Damn. I know Tiger will ask him to join us. There goes our special dinner and our privacy. But we still have two nights left, I tell myself. Tiger asks Bobby in and hauls out the seal oil we brought and some dried fish—not exactly what we wanted, but Tiger wants to be hospitable to our guest. As I eat the seal oil and the dried fish, I feel my insides and whole body warming up. No wonder the Inuits always take seal oil along on a camping trip. Despite the fact that it warms my insides, I wish we were eating steak—it's what we had both planned on. Tiger is learning a lot from Bobby, and I imagine Bobby's visit is welcome to him. Tiger and Bobby will talk all night. I do what the native women would do, just sit and listen.

When I slip outside to pee, I'm near the edge of the embankment, and before I know it, I'm tumbling down like I'm on a slide. At the bottom, the snow is deep and soft, perfect for making snow angels, but I hardly feel in the mood to do that. I stand and shake off the snow like a dog shakes off water. By the time I get up to the tent again, I look like the Abominable Snowman.

The men laugh at the sight of me.

"I told you, Tiger, one of us could fall down the bank."

I only hope I won't have to go again in the middle of the night. What if I had slipped and hurt myself? Bobby and Tiger might never know I had gone outside until much later, and by then, it would be too late. As Tiger says, I worry too much.

The next morning is beautiful, with a sky the color of blue velvet. The sun, barely above the horizon, tinges the snow with a peachy pink hue. Finally, Bobby is on his way, and Tiger and I are alone again. We take brief walks together, never straying far from the campsite. The temperature has plummeted to thirty degrees below zero, and between walks, Tiger works on his fish cache, separating the fish. They have frozen into a huge mass, and it will be impossible to feed the dogs without separating them. As Tiger works on the fish, I sit inside the tent, keeping myself warm from the heat of the Coleman stove. I try to read, but I'm not in the mood and it's hard to concentrate. It takes a few hours to separate the fish and when he's finished, he returns to the tent.

"Let's take a walk under the stars." He doesn't seem to mind the cold, although he has been out in it for several hours.

Finally! A romantic evening to ourselves. I stand up, giving him a hug, and we leave the tent. The sky is midnight blue sprinkled with silver stars. Despite the severe cold, it's a beautiful evening. And then, before I know it—another surprise. As we step out of the tent, another dog team arrives. Once again, we have an overnight guest, Lowell Sage, who lives right behind our house. Why did he have to come? Oh well—I'll just have to deal with it.

Once more, I don't participate in the conversation. I might as well not be here. The men enjoy the meal of dried fish and seal oil. I was really looking forward to steak and I don't eat much of what they offer to me. In fact, I'm annoyed at the turn of events and I've lost my appetite. Now, we only have one night to spend without someone barging in on us.

The men sit on the ground, telling stories about hunting and fishing in the depth of winter ignoring me. Tiger and Lowell talk long into the night while I lie in my sleeping bag on the ground and sulk, wishing I were back in the village, where it's warmer. The men stop by all the time to visit Tiger, and this is no different, except there, I would be sleeping in a warm bed in a warm house and not freezing on the hard ground.

Lowell leaves early the next morning. He tells us he is going to a campsite farther up the river. I share my relief with Tiger when Lowell leaves, happy to be alone together once again.

"I hope we don't have more visitors tonight. It's our last night here. Do you want to stay in the tent and talk and snuggle for a while now that we're finally alone?"

"No," he says, pulling on his mukluks. He puts on his parka and starts to go outside to feed the dogs. "Let's hitch up the dogs and go upriver to ice fish."

Ice fish? What on earth gave him that idea?

"I'm not sure I want to do that right now, Tiger. The tent is warm and comfy."

"Oh, come on. You'll love the trip, and if you get too cold, we'll turn back."

I agree to go, but the truth is, I'm beginning to believe that I'm not cut out to be the wife of an Arctic anthropologist. How did I ever think I could do this sort of thing? This is different from any cold I have ever experienced and the temperature has dropped once again.

We turn back sooner than Tiger wants because I can't stand the frigid weather. My feet feel as though my mukluks are full of ice. My hands are just as bad. As we head back to our campsite, we run into two Inuits and talk for a few minutes. Tiger asks where they're camping. "Bobby and Lowell stayed at our camp," he tells the men, "and I think they were headed toward yours. Did they ever get there?"

"We never saw Bobby or Lowell," one of the men says.

"Maybe they turned around and went home after they stayed with you. Maybe they decided the weather isn't good for camping. Sure feels that way to us all right. It's so cold now, no one else will come to your campsite," the second man says. "Our camp is six or seven miles farther upriver. We thought of going back to the village, but we decided to stay for a couple more days."

Back at the tent, Tiger lights the Coleman stove to give us some heat. I am happy to be in the tent at last, happy to savor the warmth and the privacy. For a while we are reasonably warm. Suddenly, however, the stove sputters and dies. The chill in the air quickly invades our tent and any semblance of warmth disappears. Now, I find myself shivering even though I am dressed warmly.

"Should we head home?" I ask, wishing we had never come in the first place. First, two visitors, and now this.

"There's a plug in it somewhere." Tiger takes a closer look at the stove. "I'm going to try and figure it out. I'm sure I can fix it. Don't worry. We'll be fine." He seems calm as he says this, but I can see he is struggling to get the stove lit again. "Besides, we can't go back to the village now. I don't want to travel at night. It's bitterly cold and we don't want to get lost. Nobody will be on the trail. I'm going to have to figure out what's wrong with this damn thing."

He's as worried as I am as he works for over an hour without success. In the meantime, we are both chilled to the bone. He really needs to get the stove working—and fast.

"I wish one of the natives would come," I say. "They would know how to fix the stove." I realize as I say this that I am pointing out his inadequacies. I wish I hadn't.

Tiger shrugs. "Well, that's not going to happen. No one's going to come tonight, that's for sure."

My mother used to say be careful what you wished for, or you just might get it. On this trip, I wanted time with Tiger by myself. Now, I have it and I'm scared to death. I am beginning to understand that my husband isn't quite the expert in Arctic living as he led me to believe when I agreed to move here with him. I watch as Tiger finally gives up. He can't unplug our only heat source. Now I wish we had brought a wood stove, but Tiger said a Coleman stove would be more dependable. Was he ever mistaken.

As a last resort, he decides to build a tipi-like structure in front of our tent. We brought another small tent along in case we needed it for anything, and he's going to use it now for the tipi.

"I'm going out to find some twigs to light inside the tipi. They'll help to keep us warm."

While Tiger is outside searching for branches to light inside the tipi, I wait in the tent, hoping it will serve as a buffer against the cold and wind. I have lost any concept of time and it seems like an eternity before he returns with an armload of Arctic willows.

I feel the time creeping away and think our lives may also be. I try to choke down my fear, because I think Tiger is just about as frightened as I am.

Tiger builds the tipi right outside the tent. I don't know how this will provide us with any heat, yet he assures me it will. He says we can keep ourselves warm enough for the night and head back to the village tomorrow.

There's no fire burning yet when he comes into the tent again. "It's going to take a while to get the fire going," he says, and he removes his gloves, rubbing his hands together to get them warm. "The branches are damp from the snow and won't light easily. But don't worry. We'll be fine."

He said this before, but from the look on his face, I know he's concerned. There's no reassuring smile.

The wind is howling, and it takes forever to light the fire, just as my husband predicted. Then, finally, the flames leap and dance, and we both breathe a sigh of relief. It's warm enough for him to boil water for tea. He hands me a cup and starts to fry the steak in a frying pan we brought. We've tried to cook it for the last two nights and now, he is going to cook it inside the tent. As I warm my hands on the mug, I start to relax.

"Whatever you do, don't let the flap of the tent go into the tipi," Tiger says, as he watches the fire that he has built outside our tent. He's not paying attention and pushes the flap into the fire with his foot, just as he says this to me. He tries, unsuccessfully, to beat out the flames. We are standing in the tent watching in horror as the walls of the tent burn around us. Within a minute both the tent and tipi are gone. Aside from being shaken up mentally, we are totally unscathed. I am left standing in the frigid air, holding my cup of tea. I'm not sure whether I am laughing or crying when I say, "If my mother could only see me now."

We both know that we may not survive this adventure. We are dressed in our warmest clothes because we had never taken them off after we returned from ice fishing earlier. Even our warmest clothes are not going to help us live through this night. My mind spins in disbelief. This can't be happening.

Tiger is quiet for a few minutes as he surveys the ruins of our tent. Finally, he says, "We'll head upriver to where the men we met this morning are camped. It's only about six miles and I'm pretty sure I know where it is. We won't make it back to the village. Finding the men upriver is our only hope." Tiger remains stoic as he tells me this.

He's right. We have to find the campsite, it's our only chance of survival, but Tiger has never been there before. Every native and dog knows these parts, and Tiger says that he knows his way around here. Then again, he also says winter camping is fun, but I am finding quickly that it's not. I hope he knows the way. How many inexperienced men have been lost in the wilderness and died as a result? If we lose our way, we'll freeze to death.

The weather has become our enemy as we stand outside in the frigid air. If the temperature drops any more, our chances of survival will drop as well. The wind is blowing through our clothes and we both are shaking with the cold as we start to pack up the things that were in the tent.

Filled with worry, I start to help Tiger load the sled. I lose my footing and fall, twisting my knee, and I scream in pain. Tiger rushes over to help, as I'm doubled up in agony. I can't walk. I know from experience that this will last for a day or two before I'm mobile again. This happened to me several times in high school. Why did it have to happen now? Tiger hitches up the dogs, loads the sled, picks me up, and puts me on it. He covers me with sleeping bags to keep me from getting hypothermia.

We start up the main river trail in search of the other camp-site, Tiger all the while hollering at our dogs, hoping his shouts would make the campers' dogs start barking and help him locate the way. After a time, we hear the dogs, but then the sound grows dim, and we're lost again. Earlier, I wondered what would happen if someone couldn't find the right trail. Now I know the answer. Lying on the sled, I see my life passing before me—all twenty-three years. This is what it must be like to die.

Tiger is driving the dogs and can't stop to tell me what is going on. The trail should be easy to follow, but somehow another path veered off from it. We must be heading a different way now. What if we can't find the site? All I hear is the crunch of the runners and the panting of our dogs as we try to find the right trail. Dear God, I pray, please let us find the right trail. Give me another chance and I'll try to be a better person.

Finally, we hear dogs barking, and find the tents. The men are inside, sleeping through the cacophony like babies. They don't wake when we arrive and crawl over their bodies in one of the tents. I don't even care that I am the only woman in a campsite full of men I don't know; I'm just relieved to be here.

Sleep won't come. I'm in shock, with a throbbing, dislocated knee. I crawl into my sleeping bag to get warm. I lie awake, thinking about our marriage. We have only been married for seventeen months but I am a weight around Tiger's neck. Because of me, he can't do many things he planned to do. He shouldn't have married me, but he's stuck with me now, and he's too prideful to admit that he's made a big mistake. Maybe I made a mistake too, and all I have to blame is my ignorance.

The next morning, I can't hold any food down. This is the way my body always reacts to stress. Tiger wants to head home as soon as we're able to, and believe me, I can hardly wait to get there. Right now, though, all I do is lie in the sleeping bag, feeling miserable and praying I won't have to puke again.

Throughout the day, Tiger leaves me occasionally to get fish for the dogs. A couple of men are always around to keep the tent warm while he's gone, and I'm grateful for their presence. As soon as I'm able to sip tea and not vomit, Tiger loads me onto our sled, and we head back to the village.

The temperature has risen, and we hope the trip back will be easier, but trouble hits again, about twenty miles from the village. A strong north wind rages, blowing the soft snow off the river and forcing us to travel on glaze ice. The wind knocks the sled around and pulls the dogs off their feet as we carry on, crossing the treacherous ice to safety. I have stayed reasonably warm before the wind hit, but now find myself numb, in shock, and freezing cold.

I am able to see lights from the kerosene lanterns in the village and know we are close to Kivalina. Finally, Tiger pulls our sled up to the house and starts to unload. We are home at last. But our struggles are far from over. Our stove is working, but it has almost run out of oil. The water that we store in our oil drum has frozen because the temperature inside the house is well below zero. Until we get the stove working properly, we will have nothing in the drum but ice, and the house won't get warm. The euphoria I thought I would experience when arriving home has not come.

Some of the Eskimos come over to ask about our trip, and they help Tiger get the stove functioning. It will be two hours before there is any semblance of warmth from it. Mildred Sage comes over to see if she can help. Seeing me shivering, she pulls up her parka and her dress. "Here," she says. "Put your feet on my stomach. This will help you get warm."

I'm embarrassed doing this, but in minutes I feel her body heat thawing the cold. I have learned another way the natives survive the winter's chill.

When they are confident that we have oil in the stove and the house is starting to get warm again, the villagers leave to go home. I can't help but wonder what they think about Tiger and his ability to survive in this extreme, harsh climate.

At last Tiger and I crawl into bed, happy to be under the warmth of the blankets and in the safety of our house. I toss and turn thinking about the camping trip. Our life in Kivalina is spiraling downward, and all I can see is a future as bleak as the never-ending nights. Would we be able to survive the winter?

Christmas is almost upon us. We'll celebrate the season along with the rest of the village. Friends and family in the States have sent us care packages, helping us get into the holiday spirit. The turkey is outside frozen in the storm shed. And that is how winter arrives my first year in the Arctic with a husband who is hell-bent on surviving the challenges the locals take for granted.

Winter blows in with a vengeance. The icy breath of the wind filters through all the cracks and crevices of our house. It is bitterly cold, and the nights seem endless, although the sun casts a glow on the horizon briefly. By December 21, there will be no light at all. The frigid air we experienced on our camping trip remains and is probably a harbinger of what is to come. The temperature never rises above thirty degrees below zero. I wonder how I will survive the dark days ahead, clueless about just how dark those days would become.

XXVI
DISASTER

Six days have passed since our catastrophic camping trip, and we are still struggling to come to grips with what happened to us there. Life hasn't been easy for either of us since our arrival in Kivalina. Tiger left the life of a carefree bachelor behind when he married me. He has so much he wants to accomplish for his research, and sometimes he forgets he brought a wife along to live with him above the Arctic Circle.

What did I think? Did I believe our relationship would deepen here because we were on an adventure together? Nobody prepared me in any way to live this kind of life, and I wish someone had. I've adjusted somewhat, but it's been difficult. Because it's been hard for me, it's been hard for Tiger too. My New Year's resolution is to love life in the Arctic as much as Tiger does. I promised myself on our camping trip, in spite of all the trauma we went through, that if I survived, I would try to be a better mate for Tiger.

We find time to relax and write letters. Tiger hasn't written home since early September, but I have written two or three times a week—every week—giving them a glimpse into our lives through my letters. I'm sure our families enjoy hearing his side of the story of our life here as well.

As he writes home, I indulge in one of my favorite activities. Reading for me is a welcome escape from everything: a way to absorb myself in someone else's life. Friends and family keep me supplied with books, and so far, I have read most of the classic Russian novels, such as *Anna Karenina* (my favorite), *War and Peace,* and *Crime and Punishment,* along with the current bestsellers. We keep up with our professional journals, though I'm finding mine less interesting now. I'd rather spend my time with a good book or my knitting.

The Coleman lamps provide us with the light we need to read and write letters. These lamps are lit from the time we get up in the morning until the time we go to bed. Lighting them is usually Tiger's job. Fire has terrified me for years. As a child, I used to dream that I was in the middle of a lake surrounded by flames. This dream haunted me and now, since the camping trip and the terrifying fire in the snow, my fears have returned with a vengeance. I'm afraid to light the lamps and only do it when Tiger is away from the house. I'm thankful he is home with me tonight.

To make matters worse, our Coleman lanterns haven't been reliable. Yesterday, two of them went on the fritz and although Tiger worked on them for about three quarters of an hour, he couldn't fix them. He gave up and borrowed one from the school. We need four to light our place properly; we are now down to two. And this morning, another problem arose. Our stove, which is used for both heating and cooking, didn't work. We bundled ourselves up in warm clothing and snuggled under a blanket waiting for one of the men who is an expert on such things to fix it for us. Sometimes, I wonder if there is some sort of malevolent spirit in this house who doesn't want me here. Tiger never had these sorts of problems when he lived here before or if he did, he never told me. I wonder: is it the malevolent spirit, bad luck, or just life in the Arctic? My mood, which had plummeted for a while, rises when Bobby Hawley fixes our stove and we are able to get warm.

We are sitting side by side on the couch, waiting for dinner to finish cooking. The stove is fixed, but a chill lingers in the air. I am wearing a heavy hand-knit sweater with a couple of layers underneath and Tiger has on his Irish knit sweater. It feels good to have kicked off my mukluks, but two pairs of thick socks help to keep my feet warm.

A special meal is in store for us—canned ham, peas (also canned), and potatoes that we've stockpiled. The potatoes have eyes in them, but I cut them out, slice them thinly, and add evaporated milk. They will be like scalloped potatoes—Kivalina style.

Tempting aromas fill the house, but unwanted thoughts continue to swirl through my head. I don't know if I can handle another year and a half in Alaska. Sometimes, I wonder if I'm in love with Tiger anymore. I love him, but the truth is, I hardly know him.

Tiger spends most of his waking hours focusing on his research, and even though I love to hear the passion in his voice when he discusses the study, it is the only thing we talk about. I am still physically attracted to him. My heart beats a bit faster when I look at him, and sometimes, I wonder how I was lucky enough to have married him. I am still in love with the idea of our life together. For me, that's all I need. Hopefully, he feels the same.

I put my hand on Tiger's knee. "I think I'm holding you back from having what you really love," I tell him. My stomach churns as I say this. "I'm not cut out to live the life you want to live."

Tiger squeezes my hand and smiles at me. "I have been writing to everybody this afternoon and telling them how well you are adjusting. You're not holding me back. You've done everything that I've asked and more since we arrived here. You endured the camping trip so well, and honestly, you could have just given up on life here. I'm so proud of the way you handled our near disaster. We both know we might not have survived."

His words aren't enough. In my heart, I know. Tiger loves me, but he's held back by me. I've thought about this a lot since our camping trip last week. If I wasn't around, he could do the things he wants and not worry about me. I have thought about leaving before, but it was for selfish reasons. I was unhappy and lonely, and leaving for my own wellbeing seemed the right thing to do. Now, I have to wonder if leaving Kivalina might be the right thing for Tiger.

He puts an arm around me, holding me close to him. "Do you want to go to Anchorage after Christmas? We'll take a break from the village for a few days."

"Oh, my God, Tiger, that would be the best Christmas present you could give me."

I thought he would never want to leave Kivalina. I am so happy he wants to do this, and I know it will be good for both of us. Tears well up in my eyes as I throw my arms around him. "I can hardly wait. It will be like a second honeymoon. We can sleep in, eat in good restaurants, and take long, hot baths and showers. I can even get my hair cut."

This time, we'll have the privacy we'd hoped for on our camping trip last week and have time away from the village and from our life in a fishbowl. We've lived off canned food, fish, and caribou meat all summer, although going forward we have the option of shipping better food in from Fairbanks. I haven't bathed for over a month. The thought of a warm bath and good meals makes me the happiest I've been since we got here.

The special meal that I prepared is on the table, paling in comparison to all the things I'm fantasizing about on our January trip. It can't come soon enough. I tell Tiger dinner is on the table when the Coleman lamp flickers and dies. Usually, Tiger goes outside to light it in order to keep the residual fumes remaining in the house from igniting. Tonight, however, it's so cold out that he takes a chance and lights the lamp in the house.

My fantasy collapses as he bends over to light the lamp. The gasses explode and flare up in his face. The fire dances across the floor like a ribbon, and the flame seems to taunt us, growing larger. This can't be happening again.

Tiger grabs my hand, pulling me out of the house. We're safe. When I turn around, Tiger is gone. Oh, my God—how could he do this? He went back to retrieve his notes and is risking his life for his work.

Terrified, screaming with fear, and close to tears, I wait for him to come out. When he doesn't, I'm paralyzed with fright. I don't know what to do. I want to run for help, but I can't. I am rooted to the snow-covered ground, unable to move.

He's trapped inside. If I open the door, the added oxygen will make the whole house go up in flames and he won't survive. If the door isn't opened, the fire might go out on its own, due to the lack of oxygen. I stand there frozen, afraid that at any moment, flames will engulf the house. Tiger's life is in danger, and there's nothing I can do to save him. All I can do is stand there screaming, praying that someone will hear me. I feel helpless, unable to save my husband. Ever since I arrived here I have felt helpless, but now it's so much worse.

I scream, "Help, help, help, fire!" My future flashes before me. What if Tiger dies? What will happen to me? It's silent outside. Everyone is inside of their houses, trying to keep warm. Even the dogs aren't barking. "Help, help, fire!" I cry again, as loudly as I can.

I feel as though I've been outside shouting forever, but it is only about three minutes before help arrives. Andrew, one of the teenagers in the village, appears and rushes to get others. After assessing the situation, the men rush to the armory to get gas masks. The fire is out because of the lack of oxygen, but the smoke is too thick to allow them to rescue Tiger. Knowing help is on its way, I run in the snow around the back of the house, to our bedroom, and smash the double-paned window with my hand. I don't realize that by doing this, I could ignite the flames again. But I need to do something. My worst fear is that Tiger will be found dead.

With their gas masks on, the men go into the house and find Tiger in the bedroom lying face down, as though he has accepted death. He doesn't move and is barely breathing. A piece of ash smolders on his leg, burning a hole in his jeans. I have rushed back inside the front door, forgetting that the men rescuing Tiger needed gas masks. Through the dense smoke, I can see the ash on his leg that is ready to ignite, but I don't hear him breathing. The men say he is alive, and pick him up to carry him to the minister's house. The smoke in the house is so thick that it is choking me and making it impossible to breath. I have to get out as soon as I can, but I stand there, frozen.

Some of the village women arrive to help me and see me shivering in a state of shock. They, too, find the smoke unbearable and hurry to get me out of the house.

Mildred Sage seizes my parka and mukluks, takes my hand, and rushes me over to the minister's house. The other women follow us to the house, where the minister is praying over Tiger. Several more people arrive to see if they can help. I feel claustrophobic in this small house. I wish they would leave. I don't want them listening to what I say to Tiger or watching me break down. I will myself not to cry, to be strong for Tiger. I can almost hear my mother's voice in my head saying, "Control yourself, Deanne."

Tiger lies as still as death. I go to his bedside. His eyelashes are singed and almost nonexistent. His face is visibly swelling, and he is gasping for breath. His eyes are open but unfocused. How could I think that I wasn't in love with him anymore?

"I love you, Tiger. You'll be all right," I say, hoping he can hear me speak. I need to reassure him, and myself, that he won't die.

I follow the men as they move Tiger to the schoolhouse where there is more room. They lay him on a mattress on the floor. Here, he is under the care of Jim Keating and the village nurse, both of whom know very little about burns. I sit on a couch near Tiger's makeshift bed, watching in terror as my husband struggles to breathe, hoping that each breath he takes won't be his last. His hands are in shreds and are burned past his wrists.

Jim uses the radio to try to reach Kotzebue for help. The call doesn't go through.

"Why can't you get through to anyone?" I ask, panicked as he tries again and again.

"It's probably weather-related. It's so cold that I can't reach anyone. If I can get through to Kotzebue, it may be too frigid for a plane to get here."

I sit, numb with disbelief, trying to hold back the tears that are streaming down my face.

"If help doesn't come soon, I'm going to have to cut a hole in his throat. He can't keep breathing like this much longer," Jim says.

God, no. Jim can't do this. Jim isn't a doctor. He doesn't know how. It's not sterile here, and if he cuts a hole in his throat, it will kill him. Please, please, let the plane come. Don't let Tiger die here.

Finally, Jim gets through. They tell us that they will send a plane up as soon as the ice fog has lifted. I only hope Tiger can hold on long enough.

Fourteen hours pass like this, without assistance. If a plane doesn't come soon, Tiger will die. He's in pain; he can barely get air into his lungs. Jim knows more about burns than I do and tells me that he has lost copious amounts of fluid. There is no way to hydrate him, which is what Jim says he needs right now. Obviously, the only way that he can be hydrated is intravenously because he can't take in fluids by mouth. Tiger is unconscious, oblivious as to how badly injured he is. I'm grateful for this. Around ten o'clock, sixteen hours after the accident, we hear the distant sound of the plane. Thank God, help will arrive soon.

The men take Tiger out to the plane, and I walk out with them. I feel as though we are leading a funeral procession, as the rest of the adults in the village follow close behind, lending us their support. We board and I am alone on the plane except for Tiger and the pilot. I pray we will make it to the hospital in Kotzebue.

An ambulance meets us in Kotzebue. Tiger's face is swollen and charred, and he gasps with every breath he takes. A doctor in the ambulance says, "No sense in putting the siren on now." Does this mean Tiger is dying? The ambulance plows through the snow to the hospital. It's not far from the airport, but it seems to take an eternity to get there. I'm afraid that every breath Tiger takes will be his last.

We make it to the hospital. I breathe a sigh of relief. We made it. He's going to be all right. The doctors here can take care of him. But I'm wrong. After one look at Tiger, the doctors know his injuries are too severe for them to deal with at this small hospital. Tiger has to be flown to Anchorage to have a chance to survive. A morphine injection is administered to ease the pain, and he is given fluids intravenously. Arrangements are made to take a plane out of the Kotzebue airport to Anchorage.

Heavy ice crystals hang in the air, just waiting to wrap the village in a fog as Tiger is loaded onto a stretcher and put onto the plane. A doctor accompanies us, and we are the only passengers. From my vantage point, a few seats behind Tiger, I can see he is still alive. Every so often, the doctor gets up and checks his vital signs. He says nothing to reassure me and doesn't tell me how Tiger is doing. He goes back to his seat and sits down. I feel powerless and frightened, not knowing what lies ahead for either of us.

The plane stops in Nome.

"I think you should call your parents from here," the doctor tells me, implying that Tiger's life is hanging by a thread and he wants someone with me if he dies.

I am desperate for my parents to be with me but know Tiger's parents should be the ones to come. "His parents are very close to me," I say. "I've known them since I was sixteen. Should I call them instead?"

The doctor agrees it would be better if Tiger's parents come. I pray they can. I'm not strong enough to handle this by myself.

It is the night of December seventh in Harrisburg, and it doesn't occur to me the Burches might not be home. The phone rings incessantly. Please, dear God, let someone answer. Finally, Mom, as I call my mother-in-law, answers and accepts the charges for the call. Her excitement is obvious when she hears my voice, and it's hard to do what I'm about to do. I am crying as I try to tell her. How awful it must be to hear that your firstborn child is on the brink of death.

"Tiger has been badly burned. The doctor doesn't know if he is going to live. I'm calling from Nome, but we're on our way to Anchorage."

Tiger's mother remains calm. She says Dad is at a meeting and she will get him away from it. They will leave for Anchorage as soon as they can. I tell Mom I'll see them when they arrive there. Thank God they are coming.

I am alone, scared, and being taken to a city where I know no one. The doctor tells me the name of the hospital where they're taking Tiger. Meanwhile, he has called back to Kotzebue and learns that the weather has changed for the worse. Planes are not arriving or departing. It was by the grace of God a plane picked us up in Kivalina and we were able to go on to Anchorage.

When we arrive in Anchorage, I feel as though I have been traveling forever. I smell of smoke and my face is streaked with tears. The doctor escorting us makes a reservation for me at the Westward Hotel. Suddenly, I remember that I have no money and no credit card with me. Tiger never gave me money in Kivalina. There was no need. Without money, there isn't a way of taking a taxi or paying for the hotel.

The doctor from Kotzebue leaves Tiger with the doctor who is in charge. Totally abandoned now, I sit in the waiting room, wondering what is going on. At least before we arrived here, I knew Tiger was alive. Now, his fate lies in the hands of this doctor, whom I have yet to meet.

It seems like hours pass between the time Tiger is wheeled away and out of my sight. Finally, the doctor arrives to tell me what is happening. He shakes my hand and introduces himself to me.

"I'm Fred Hillman. I've just performed a tracheostomy on your husband. A tracheostomy is a hole in the throat, which will help him to breathe better."

I remember that Keating was going to attempt to do this and am thankful a doctor did it instead.

"Right now, his condition is critical. I wish I could give you better news, but only time will tell. He has lost a lot of fluid and his lungs are badly damaged. He has severe burns on his head, face, and hands. He's lucky not to be wearing a wedding band. His hand is swollen, and we might have had to amputate to get the ring off. We need to test his eyes at some point to see if he'll lose his sight."

I think of those beautiful blue eyes of his. Will he ever see a sunset again? Will he ever see my face or the faces of his loved ones? Will he even survive? If he was blind, would he even want to survive?

I voice my fears to the doctor, and he looks at me with compassion.

"I hope you didn't marry him because of his eyes."

Dr. Hillman is trying to tell me that if he survives, my husband will never look the same again.

"Where are you spending the night?" he asks.

"At the Westward Hotel; my in-laws are flying from Harrisburg to be with me." I don't want to add that I'm not sure how I am going to pay for it and am afraid that I might end up spending the night in the chair I'm sitting on.

"You can't stay there by yourself. I'm taking you to my home. You'll stay with us until your in-laws arrive."

His compassion overwhelms me, but I'm too tired and in too much shock to protest. At twenty-three, my life has changed forever. I want to shout to the heavens: Why? Why did this have to happen? Will life ever be normal again? What is going to happen to the life Tiger so carefully planned? Is he going to live? What will he be like if he does live? I curl up in the fetal position on a couch in the waiting room until Dr. Hillman comes to take me to his house.

At Dr. Hillman's house, I meet his wife, Louise, who is also a doctor. She looks at me, taking in my uncombed hair and the clothes I've been wearing for two days. She gives me a pair of pajamas, and then takes my dirty clothes to the washing machine. I must look like a fright.

On the way to my room for the night, Louise says, "There's a shower down the hall. We have unlimited hot water and you can take one for as long as you want." I haven't washed in three days and can't remember the last time I had a bath. I probably smell, but she's too kind to say anything.

"A hot shower and clean sheets will make you feel human again." She gives me a sleeping pill and sends me off to a comfortable bed. I haven't slept for over two days, but I'm afraid to. I should be keeping vigil by Tiger's bed. I need to be there in case he wakes up and wants me. Worse still, I must be there in case he dies. I don't want him to die alone. Sleep is elusive and despite the pill, I toss and turn all night.

The next morning, I am up early and stumble to the kitchen, where there is a glass of orange juice waiting on the table. Orange juice should be a treat, but I can't drink it. I haven't eaten since we left the village; the thought of food makes my stomach turn. My only wish is to be taken to the hospital.

Louise is bustling about. "Fred called. Tiger is holding his own. I paged the airport and your in-laws have arrived and will meet you at the hospital. I'll take you there as soon as you eat some breakfast."

What does it mean, *Tiger is holding his own?* How could my in-laws possibly be here already? I called them yesterday at six in the evening, Harrisburg time. It is only nine in the morning here. Does she really think I can eat breakfast right now?

I can't believe they have arrived already, but I'm relieved because now, I can let go. I can be a little girl and let them take care of both of us.

Louise drives me to the hospital and stands by as Tiger's parents greet me with open arms.

"Your dad and I were so worried about you. We knew Tiger was getting help, but all we could think about was you. We knew you were by yourself and terrified. When we found out that the Hillmans were looking after you, we were relieved." She smiles at Louise as she says this. "We haven't seen Tiger yet. We were waiting for you to get to the hospital."

I don't know what to say to them. I'm just thankful they are here. Overwhelmed, I burst into tears and my mother-in-law holds me in her arms as I sob.

We go together to Tiger's room, which is in the ICU. None of us know what to expect, and when we see him there, full of tubes and catheterized, it's heartbreaking. His hands are bandaged, but his face isn't. It's black, swollen, and charred, and resembles a burnt marshmallow. He's conscious.

Mom says, "No, that's not my son. My son isn't black. Where is he?"

"Severe burns cause the skin to blacken and char," the nurse explains. "This is your son."

I am amazed at Mom's control. She goes to Tiger's bed. "I'm so sorry this had to happen, Tiger, but you're going to be alright."

Meanwhile, my father-in-law is standing by her side and holding her hand as she speaks to Tiger. I'm not sure that he knows what to do or say and it is unusual for him to be at a loss for words.

Tiger tries to speak, but his throat is swollen, and he can only croak. It is difficult for him to talk because of the trachea tube. Tiger is shocked when he sees his parents. Until his parents arrived, he would later tell me, he had no idea of the severity of his situation. He thought that he would be able to go back to Kivalina in time for Christmas. No one has told him just how badly he has been burned, and he hasn't been conscious for most of the time. Now, seeing his parents, he realizes how serious the accident was.

I want to take Tiger's hand as I did the other night, before all of this happened. I wish I could turn the clock back to the time he said we could take a holiday in Anchorage after Christmas. Now we are here, and no one knows what the outcome will be.

We don't stay at the hospital long because Tiger is too weak for us to stay for any length of time. The nurses and doctors come in and out, attending to him, and we are in the way. Mom and Dad have reserved rooms at the Westward Hotel. The rooms are sumptuous and welcoming. The view from my room of the mountains and ocean is magnificent. The huge bed is filled with pillows and I wish I could bury my head in them and pretend that nothing ever happened.

We were supposed to be in Anchorage after Christmas, not now. How dare I love the room or the view? I shouldn't be here. Tiger and I should be back in Kivalina, preparing for the

Christmas feast. It feels wrong for me to appreciate the room and the view.

There is not much anyone can do for Tiger except pray, but Mom knows what to do for me. My sweater smells of smoke, and I have been wearing it since the accident. After lunch, we hit the stores. She buys me sweaters, slacks, and underwear. They are the nicest clothes that I've owned since before we left for Alaska. Our next stop is the beauty salon for a haircut. When I emerge, I feel more like the girl I left behind seven months ago. I know Mom is doing this for Tiger, as well as for me. If he sees me downtrodden, he will worry. If he sees me carrying on, he'll think that he's going to be alright.

Walking along the streets in Anchorage, I'm drawn to a painting in a store. It's an oil painting of four children against the backdrop of a late-autumn sunset. The background is orange and the children's faces reflect the soft colors of the twilight. The only other colors are the colors of their hats, each different. The artist is Eskimo. I point it out to my mother-in-law. "Mom, look at this painting. It reminds me of the children in Kivalina." The artist has truly captured these four little girls. I love it.

For a moment, I feel a pang of regret for all I have left behind—the people in the village, the children who visited, and our plans for the Christmas feast. Most of all though, I feel a deep sorrow for all of Tiger's dreams which will never come to fruition.

As we trudge along the snow-covered streets, I tell her a bit about the children in the village, with their dark hair and almond-shaped eyes, and about the times they would press their noses against my window or come inside to just watch me. I tell her how I was looking forward to Christmas there, with the children dressed in their best clothes and running around the armory like they did at Thanksgiving. "We were both looking forward to the Christmas celebration there," I tell Mom.

Mom sighs and puts her arm around me. "I can't begin to imagine what you are thinking about right now. Now, all we can do is pray that he will be all right."

The shopping and window shopping are finished, and it's time to end this luxury and get back to real life and the tragedy that is unfolding before us.

Back at the hospital, we find that Tiger is still in critical condition. We are playing a waiting game. Dr. Hillman has tested his eyes. Thankfully, the burns have not affected them; he will be able to see. Part of his nose is gone, and his ears have sloughed off. He is conscious, but he speaks little, because the pain is excruciating.

We take the Hillmans to dinner, and Fred Hillman explains the situation. "If we get him stabilized here, you can take him to a hospital specializing in burn cases. Find out what options are available to you in Harrisburg. I'll locate a nurse to accompany you back. I hope that he'll be able to travel in eight or ten days, but I'm warning you, taking him back is full of risks because his lungs are so badly burned. He is apt to get pneumonia, and there is always the risk of infection to the burned area. He has months of surgeries to go through and will need round-the-clock care in the hospital."

If we get him stabilized here? What will happen if they can't?

I am still in a state of shock when we return to the hotel after dinner. I knew this was a very serious situation, but now I am aware that it will be months before Tiger is well. Then, Dad hits me with his bombshell: "Deanne, you and I are going to Kivalina to assess the damage. We'll go tomorrow, stay overnight, and be back in Anchorage the next day."

I don't want to face this. "Dad, I can't go. Can't we just let the teachers help? I know that they'll do it." My voice breaks. I don't want to go there ever again. I can't be away from Tiger for more than a few hours, let alone two days. What if he dies and I'm not there with him?

"No, you can't let others take on your responsibility. The dogs need to be taken care of, and you have to see what repairs need to be made to the house. We'll leave tomorrow."

I have to accept this, and I steel myself to face the days ahead. I close my door and lie on the bed, still in the clothes I wore to dinner, trying to get used to the fact that Dad and I will be returning to Kivalina.

Later that evening, Mom comes into my room. "Why don't you call your parents and ask them to come to Harrisburg for Christmas? They'll be a support to you, and we hope that we will be in Harrisburg by then. She hands me the phone, and I dial home. I haven't spoken to my parents since August. I remember how desperately I wanted my parents to be the ones with me in Anchorage. My heart is pounding hard. If we are able to come home, I want my parents to be there with me. The Burches have been wonderful, but I need my parents to help me through this.

Mom picks up the phone. She hasn't heard from any of us since Mom Burch called her on the seventh of December. I tell her about Tiger, holding back tears as I try to describe how he looks. "Mom, you're not going to recognize Tiger. His face is black and swollen, and he has a tracheostomy tube. He can't talk. He's in critical care, but the doctor hopes we'll be able to leave by the sixteenth. Mom B. invited you and Dad to come to Harrisburg for Christmas. Please come? I need you."

I'm met by dead silence on the line, and then she answers. "Dear, we've been invited to David and Peggy's for Christmas. It's Judy's first Christmas. I don't think we'll be able to."

The tears stream down my face. I'm flabbergasted. Her response is more than I can take. I want to scream at her, "My husband is dying, but you want to spend Christmas with David and Peggy, and not with me? How can you possibly do this to me?" I haven't seen them for seven months. I understand why they want to be with the first grandchild for Christmas, but she's only six months old. She won't even know the difference.

"Okay, Mom. Fine," I manage to say. Then, I slam down the phone and burst into tears. I don't know how much more I can tolerate, but I don't have the energy to say anything more to her.

Mom Burch runs a bath for me and puts me in the tub with a glass of bourbon. As I drink the liquor and start to relax, the phone rings in my room. Mom answers it. "No, Ruth, you can't talk to her right now. She's taking a bath and trying to calm down." Her voice is cold, not upbeat. A couple of minutes pass and then I hear her say, "Well, I'm happy you changed your mind. We don't know if Tiger will live when he gets back to Harrisburg, and Deanne needs you with her."

I sit in the bath and let them talk. They have been friends for years. I don't want to talk with my mother right now. I'm angry and hurt, and although I'm glad she changed her mind, I wish she had never hesitated. I wonder if I will ever be able to forgive her. By the time Mom Burch hangs up the phone, the bourbon and hot bath have worked their magic and I'm tired. Tomorrow, we will go to see Tiger and then I'll head back to the village with Tiger's father.

It's morning now, and Dad and I are ready to leave for Kivalina. We enter the critical care unit where Tiger is. He is hooked up to IVs to hydrate him. I feel sure, although I don't ask, that antibiotics are in one of the IVs. I hope so. He is catheterized and I know if he could, he would rip the catheter out and try to make his way to the john. Right now, he doesn't have the strength.

His hands are covered with huge bandages to prevent infection but his face, still charred and swollen, isn't. He opens his eyes and sees us standing there. I go over to the side of his bed and tell him that his father and I are going back to Kivalina to see what damage has been done. I tell him that we'll just be there overnight and that I love him. He nods his head and croaks out an okay.

There hasn't been any improvement. As I leave the room, I realize I might never see him alive again. I don't want to go back to Kivalina.

XXVII
TRAPPED

As the small plane makes its descent into Kivalina, I watch out the window and see the dots of houses covered with snow. A week hasn't even passed since the accident. I can't believe I'm back. We'll stay with the Keatings overnight and leave for Anchorage tomorrow.

The weather is frigid, and I can see an ice fog starting to build. It would be awful to get stuck here or in Kotzebue because of the weather. Jim takes us over to the house to see the damage. I'm afraid to go inside. I enter slowly, not wanting to look. Apart from soot on the walls and a charred swath across the floor, the house looks much as it did when we lived here. Even though Jim brought a flashlight, it's dark in here. The flashlight doesn't provide enough light for us to see properly. It's possible that there is more damage than I think there is. I hope not. My fur parka, which was hanging near the burned area, has been destroyed. Sadly, I can never wear it again.

Dad stands in the house looking at the damage. He doesn't say anything and just shakes his head in disbelief. I can't tell if he is upset because it is not as bad as anticipated but it has nearly killed his son. Or is he appalled at the way his son and wife are living? After all, he and my mother-in-law never lived like this. In fact, I'm sure he doesn't know anyone who has lived in a place like this. I can tell by the look on his face that he is dumbfounded and doesn't know how to react.

How could the house be intact and Tiger be so damaged? I see a couple of envelopes on the desk, stamped and ready to mail. Tiger's notes are lying on his desk in the loose-leaf binder he kept them in. They appear to have very little fire damage, and we pack these things to take home. Seeing those notes, I want to scream. He went back in to save them, and he may die because of that hasty decision. This representation of his life's work is lying here undamaged, as though the fire never happened. They would have been here even if Tiger had not run back to retrieve them. Didn't he know that the fire might die because of the lack of oxygen in the house to feed it? Could he have been burned when the gasses ignited and flashed in his face? Was he in shock and not able to think clearly? I still don't know what happened in the house when he went back in, but I imagine I'll find out, if Tiger lives.

Outside, the dogs are howling, waiting to be fed. I need to find Amos to look after them for the winter. I know Amos well enough to know he will have taken care of them for the last few days. In fact, I think any of the men in the village would have done so. If we never come back, the dogs will be Amos's to keep. But what will I do about Bubbles, my pup? She's not old enough to pull a sled, and she might not be of any use to Amos. Dad seems to read my mind because he suggests we bring Bubbles home with us. We'll take her on the plane with us to Anchorage and put her in a kennel until we leave.

I don't bother to pack any of our clothes. I'll leave them behind and if we don't come back, I'll tell Mildred that she can have them and give them to anyone who can wear them. They probably smell of smoke anyway.

I asked Dorothy to distribute our canned goods to everybody in the village. She can keep our turkey and any of the cookies that are in the house. Tiger will want to come back here if he is able to. I wonder though, will we ever come back? Will we ever see the village and these people again?

We leave the next morning. Most of the people in the village dropped in at the Keating's house when we were there, asking after Tiger.

We trudge out to the airstrip in Kivalina with the whole village behind us. Once again, I am grateful for the love and support they show me. We arrive in Kotzebue to find that our plane to Anchorage is delayed. The airport is small, but there is a building where Dad and I sit and wait. We don't talk much, both of us lost in thought. Two hours pass, and then the plane is canceled. The ice fog prevents planes from flying anywhere. I am biting my lip and trying not to cry. My father-in-law says, "Don't worry. I'm sure we'll be able to leave tomorrow."

I sigh and say, "I hope so too."

We phone Mom from a pay booth. Tiger is the same, she says, but he is beginning to talk. Regrettably, we tell her we are delayed indefinitely, waiting for the weather to improve.

The best hotel in town is open for the winter months, I'm relieved to learn. It's clean and warm. The hotel has no guests, and often the reception desk is unmanned, so I sneak Bubbles up to my room. I take her out as often as I can and hope that she doesn't have an accident in the middle of the night.

There is no restaurant at the hotel, and so we make our first trip to Art Fields's restaurant for a meal of burgers and fries. I can't eat much. I'm numb with shock and trapped in a place I don't want to be. Tiger's dad loves adventure, and I think he is getting vicarious pleasure out of this in a way, despite his son's accident. As usual, we are regaled by tales of many of Art's escapades. I have heard them before when Tiger and I were in Kotzebue last spring. I don't want to listen. At night, I can't sleep. I'm tormented by worry about what is going on in Anchorage.

We are up early for breakfast after our first night in Kotzebue, once again at Art Fields's. It is the only place to eat in town at this time of the year. The place is so small that it only has a counter where we sit to eat. We walk to the airport for our flight to Anchorage; each of us bundled up to ward off the cold. I at least have my parka with a fur ruff, but Dad is totally unprepared for this type of weather and has only his down ski jacket for warmth. Fortunately, he has a ski cap and the jacket has a hood. I watch him shivering as the temperature is in the minus thirties. I hope he doesn't catch a cold.

The cold sears our lungs, making it hard to breathe. The sky is enveloped by an ice fog composed of tiny ice crystals, making it difficult to see. I ask my father-in-law if he thinks the plane will be cancelled. He doesn't answer me, maybe because he thinks we won't be leaving today.

When we arrive at the airport, we are told the plane is cancelled. My heart plummets at the news. I want to scream, but instead I retreat into myself, building a wall around my feelings. I am determined to get through this.

We head to Hanson's, the general store, buy a leash for Bubbles, and then I search for a book, any book. Throughout the entire time that we were in Kivalina, I could shut out the world and retreat into a different one. Here, there are no books. There is no world that I can find as a means of escape. It's almost Christmas and yet the store doesn't look as though the holiday is even close. It's desolate and unwelcoming.

We go back to our hotel and I open my suitcase, which is full of Tiger's notes, and the burnt envelope containing the last letter he wrote home and never had a chance to mail. I lie on the bed and read the letter. Bubbles lies on the floor close to the bed.

December 6, 1964 (excerpt from a ten-page letter)

Dear Everybody,

At long last, I am getting around to writing. I can't tell you how sorry I am about my long silence. I am sorry on the one hand because I should write like ten times more often, and on the other hand because when I wait so long it takes about six hours to write an even moderately adequate letter. Anyway, here goes.

You are all sure to be interested in Deanne's condition. It can be said without equivocation that she is feeling much better than she was last September, but she can still go a bit further before she can be considered in perfect shape again. She was in pretty bad shape when we first got here, but improved considerably over the summer. When I returned from my dog-buying expedition to Kotzebue, she was more self-sufficient and surer of herself than I have ever seen her.

My research has been totally defunct since August, and I am horribly discouraged about it. So many things have fouled up my plans that I can hardly believe it. I had allowed for two weeks of fishing and two weeks for the sled. However, I told you what happened to the sled and, just when I got that finished, I broke two pairs of glasses within a couple of days of each other. That finished me for three weeks more. I had planned to write this letter then, but could only type for a few minutes at a shot without my eyes hurting, so I had to forgo it, and lots of other work. In addition, everything that could go wrong around here seems to be going wrong. Everything breaks or something so that three-quarters of my time is spent repairing things and the other quarter doing the regular chores of Arctic living. Tonight as I was typing this letter, two of our Coleman lanterns just quit and although I wasted three-quarters of an hour trying to fix them; they just won't work. If I hadn't been able to borrow a lantern from the school, I would have had to postpone this even more. If it hadn't been for Deanne, who seems to get a tidbit of information every day, I wouldn't have gotten any information at all for the last couple of months. I certainly hope to rectify this situation in the near future—I have to.

It is now the next morning and a new trouble has arisen. Our heating and cooking stove seem to be on the fritz—the house was just freezing this morning. I managed to fix it a bit, but I'll have to wait until one of the men (an expert on such matters) returns from camping before I can do the job properly.

I don't know how much more bad luck we can survive. Our troubles are not inherent in Arctic living; they are a clear case of very bad luck. I want to take Deanne on a trip to Anchorage for a short holiday. I am going to tell her tonight, but if things keep up like this we will probably be very afraid to get on a plane. Only two things are left that I can think of—one of us will get frostbite (I don't

know how Deanne missed out on our camping trip) or the house will
burn down. And on that optimistic note, I am finishing this letter.
   Love,
   Tiger

By the time I reach the end of the letter, I am weeping,
filled with sadness for what will never be, guilty for any role
that I played in the troubles he experienced over these last seven
months, and sure of what I never was sure of before: Tiger loves
me and sincerely wanted me to love this place as much as he
does. Why wasn't I aware of how much he loved me? Perhaps,
he was afraid to show his feelings to me. But now I know, and
that's all that matters.

I vowed on our camping trip that if we survived, I would be
a better person. I am determined to be the wife Tiger has always
wanted.

Photos show some of the wonderful faces I encountered in Kivalina.

Boating with the Hawleys

Child enjoying flipper

Martha Swan

Some of the children in Kivalina

Fixing the seining nets

Children visiting our tent

Just one of the boys

Edith Kennedy beside her house

Regina Swan

Tommy Sage

Unknown elder

Orin Knox

(possibly) Milton Swan

Mother and child

Martha A. Swan

Sarah Hawley

Photographs capture a memory and a time never to be forgotten

PART II

XXVIII
HOSPITALIZATION

We are met in New York by a private plane that takes us to Harrisburg. A young doctor is on board to look after Tiger. I breathe a sigh of relief when I see him. At least now, there is someone on this plane who knows what he's doing—a far cry from our flight from Anchorage.

When we land at the New Cumberland Airport, an ambulance is waiting to take Tiger and the doctor to the hospital. I want to go with them, but know that there is really nothing I can do. As the ambulance whisks my husband away, I pray that we made the right decision in bringing him home. Back in Anchorage, Dr. Hillman warned us the trip back would be full of risks, and an infection was one of them. But we had to take the chance—we had to find a good plastic surgeon.

The last few days have been a challenge. Tiger's dad and I were trapped in Kotzebue for three days. During that time, he experienced a medical emergency which scared both of us. We felt isolated from Tiger and everything going on in Anchorage. Fortunately, we were not trapped in Kivalina; at least in Kotzebue we could contact Mom to find out how Tiger was. Her reports were more optimistic, and she had bought first-class tickets for all of us and hired a nurse to help with Tiger's care on the way back to Harrisburg. On the airplane, people smoked the whole time, even though Tiger was on oxygen. The nurse that Mom hired was useless. I wanted to help her, I was unable to. The flight attendants ordered me to stay in my seat with my seat belt on. No food was served, and it was obvious that there was something wrong with the plane, although we were never told about it. Luckily, the plane landed safely in Chicago, but we had to deplane and take another plane to New York. People stared at us as we wheeled Tiger through the airport. We worried that since we had to change planes, this might increase the risk of Tiger getting an infection.

* * *

Tiger's real treatment will begin tomorrow. Dr. Hillman had been trying to get him stabilized so we could go to Harrisburg, where he could be treated by a plastic surgeon. I lie awake most of the night—fearful for Tiger's well-being and the treatment that he is about to start.

The next day, I go with Tiger's parents to see Tiger at the hospital. He has a private room on the critical-care floor, with round-the-clock nurses. Before we enter his room, we're given masks and gowns to wear; Tiger's risk of infection is high.

Tiger's plastic surgeon, Dr. Harding, has put many soldiers back together after the Korean War. He is known to be an expert in his field, though I will come to find that he lacks good bedside manner, but this might just be because he is shy. Dr. Harding barely makes eye contact with me or Tiger's parents, but his expression is compassionate. Tiger and I are so young to have to experience this immense tragedy. He isn't particularly communicative about Tiger's condition and how he plans to treat him. This isn't encouraging.

Meanwhile, Tiger drifts in and out of consciousness. The general practitioner, Dr. Moyer, comes in to talk with us. He has news for us, and it is not good. Tiger has a lung infection. "It will be a few days before we know whether he'll survive the infection," the doctor says.

Mom and Dad and I look at each other. Mom puts her arm around me and says, "Dr. Hillman warned us he might get an infection. He's going to be all right." I love Mom for her optimism, but I'm in shock and cry constantly. The news of a lung infection that Tiger may not survive has only made things worse.

The doctor explains the treatment. "Before anything else can be done, the dead skin will be removed. He will have to have skin grafts on his hands and forehead, where the burns are the worst. We'll have to wait and see if he needs grafting in other places. Where we don't graft, he will have a great deal of scarring. At some point, he will need to have new ears built. It will be up to him whether he wants to continue with scar-tissue removal. This could be an ongoing process."

I am sobbing as he tells us this, but the Burches remain calm. Is this New England stoicism? Or are they just acting brave for me? After some time, with the doctor and nurses bustling in and out, we decide to go home. We are in the way here.

Harrisburg, and the comfort and warmth of the Burches' two-story home are a far cry from our tiny house in Kivalina. It feels strange. It's winter here, with temperatures hovering in the mid-forties. There is no snow on the ground. In Kivalina, this would be a mild spring day. Although we are nearing the shortest day of the year, darkness doesn't fall until about four thirty.

Mom and Dad go about their daily routine while I just sit and worry. I can't concentrate enough to read. I can't even knit, my usual therapy. I stay in my room a great deal of the time —the room Lynn and I shared before I was married. What happy times those were, giggling with Lynn about my future as her brother's wife. Right now, Lynn is in California, but she'll be home soon for Christmas and I can hardly wait to see her.

One afternoon, I tell Mom Burch that I need someone to talk to. "We know a minister," she says, "I'll make an appointment with him for you." I meet with the minister, but this family friend of theirs turns out to be of little help. I can't talk to him about anything that I want to. I can't explain our life in Alaska and how lonely I felt living there. I just tell him I am depressed.

"You're suffering from survivor's guilt," he says. "After a serious accident, a person who isn't hurt or doesn't die often has these feelings of self-reproach."

"Could be," I say. But I know it's much more than that. I wish I could have done more to save Tiger. But I also wish I had tried harder to fit into his world. I wanted to be more than the wife who let him chase his dreams. I wanted to be his soul-mate and partner. I am filled with regret about how our life in Alaska turned out. I leave the meeting with the minister, certain I need someone else to talk with, someone skilled with relationships, someone who could actually help. A minister who knew the family couldn't help me with all my anxiety. I wanted to learn how to accept all that had happened and learn how to go on with life.

Bubbles was put in a crate to join us when we flew from Anchorage to the Burches' place. Having Bubbles in Harrisburg is my salvation. She is company for me, and I'm hoping that she'll be a good distraction for Tiger while he's healing, take his mind off his pain.

Now that I know Bubbles will never be a sled dog, I can spoil her as much as I want. She sleeps next to my bed and follows me around the house. I take her outside to play behind the house, and she immediately tries to dig a hole. While I watch, she stops digging suddenly and lies still, panting. The poor dog is suffering from the temperature! Maybe she thinks a hole will help her stay cool. It was thirty-five degrees below zero when we left Kivalina. It's forty-five degrees above zero here. Her winter coat is thick and heavy and it will take her time to acclimate.

And it will take me time to acclimate too, for different reasons. I feel useless. My parents will arrive next week for a few days, and Lynn will be here as well. Mom Burch has been an incredible support, but it's easier to talk to my mother about things that are troubling me. I need her with me. My dad will be a silent but sympathetic cheerleader.

On December 18, two days after our return, outfitted in gowns and masks, Mom and Dad and I go in to see Tiger. He is lying in bed completely motionless, and the doctor gives us bad news. Tiger has pneumonia and it could be fatal. They have him on a strong antibiotic. "He'll likely sleep most of the day," the doctor tells us. I dissolve in tears. Have we come this far, only to have Tiger die in Harrisburg?

The rest of the day is a blur. The Burches go back home, leaving me at the hospital. They will return if things get any worse. I've decided to stay nearby. If my husband is going to die, I don't want him to die alone.

For hours, I sit at the end of the hall, terrified, waiting for any news. I can't distract myself no matter how hard I try. It hasn't even been two weeks since the fire; I feel traumatized by all that has happened in the past twelve days. When I can't endure the waiting anymore, I put on the gown and mask and go into Tiger's room. He can barely acknowledge my presence. I'm not sure if he even knows I'm here. The doctor tells me that Tiger hasn't eaten and keeps losing fluids. Kidney failure has become a possibility. I begin to wonder not only whether or not he will survive, but if he wants to.

Tiger's parents pick me up late in the afternoon, and we leave the hospital, praying that Tiger will turn the corner tonight. None of us sleep that night. Thankfully, the phone never rings.

At the hospital the next morning, we gown up without knowing what to expect, and when we enter Tiger's room, we're overjoyed by what we see. He has turned a corner. His eyes follow us around the room and he is more alert than I've seen him yet. He even tries to smile at us. I want to rush over and hug him, but he is so full of IVs to keep him hydrated that all I can do is go to his side and pat him on the shoulder. His hands are covered in bandages.

"Tiger, thank God you are better. You seem to have improved so much since we first saw you." As Mom speaks, Dad takes her hand and nods in encouragement.

We don't speak of his appearance. It's not a subject for discussion at this point. Tiger was a very handsome man. I think he knows he will look very different after all of his surgeries.

This evening, we visit again and find Tiger awake and watching TV, something that he never did much of in the past. He's watching *The Red Skelton Show* and looks amused by it. This show will become one of the things that he will look forward to doing during his long months of healing.

Two days after what we have come to refer to as Black Friday, the day Tiger almost died of pneumonia, we visit Tiger. Mom and Dad for some reason have taken separate cars.

"Your mom and I are going to a party at noon," Dad Burch explains. "We'll leave a car for you to drive back by yourself." He hands me the car keys.

My hands are shaking. I am terrified of driving. When I was sixteen, my father gave up on teaching me to drive when I stepped on the gas pedal instead of the brake and drove us through a hedge. When Tiger and I married, I still didn't drive. Tiger sent me to driver's school in Chicago, and I passed my driver's test, but I rarely drove in that city because there were alternatives. I could usually walk or use public transportation. After seven months in Alaska, I scarcely remember how to drive.

The Burches live in the country, about five miles from the hospital. "I don't know the way," I tell him, holding the keys. In the days we've been visiting Tiger, I've barely paid attention to the route we've taken. I assumed the Burches would always drive me. Suddenly, I realize I can't be dependent on them the entire time Tiger is in the hospital—however long that will be.

"I'll give you directions," Dad Burch says, and he writes them down quickly and hands me the paper. It sounds simple enough, but I'm nervous.

His parents and I enter Tiger's room to visit and find him playing with a toy one of his buddies has brought him. He laughs, watching the bird bob up and down in a glass of water. The silly toy enchants him, and it's good to see him amused. His parents leave after a few minutes. I say goodbye and tell them to have fun. I stay for a while without saying much, and then get ready to leave to make my dreaded journey home.

"I'm driving home by myself," I tell Tiger. "I'll see you tomorrow."

192

Tiger can't speak without taking the trachea tube out of his throat. He raises a hand and tries to wave goodbye. I doubt he understood the full impact of what I said anyway.

I'm tense driving to the Burches' house and grip the steering wheel tightly. Traffic is light and I make it without incident. What a relief! Now I can visit Tiger whenever I want. Dad Burch gave me the gift of independence when he handed me those car keys. I wonder how many visits I'll make to the hospital from my in-laws' home and what the future might hold.

XXIX

CHRISTMAS

The next day, I drive to the hospital and suit up with a mask and gloves to enter Tiger's room in the ICU. Dr. Harding, the plastic surgeon, is here to start the debriding process. He will remove the dead skin from Tiger's hands to promote healing and decrease the chance of infection. I sit across the room and watch the gruesome procedure while a couple of nurses stand by ready to help.

There is a lot of pus as the doctor works, using an instrument that looks like a pair of scissors. Infection is already setting in. Once the dead skin is removed, the doctor will assess the skin underneath to see whether grafting is necessary.

Ordinarily, this procedure would be a surgical one, done under anesthesia. Because of Tiger's severely damaged lungs, however, he can't handle anesthesia unless it is absolutely necessary. Unfortunately, he is awake for this. I'm told that the burns in his hands and wrists are very deep, and the nerve endings are dead, so there should be no pain. Sadly, though, I can see that Tiger does feel pain. He doesn't shout out because of his trachea tube, but I can see that he's gritting his teeth and he seems to be writhing in agony. It's torture to watch and be unable to help.

After about half an hour of this, the doctor cleans the delicate underlying tissue and wraps Tiger's hands in fresh bandages. There will be grafting done, but first, there will be several more debridements, Dr. Harding tells me. No more work will be done until after Christmas. Before I can ask any questions, he gets up and leaves the room. I had wanted to wish him a Merry Christmas; he is one of our saviors.

Alone now with Tiger, I go to his bedside and look into his beautiful blue eyes. I wish I could do more than touch his shoulder, but it's all I can do with so many tubes attached to his body. "That must have been awful, Tiger."

He nods in agreement, and then croaks out a few sentences. "The minister from Trinity Lutheran came in yesterday. He just stood in the doorway and stared. Then he said, "It must hurt."

The minister must have been stunned by Tiger's appearance, but I wish he had done something to console Tiger instead of just showing distress at his appearance. I can't tell Tiger that. Instead, I blow him a kiss and tell him I love him as I leave the room. This was not the minister who counselled me, but I am sure he would also be shocked by Tiger's appearance.

As Christmas nears, quiet celebrations start at the hospital. Christmas carols can be heard in rooms and down the halls. A choir from one of the churches has come in to sing and bring some joy to the patients. The nurses' station is piled high with boxes of candies from the grateful relatives of patients. The hospital lobby is full of poinsettias. I don't feel any of the happiness I usually feel at this time of year.

Lynn is coming home for the Christmas holiday. I can hardly wait to see her. She hasn't written since we moved to Alaska, and before that, we were close. I've learned from Mom Burch that Lynn is having emotional problems and is seeing a psychiatrist. I worry about her seeing the way her brother looks and hope she can handle it.

I go with the Burches to pick up Lynn at the airport and she greets us smiling and carrying a huge papier-mâché figure of Friar Tuck. She's brought a bit of Christmas with her. Mom Burch puts the holiday decoration in the front hallway so everyone can see it as they enter the house. Years later, every Christmas, Lynn's gift sits on my table in the hall, reminding me of the Christmas the year that our lives changed forever.

Lynn has brought a ray of sunshine into the house. We sleep in the same room again, and talk long into the night, like two sisters. She's focused on Tiger and his well-being.

"I wonder what he'll look like after all his operations. What does the doctor say?"

"Not much. And your parents and I don't talk about it either. Tiger hasn't even asked for a mirror. It's going to be hard for him when he does."

"I remember that you always thought he looked like Paul Newman."

"He'll never look like Paul Newman again; I know that much. No one knows what he'll look like after all the surgery he needs. I'm afraid for him, but I'm afraid for me, too. What will our relationship be like after all this?"

Lynn sighs deeply, and I do too.

"It's good to have you here," I tell her.

Lynn comes with me to visit Tiger at the hospital the next day. It's difficult for her to see her brother this way. She was warned about his appearance, but she couldn't understand until she saw him. Nobody can.

That night, the four of us sit quietly in front of the fire in the living room. None of us have the Christmas spirit. Mom gets up to answer a knock at the door and finds a family standing there, waiting to be asked in to sing Christmas carols. Apparently, these neighbors visit their friends every year and treat them to a few songs. Mom looks reluctant, but she asks them in. I wish they hadn't come. I feel as if they're forcing Christmas upon us. The family stands together in front of us and sings a couple of carols while we listen politely, but they don't stay long. A pall hangs over the room. They must know about Tiger's accident; the grapevine moves swiftly here. Did they really think they were going to bring us joy right now? The future looks so bleak for Tiger.

My parents arrive two days before Christmas. They will be staying here and not at a hotel. I drive them to the hospital to visit Tiger, which pleases my dad. He is surprised because he has never seen me driving before. We put on sterile gowns and masks and enter the room to see Tiger lying in the bed. His face is not bandaged, and they can see where his ears should have been. Mom and Dad don't see his hands without bandages, but his face shocks them. His burns are far more severe than they anticipated, although on the way to the hospital, I explained what to expect and told them that he doesn't look nearly as bad as he did in Anchorage, when I phoned not long after the accident.

"Tiger almost died the other day from pneumonia. Sometimes, I wonder if he'll even want to live when he realizes that he will never look the same," I tell them.

On our way back to the Burches', my mother says that she understands now why I didn't want them to spend Christmas with my brother and his family. "I didn't realize it was so bad," she says.

"What did you expect, Mom? I tried to tell you on the phone." I want to tell my mother that she never should have hesitated about being with me, but I know she'll only defend her actions. I resolve that if I ever have a child, I'll be there right away when I'm needed, no question.

Soon, family will surround me. My brother, Robert, comes in on a bus from Pittsburgh instead of flying due to heavy fog. Tiger's brother, John, won't be here, but with Robert here, we'll have enough family to make it as festive as possible under the circumstances.

On Christmas Eve, after a hospital visit, I ask Lynn if she'd like to go to church with me and thank God for helping Tiger pull through pneumonia.

Lynn's answer surprises me. It's the first time on this visit that she has spoken about her own issues. "I don't really want to. I feel like God has let me down and He has let you and Tiger down as well. I'm not sure that I believe in God right now."

I share my own thoughts, too. Sometimes I don't believe in Him anymore. I question the value of praying. Why would He let this happen to us? Is there a predestination? Maybe our whole life is carved out for us and we have no choice in what happens. But is it God who is giving us no choice?

We decide not to go to church.

I wake on Christmas Day to the aroma of sausages cooking and fresh-brewed coffee. I wander downstairs to grab a cup. Mom Burch will serve country sausage and coffee cake. I don't have much appetite, but everyone is making a special effort today.

The house is festively decorated, and a large tree with beautiful decorations and twinkling lights stands against the bay window in the living room. For the last few days, Mom Burch has labored to make it a celebration. Presents are stacked under the tree, gaily wrapped and waiting to be opened. I don't have presents or cards for anyone. The best present that I could have would be to wake up and find this whole thing was a nightmare.

Mom Burch has made Christmas cookies—sand tarts, ginger-bread men, and bourbon balls. My mother has made shortbread cookies—my old favorite—and sugar cookies cut into the shape of stars. At noon, Dad Burch will make the eggnog he's famous for and serve it in tall glasses topped with a sprinkling of nutmeg. My dad will be the official taster and they will both get a bit drunk on the potent drink.

We sit to open gifts, and Mom Burch hands me a beautifully wrapped present. It is large and wrapped in green paper with a gold bow. Everyone watches as I unwrap it. It's the painting of four children we saw when were together in Anchorage, a few weeks—or a lifetime—ago. I burst into tears at the sight of it.

"Oh, my God, Mom, I can't believe that you did this for me."

How could she think to buy this for me when she must have been so preoccupied with her son's tragedy? I love the painting but don't want this reminder of Alaska if Tiger dies.

She smiles. "It's for you and Tiger, a gift for the future. I hope that you'll hang it in your home someday and enjoy it for many years."

More than fifty years later, the painting still has a special place in my home.

On Christmas night, I take Robert with me to visit Tiger. Tiger tries to smile at him and croaks a greeting. Robert is so shocked by Tiger's appearance he can hardly speak.

In the elevator on our way out, he puts an arm around me. "Deanne, I didn't know it was this bad. Are you sure you're able to handle this?"

"I'm doing my best," I tell my brother. "Every day is a challenge. Sometimes I think he wants to die. We don't talk about it. I just want him to survive. I love him."

Everyone but my mother leaves for home a few days after Christmas. Now, I am facing a new year, a new life. Last year, we had so much to look forward to. Now, our dreams are shattered.

XXX

AFTER CHRISTMAS

The hospital is a beehive of activity. Tiger is still in the intensive care unit, with round-the-clock nursing care. His day nurse, Mrs. Lilly, is an old battle-ax with a soft heart. She allows Tiger very little pain medicine. She remembers the soldiers who became addicted during the Korean War, and she refuses to see Tiger become an addict on her watch. Tiger will later tell me his first shot of morphine took him to the moon. The next shot didn't take him nearly so far, and by the third, he felt very little. Thank God for Mrs. Lilly. The nurses prepare food for him, too, food he likes—sausage and steak. He is getting better, and he tries to smile and talk more. He's still in a lot of pain, but each day he is getting stronger.

One day, when I walk into Tiger's room, there is the distinct smell of Lysol. It's unusual to smell this because the ICU is kept scrupulously clean at all times. I ask Tiger about it, and he points to Mrs. Myers, his afternoon nurse. I see by the look on his face he is shaken up. I ask the nurse to leave the room for a few minutes and she does.

"What's going on, Tiger?" I ask.

This is what he tells me. Mrs. Myers came into the room and proceeded to wipe down everything with Lysol. She asked him if he had looked in a mirror. He hadn't; we had had the mirrors removed for the time being, fearing that his seeing his face would cause a setback. She told him he would look like a monster, even after plastic surgery. She said people would stare at him and avoid him. I want to kiss away his tears, but I can't even wipe them away with a Kleenex, because it may not be sterile enough. How could anyone be so cruel? That mean and sadistic woman doesn't belong in the nursing profession.

"I want to see what I look like. Is there a mirror anywhere?" he asks me.

"Right now, your face is raw and swollen, and your eyes are still slits. The swelling is going down, and I see improvement every day. I think you should wait to look in the mirror until after you have the surgeries. And know I will love you no matter what you look like."

Tiger doesn't say anything. I know he'll keep asking now for a mirror. I can't fire Mrs. Myers fast enough.

Throughout January, Tiger has countless operations. Skin is grafted from his thigh to his forehead, and to his hands and his fingers as well. I sit at the end of the hall as he is wheeled to and from the operating room, knitting to pass the time, like Madame Defarge in *A Tale of Two Cities*.

The days blend into one another, with Tiger showing more improvement every day. Mid-January, he is no longer under the strict sterile conditions and his room is filled with flowers. It appears that flowers are being sent by almost everyone we know. Someone has even sent a small aquarium with fighting fish in it. Tiger had an aquarium as a young boy, and this seems to soothe him. I hope the cheer the fish and flowers bring will speed up his recovery.

Tiger spends most of his days lying in bed. Occasionally, I take him for a short walk down the hall, helping him with the tubes he has to take along. I'm happy to see him somewhat ambulatory, but this doesn't help his somber mood. I wonder if he is depressed and if he is thinking about his future. I want to know, but I don't ask. These conversations upset him.

One day, hoping it will make him feel better, I decide that it's time to give Tiger his notes from Kivalina.

"They're in great shape," I say, handing him his notebook. "Just a bit of smoke damage around the edges."

He looks at the notebook in my hands and asks me to put it on the table beside the bed. I can't believe he's not even going to look at them. Isn't this what he almost died trying to retrieve?

"I think you'll be amazed to see how much information we collected."

He finally takes a cursory glance at them. "Put them back on the table. I want to go back to Kivalina to finish the study," he says somberly.

"Don't you think we already have a lot of good information?"

"No. We're going back as soon as the doctor says I'm well enough. I want to rent Jakie's house and spend another winter there."

I wince at the thought, but say, "I'll support whatever you want to do." Tiger will be in danger of pneumonia every time he catches a cold. With his badly burned lungs, he'll be susceptible to everything. Then, there's the problem of having no proper medical help nearby. Maybe he'll come to his senses and change his mind. It's possible that thinking about our return to Alaska is the only way he can get through this ordeal.

One day, my mother decides to give me some advice. I have just come home from visiting him at the hospital.

"You know, dear," she says, "when Tiger comes home from the hospital, you must pretend that everything is the same as it was before he was burned. You can never let him know how different he looks, and you can never let him know that it bothers you."

I wonder if I can do this. He'll never look the same. His hands aren't even the way they were before. They won't feel the same when he touches me. And there are more problems, too. I need more in our relationship. I wish that I had a therapist to help me accept what has happened. It's not just accepting the accident and its aftermath. I also have to accept our two very different personalities. Even under these extreme conditions, Tiger is focused on his work. Sometimes I feel as though work is his wife and I am his mistress.

I consult with my mother, who is leaving the next day for Toronto. "Mom," I say, "why did this happen to us? It's not fair."

"Well, dear, no one ever said life is fair. You're just going to have to deal with the cards that you have been given."

Nobody should have to deal with this deck, I think to myself, but I vow to try.

By the time my mother leaves to go back to Toronto, I have a literal lump in my throat that I can't swallow. It never goes away, and I worry that I might have a thyroid problem, or cancer. Whatever it is, I don't tell anyone. There is enough to worry about.

Living with Tiger's mother, I focus on new things to help lift my spirits. In the evening, we take turns cooking. She is an excellent cook, and I learn new recipes and techniques from her. She shows me how to flatten the veal for veal scaloppini, and she makes a mean Caesar salad. One night, she experiments with making a liver meatloaf. I didn't particularly like it, but if we have seal liver this summer, I can try to make one.

Something that I'm trying to learn from Mom Burch is optimism. She bustles around the kitchen, always cheerful no matter how she feels inside. Before I leave for the hospital in the morning, we sit and drink several cups of her coffee. I am used to the more robust Alaskan coffee, and crave a strong dose of it, but I appreciate getting ready for the day this way. I'm ready to face what lies ahead of me, ready to focus on Tiger's well-being.

During early February, Tiger is much stronger, and he improves more every day. He starts physical therapy on his hands to keep the muscles from atrophying. Most of the time, he squeezes a small rubber ball.

David and Peggy visit, and their timing couldn't be better. Tiger can enjoy the visit, as many of his grafts are finished and the trachea tube is out. He is able to talk normally. Their visit is a treat for me, too. Peggy looks on the bright side of things and makes me laugh. She is a nurse and has seen other burn cases. She knows what to expect, which I'm thankful for.

When she and David enter Tiger's hospital room for the first time, the doctor is cutting away some of the scabs around

Tiger's eyes. This is done daily because his eyelids are still badly swollen. We visit for a while, and then Peggy and David leave so I can say goodbye to Tiger. Tiger says, "Peggy wouldn't look at me when Dr. Harding was cutting away the dead skin. Do I really look that awful?"

"Of course she doesn't think that you look that bad. And even if you did, I'd love you anyway." I need to reassure him all the time that no matter what, I will still love him.

When I join David and Peggy in the hall, I tell Peggy what Tiger said.

"Oh gosh, I feel so awful," Peggy says. "I only averted my eyes because I wanted to give him privacy."

The next day, David and Peggy bring a Barbie doll for Tiger to squeeze when they visit. Tiger laughs. "This would be more fun if her boobs were rubber instead of plastic. And they could be bigger, too!"

Tiger needs blood transfusions, and both David and Peggy offer to replenish the blood bank for them. I decide to do it as well. We are tested and find that only David can donate because Peggy has an Rh factor complication and I have allergies and a high stress level. David is terrified, but he does it. He reminds me of the football players at university who fainted while giving blood. Their visit ends much too quickly, but it was a bright spot for both of us, especially for me.

Itching from the grafts and donor sites plagues Tiger. A doctor has recommended a small amount of liquor to relax him, and he looks forward to his nightly libation. One day, an older dentist arrives as a patient. He has managed to smuggle in a case of Wild Turkey. He and Tiger imbibe together from time to time. I'm surprised, but I figure that if drinking with the dentist makes him happy, it's fine. Right now, it's all I care about.

XXXI

NEW BEGINNINGS

Two months after he was admitted, and just in time for Valentine's Day, Tiger is released from the hospital. The doctors say he has made a remarkable recovery because he was healthy before the accident.

The first thing Tiger sees when he gets home is Bubbles. He stoops down to pet her, and then looks at me with a smile on his face.

"She's gotten so big," he says. And then, sadly, he adds, "She would have made a great leader on the team." I nod, knowing she'll never be a leader now. She has been my pet for two months.

I follow Tiger upstairs to his old bedroom. It's our room now, and Mom B. has made his two single beds into a king-size bed by putting a piece of foam rubber over the top of them. I am uneasy as to how it will feel to sleep together after all this time. Later, when we go upstairs for the night, I am nervous, not knowing what to expect or what I should do. I snuggle up to him as though we are in the twin bed in Kivalina and we sleep that way through the night. Having him out of the hospital is the best Valentine's Day present I could have.

As I lie next to Tiger trying to sleep, I think about our life together. It's depressing to know that every time he looks in the mirror, he'll remember what he's lost. Every time that I look across the room at him, I'll remember the handsome young man I married—a man who will never look the same. Tiger's face is bright red where no grafting has been done. It will always be badly scarred. The graft is a different color than the rest of his skin. He's lost part of his nose, and eventually will have his ears reconstructed. He has almost no hair, but the doctors assure us it will grow back soon because the hair follicles weren't destroyed. His head is covered with burn scabs, and he wears a cap to avoid infections. He'll never be able to use his hands the way he did. Typing will be difficult, and playing the piano and the accordion, two things he loved, will be challenging. I remember him playing his accordion in Kivalina, a smile on his face as his fingers jumped over the keyboard. He will have physical therapy on his hands daily. The only thing that is the same are his piercingly blue eyes. We don't talk much about the night of the accident. I hope that it won't always be this way.

Right away, Tiger starts a regimen to strengthen himself. He has been home from the hospital for two weeks. Today, after walking Bubbles, he says to me, "I'm starting to get my strength back. I can hardly wait to go back to Kivalina."

I gulp. I have a deep sense of foreboding about our return, but I can't tell him this.

Tiger enjoys the solitude of the property his family lives on. The Burches own several acres of property and it's a peaceful area for walking Bubbles, which he does every day. I don't know what we would do without Bubbles. She is a reminder of our life in Alaska, and she brings us both so much happiness. Bubbles is a beautiful dog, a malamute mix with gray and black markings. Her fur is tipped at the end with silver, a touch of the wolf in her. Bubbles is a great companion, a very gentle dog.

Tiger doesn't leave his parents' property much. Neither of us does. I suspect we are avoiding the inevitable—Tiger's first time in public. Tiger is quiet about his looks. I pretend everything is as before and his appearance doesn't bother me, just as my mother has told me to do. But in truth, it's hard to get used to.

When a month has passed since his release from the hospital, we realize that we can't isolate ourselves from the world anymore. It's time for Tiger to get used to going out in public. We start with Howard Johnson's. Tiger has been craving a Ho Jo hot dog and ice cream since he left the hospital.

On the way to the restaurant, I'm apprehensive. Will people stare and whisper? How will we handle this? Can I handle it for Tiger? He looks as though he has just returned from the war and I am the wife he has left behind.

At the restaurant, we find a booth, hoping for a bit of privacy. There are not many people around. So far, so good. A young woman with her son walks in and settles into a booth across from us. She sits down, sees Tiger's face, and looks away. Is it horror, disgust, or empathy that I see in her eyes? Her son, who is about four years old, sits, staring at Tiger. Finally, just loud enough for us to hear, he says, "Mommy, what's wrong with that man's face?"

His mother ignores him. She's probably embarrassed.

He repeats his question. "What's wrong with that man's face?"

She continues to ignore the child.

Finally, he shouts. "Mommy! What is wrong with that man's face?"

The woman's face turns beet red, and she whisks the child away with her to another booth.

We try to go ahead with our meal of hot dogs and ice cream, but our hearts aren't in it.

These issues will continue. A year later, in Harrisburg, I'll become friendly with a woman who invites us to dinner a few times. One night, privately, she surprises me by saying, "Do you know why I am being so nice to you?"

"No, why?"

"When you move away from here, you're going to have a difficult time. People won't want to be seen with Tiger. It's going to be hard for you to make friends because of him."

Her words are upsetting. It's hard to imagine a life in which I will hear hurtful words like hers wherever I go. Will Tiger always be an object of scrutiny? In forty years, I'll have an answer to that question. A nine-year-old grandchild at a friend's family dinner will say, "Mom, what's wrong with that guy's face?" We'll ignore his question. Later, I'll wish I had spoken up.

In March, we visit my family for a couple of weeks. There is an excellent physical therapist in Hamilton, and Tiger can have rehabilitation at the hospital there. He says it is better than the treatment he is getting in Harrisburg.

I overhear my mother on the phone one day, telling a friend about me and Tiger. "It's like nothing ever happened to him. She just sits on the couch holding his hand. She is remarkably strong through all of this." Doesn't my mother have a clue about what I am trying to keep inside? I am trying to pretend that everything is the same, like she told me to do. I'm trying to avoid thinking of how my life with Tiger is forever changed, and about the accident that will plague us both for the rest of our lives.

Friends in Toronto were a great support to me when we were in Alaska. Now that we're here, few of them have us over. None of them ask me much about the accident. Scarcely any of them are there to support me; they don't ask questions, don't want to hear about how I feel or let me vent. Some have even asked me not to talk about it. Are they afraid that my bad luck will trickle into their lives? I can see now that they don't understand what my life in Alaska was really like, and frankly, they aren't interested. Our conversation focuses on buying a house, having children, and discussing upcoming weddings. I want to be part of their lives but they aren't interested in mine.

One friend, Sue, invites us to dinner. Sue was my bridesmaid, and her husband was an usher. Before we come over, Sue tells me she is nervous.

"Sue," I say, "think about how Tiger feels. He knows he looks totally different from the man you knew a year ago. He's just as nervous as you are."

Dinner goes well that evening, and I'm relieved. Tiger needs to start seeing people that we knew before, people from our other life. It's a good beginning.

The lump in my throat isn't gone, and I know I am going to have to deal with it. It feels like I have swallowed a golf ball. I haven't told Tiger. He has enough on his plate without having to worry about me.

* * *

Last summer, the Burches built a small cottage on the property where the larger one is. The "big" cottage, as they now refer to it, is a magnificent structure with huge rooms, a winding staircase, and seven bedrooms, each with its own bath. When I'm there, I feel like I'm living in a castle. Built in 1908, the home is called Ardencaple, perhaps named after a castle in Scotland built sometime in the late twelfth century. The new cottage is small and cozy, with two bedrooms. The living and dining areas are a single large room, and a stone fireplace is at one end of it. The cottage is winterized, ready for the elements. It almost sits on the lake, and we can watch the sunrise and the moonrise through its windows. I'll find out later, when we spend summers here, that we also get the spectacular afterglow of the sunset, with brilliant colors streaking across the sky.

A weekend at the lake in early March is a welcome respite from the daily hardships of trying to adjust to our new lives. David, Peggy, and Judy will join us. They are good company and will take my mind off of Tiger's plans to return to the north.

The weather is cold and beautiful when we arrive at the lake for our weekend. The snow drifts down in large flakes and the lake has a coating of ice deep and sturdy enough to walk on. The temperature and wind here are not as extreme as they are in Alaska, but it's a good test for Tiger's tolerance of the weather in his current condition.

We take walks across the ice to some of the nearby islands, peeking into the windows of some of the empty cottages for fun. In the late afternoon, we sip hot chocolate by the fire or drink hot rum toddies. I ached for this type of companionship when we lived in Kivalina, talking, laughing, feeling good. Feeling at ease.

After a wonderful weekend, we return to my parents' house in Toronto. Unfortunately, the lump in my throat is worse than ever. I can hardly swallow, and I can't eat. I decide to tell my mother, and she makes an appointment with the doctor.

What happens next is a curiosity. The doctor can't find anything wrong with me. I ask him if he thinks the lump in my throat could be caused by stress.

"Why on earth are you stressed?" he asks. "You're a young bride. This should be the happiest time of your life." Dr. Ross knew me before I was married, and he knew I was going to live in Alaska. I tell him about the year there, how hard it was, and all the times I was sick after bottling up my feelings. Then I tell him about the accident and what happened to Tiger. I share my thoughts about going back to Alaska, tell him I'm frightened to return. "I'm depressed and I'm scared," I say. "I can't even think about going back for a winter up there, and it's all Tiger talks about."

"I'm sorry," the doctor says, frowning. "But I can understand why you would be stressed. The lump in your throat is called globus hystericus, caused by anxiety. I'm giving you a prescription for Valium. The pills will help you relax. They may even lift your spirits."

He says he has given me enough Valium to last while we are in Alaska, and he's not kidding. The bottle of pills turns out to be the size of a jar of spaghetti sauce! I look at the blue tablets through the glass, wondering if they truly will be my pathway to contentment. I'll come to refer to these pills as my "happy pills." I remember reading *Valley of the Dolls* while we were in Alaska, and I wonder if I could become addicted to them. The doctor doesn't warn me of that possibility.

When I'm home again, my mother is sitting with Tiger, who doesn't know I have a problem. "So, what did Dr. Ross say? What's wrong with you?" my mother asks.

I don't mention the pills. "Oh, he just said I'm suffering from stress," I tell her. "He calls it globus hystericus. He said I need to learn to relax."

Tiger comes over and puts his arms around me. "We've both been through hell. We'll be fine once we get back to Alaska."

I tremble hearing this, but don't say a word.

Spring comes, with blooming yellow daffodils and deep red and purple tulips brightening the gardens. Soon, the flowering trees will blossom, and the weather will be warmer. But I can't enjoy the season here, I can't settle into a life that feels comfortable to me. If we can rent the same house, Tiger is planning to spend the winter in Kivalina.

We leave Canada, say goodbye to family and friends once again, and get ready to return to Kivalina. No one asks how I feel about it. I keep my thoughts to myself and start taking the Valium. Like magic, the lump in my throat is gone. What a relief! I am feeling like my old self again by the time we arrive back in Harrisburg to get ready for Alaska.

Tiger and I take a vacation weekend in New York visiting old friends. When we come back, Mom and Dad pick us up at the airport and I chatter away happily about our weekend. It had been a wonderful weekend, a reprieve for me at least as to what lay ahead. A pall seems to hang over the car and finally, Mom turns around to tell us that Bubbles ran away while we were gone and was found dead on the road. This news is more than we can bear, and we both burst into tears. Tears have been a long time coming for Tiger, and we have never cried together. Bubbles was the best thing that happened to us in Alaska and she's been an important part of our life during the months in Harrisburg, too, our support and comfort in so many ways. Her death would make a huge void in our lives. Why are we being tested?

Before Tiger and I leave for Alaska, Lynn comes from California to say goodbye. She asks if she can visit us in Kivalina in early September.

"We'd love it," I tell her. "But right now, we don't even know if we'll be able to rent the same house. Maybe we'll be in a one-room house. Maybe we'll even be in a tent. Are you okay with this?"

"Yes, I want to experience what you both have experienced."

We say goodbye to Mom and Dad and thank them for all they did for us for the last six months. We couldn't have gotten along without them. I miss Bubbles. We should be taking her back with us, though having a dog as a pet would differentiate us from the rest of the village. Neither of us thought about this when we made plans to go back to the village. I don't care if we are different from the rest of the villagers. If we want to raise a dog as a pet, we should. I'm tired of living exactly the way the natives do. Tiger is talking about looking for a malamute when we are in Anchorage, and he may be planning on having it as a pet. I'm sure he wouldn't raise it as a sled dog, but I haven't asked him.

Before we leave, hoping I won't regret it, I dump my "happy pills" down the toilet. I probably polluted the water system, but what else could I do with them? I'm afraid of becoming addicted, and I know in my heart that medicating my pain is not the right thing to do. I need to face whatever lies ahead.

XXXII

BACK TO ALASKA

Back in Alaska again, we start in Anchorage, spending the first night in the Westward Hotel. Spring is making a spectacular appearance with melting snow and pots of pansies lining the streets. After sleeping off our jet lag, we rent a car and drive some country roads, hoping to see some of the wildlife around at this time of year.

"I'd love to see a moose," Tiger says, as we drive. Moments later, as we round a bend, we see a moose wading in a creek near the roadside. Wish granted! It's the first time I have seen a moose, and I have to agree, it's a magnificent creature.

Driving around a suburb of Anchorage, we see the devastation caused by the 1964 earthquake. We see remains of houses that fell down the cliffs and trees that were destroyed by the earthquake. Debris litters the hillside. I shudder. "Earthquakes must be terrifying. I would hate to live through one," I say.

Tiger feels differently. "I'd like to know what it's like," he says. "I'd even like to experience a tidal wave."

"Are you serious?" I can't believe what I'm hearing. "We've had enough excitement for a lifetime."

That night at the hotel, I'm wakened suddenly by a thunderous sound. The bedside lamps are swaying. I can even hear the water swishing in the toilet. It's an earthquake.

Tiger takes my hand and I lie as still as I can, trying to wish it away. The seconds seem like hours before the shaking stops. It isn't a serious quake—the building isn't crumbling.

"No more wishes, Tiger, okay. You wanted to see a moose and you saw one right away. You wanted to be in an earthquake and now we've had one. I don't want to worry about a tidal wave."

Our few days in Anchorage are pleasant. It's a beautiful city, with a lot to do. Last December, it was a safe haven for me, though I was in too much shock to remember much about it. This time, when I look out the window of our hotel and see the mountains and the ocean, I don't feel guilty. I'm happy to be here with Tiger and getting a second chance to be a better wife.

We call the Hillmans who welcome us back and invite us to meet them at a restaurant in town. After dinner, we are their guests at the symphony.

"I'm pleasantly surprised with Tiger's appearance," Louise says to me. Fred doesn't say a word about it, and I'd like to know what he thinks. He was the first doctor to treat Tiger, and maybe his expectations were higher. Perhaps he thought that the surgeon could have done a better job.

After enjoying time with the Hillmans, the next day we visit Providence Hospital, where Tiger spent the first ten days after he was burned. He wants to thank the staff who looked after him. This is important to him. I appreciate the strength and integrity Tiger has. As it turns out, however, very few members of the hospital staff remember him. We are told burn victims are treated at the hospital all the time. His accident was just one of many. I think this surprises Tiger. He assumed that he would be remembered.

I attempt to reassure him that what he's done by going in to thank the staff was meaningful. "I think they appreciated you going in to thank them. It probably doesn't happen very often."

Tiger takes my hand. "I'm happy to see where I was last winter. I'm sure they saved my life. We can go."

Wandering around downtown Anchorage later that day, we run into some of the crew who were on our flight out of Alaska. We recognize each other and stop to say hello.

"That was a terrible flight," I tell a flight attendant who I remember well. "Nobody would help us, and nobody would let me get up to help my husband. He was on oxygen and all around him, people were smoking. What was going on?"

"You don't know the half of it," she replies. She won't elaborate, but I have a feeling we were lucky to have landed safely. I wasn't happy about the flight back then, and I'm not happy remembering it now. We bid her goodbye and move on.

We start looking for a malamute, hoping to find a dog that resembles Bubbles. Quickly, however, we learn that there are no breeders around. People go to Washington or Oregon for a malamute.

"I guess we'll have to find a dog when we get to Kivalina," Tiger says, with a sigh. "I want to get one as soon as we get there."

"Let's hope Bubbles' mother is having a litter soon." I answer.

In Anchorage, Tiger tries to find Jakie Sage to see if we can rent the house again. When Tiger can't find him, he sends him a check for five hundred dollars, which Jakie promptly returns to our hotel. Tiger thinks that Jakie doesn't trust him.

"I was going to offer to put a generator in for us if we could rent his house. I'm tired of kerosene lanterns and Coleman stoves," he tells me. Why couldn't he have bought one last year? This would never have happened.

"We'll have to find a different house to rent," Tiger says. When I hear him say this, I know he is determined to spend another winter in Kivalina.

I don't want to rent a one-room house. I don't want to spend another winter in Kivalina.

"Yeah, maybe," I say. Why can't I communicate my feelings about this whole venture?

XXXIII

KIVALINA, AGAIN

We arrive in Kotzebue and hire Nelson Walker to fly us up to Kivalina. Jakie has allowed us to stay in his house temporarily while we make repairs. This will give us about six weeks before we have to be out of there.

When we arrive in the village, people are waiting at the airport for the school kids who have been away at school since Christmas. They don't know if today is the day that they will be coming home, but they don't look disappointed to see us emerging from the plane instead. They knew we were coming back soon, because Tiger had written to Clinton Swan to ask him to start repairs on the house.

A chorus of "Welcome home!" and "Good to see you again!" greets us as we step off the plane. I feel happy to be received so warmly. Sarah Hawley throws her arms around me, a gesture that's quite out of character for her. "Come in for coffee and visit for a while," she says, with a big smile.

Half of the village joins us at the Hawley's. Everyone wants to let us know how pleased they are that we have returned.

Sipping coffee at the table and looking at the beaming friendly faces, it feels good to be back. What a difference from the last time I arrived here when I knew nobody and everyone was a stranger. No, I don't want to spend a winter here, but it helps to know I can count on the support of so many people if we do stay.

Eventually, it's time to leave the warmth of the Hawley's house and go to assess the damage done to our house. Many of the people that we've been visiting with follow us.

As we walk, one of the men nudges Tiger, saying, "Your wife sure looks good, alright, Tiger. She's gotten a little fat."

Later, Tiger will tell me the man was paying me a compliment. "The natives are all heavier than you. Being heavy is their perception of beauty."

I feel as though I fit right in, even if it isn't true.

Some of the men carry our suitcases as we walk to the house. They are very solicitous because of Tiger's health. After depositing the suitcases in the shed, they leave us to have a look at the damage the fire did to the house.

Charlotte and Clinton Swan have worked for several days, scrubbing the soot from the floors, walls, and cupboards. They've cleaned every room. Charlotte has painted the walls and only one wall that needs repairing remains. It was the wall suffering the most damage in the fire. We will order a piece of lumber to finish the job. We'll reimburse the Swans, too, for everything they've done for us to make the house ready for our return.

Still, Tiger is clearly shaken by the damage. He walks into the bedroom. Does he remember lying there, face down? Was he even conscious? I watch for his reaction, but there isn't any.

"This is where you ended up in the house. It looked like you were getting ready to die." He almost shakes as I tell him this. He says, "I don't remember," and pauses for a moment, thinking. Then, for the first time, he tells me about his experience of the fire. "When I was lying on the mattress at the Keating's, I knew that I was in trouble. I could barely breathe. I think most of the time, I was unconscious. But when I was conscious, I thought that we'd get to Kotzebue and they would patch me up. I honestly thought that I'd be back here for the Christmas feast."

"How could you have thought that?" I ask. Then, I realize that he couldn't face the fact then, and maybe can't face it even now. I wonder how he'll feel tonight, sleeping in the house where he almost died. I know I won't feel comfortable.

During our first day back in Kivalina, Tiger goes over to Amos's house to hitch up the dogs to go upriver and get ice for water. Amos looked after our dogs for the winter, not knowing whether we would return. Amos has the sled too.

While Tiger's out, I stay at the house, surveying the repairs the Swans have made. Then, I try to do more cleaning. The windows won't open, and there is a lingering smell of smoke because the house has been closed all winter.

As I clean, I hear a commotion just outside the door. It's Pepper and Coco! The dogs are pulling the sled toward the house. They look ecstatic to be here, despite the fact that Amos has been with them for longer than we were. I go outside to greet them, and Pepper gives one of his happy growls. I melt after hearing this and run to bury my face in his fur.

Later that day, Tiger tells me about Pepper. "Amos used Pepper on his team all winter and thinks that he's fast and strong and a very good sled dog. If we stay, he might even be our leader." However, Amos also told him that Pepper's fur isn't suited to Arctic conditions. It's not thick enough for the frigid weather. Pepper was lucky to have survived the winter.

We both know that we may not be able to find a house for the winter. If we can't stay for the winter, we may bring Pepper home with us. We are probably crazy to think we can make a sled dog into a domesticated pet. He is hardly dainty. Although he's not large, he is built like a barrel and very strong. I remember last year when we raised Pepper and Coco. Coco was always the fearless one, ready to get into trouble at any moment. We thought he would be the one Amos would talk about.

* * *

It is mid-May, a few days after our return. The Keatings are leaving for the lower states until late August. When they come back, Tiger would like to go over old papers that former teachers have written up. He hopes to get a history of the school since its beginning. Before they leave, they show us photographs taken the night of the fire and help us reconstruct what happened that night. I didn't need reminders, but it's good for Tiger to hear their version of that night.

Jim tells us that Lowell Sage said when they took Tiger into the minister's house, his hands looked like rubber gloves hanging in shreds. He touched his mukluks and they just disintegrated. Jim says, "Lanterns should never be lit indoors." He's preaching to the choir.

"I guess I had to learn the hard way," Tiger says, with a deep sigh. "I knew this could happen but honestly, I didn't think it would happen to me."

Back at the house, after that visit to the Keating's, I decide that it's time to talk with Tiger about the night of the fire. I have wanted to talk about it for five months, but it's been a taboo subject. It shouldn't be the elephant in the room.

I start by telling Tiger that I think he was burned when the kerosene lantern flared up in his face.

"No, I wasn't." He is certain about this. "When I went back in, I tried to use the fire extinguisher, but it wouldn't work. I tried beating out the fire with a blanket. Then I had to walk through a wall of fire with my hands over my face."

"Tiger," I say, "look at your hands." Besides the discoloration from the skin grafts and the scarring, many of his fingers are bent because there was damage to the tendons, bones, and joints.

"I think that my hands protected my face from being burned worse than it was."

"Maybe they did, but I think you were burned initially and went into shock. I don't think that putting your hands over your face made any difference at all."

Tiger shakes his head, disagreeing with me vehemently.

Part of his memory of the events makes sense to me, but the rest doesn't. The night of the fire, he was wearing an Irish knit sweater. His hands were burned only as far as his wrists. The sweater protected his arms, but his hands were burned because he was trying to shield his face. His ears were unprotected and were burned so badly that the tissue shed right off. I believe that he was burned by the lantern, went into shock, and couldn't

219

think properly when he went back into the house. That is why he couldn't use the fire extinguisher or beat out the flames with a blanket.

Slowly, we learn more about the night of the fire. Many people helped us, but I was in such a state of shock, I wasn't even aware of that. Andrew Baldwin, the teenager, heard me shouting for help and went for the minister. Another boy saw the flames through the window and went for help. The "wall of fire" that Tiger ran through was out by the time his rescuers came and found Tiger unconscious on the floor. They had to use gas masks because the smoke was so thick. Tiger had been on the floor for about thirty minutes, which is probably the reason his lungs are so badly damaged.

Dreams of that night will haunt us for the rest of our lives. I will be afraid to light candles or matches. Tiger will be claustrophobic entering a room full of steam at the Y because he is unable to breathe or see.

Appearances aren't as important to the Eskimos as they are to people at home. Mildred, the postmistress, says, "As long as he has the same smile and laugh, we don't care how he looks." At home in Harrisburg and Toronto, Tiger was an object of curiosity. People openly stared.

Mildred Sage: Postmistress and good friend

The most Bobby Hawley says to me one day is, "Tiger sure looks different. Too bad he had to go and get himself burned."

"His whole life has changed, Bobby," I tell him.

Later that summer, I overhear Bobby and Tiger laughing together, chanting the words of a Johnny Cash song. "I fell into a burning ring of fire..." I'm surprised but figure it's a good thing for Tiger to be able to make light of the situation with a friend. Kivalina will be a healing place for Tiger. I hope in some small way, it will become a healing place for me too, that I'll come to accept we are not the same people that we were before the fire.

Two weeks after we're back in Kivalina, Tiger comes back from a visit with Amos. He has a puppy with him. The dog is tiny and fits into Tiger's hand. "Amos knew how much we wanted a puppy and he gave us one of his females for us to raise," Tiger tells me, smiling.

At first, I'm disappointed. I wanted a dog related to Bubbles. (As it turns out, another female dog will attack Bubbles' mother's new litter and kill all of the pups.) Before long, I fall in love with this deep brown ball of fluff with tan dots over her eyes and down her legs. She will never be the beauty that Bubbles was, but I can already see that she has more spunk and will be a much better pet, if Tiger allows me to have her as a pet, that is.

Tiger suggests we give her an Eskimo name. "Why don't we call her Aklark, the Eskimo name for brown bear?" he says.

I suggest that we call her Lucky. "It's easy to say and she could be our good-luck charm."

Tiger likes the name even better. "And guess what?" he says. "This time, we are going to raise her in the house. You can have her as a pet." I can't believe what I'm hearing. I can hardly wait to take Lucky into the house and play with her.

I worry: by calling her Lucky, are we tempting fate?

XXXIV

A NEW HOME

It's June first when Mildred visits to see how we're getting along. "We're repairing Jakie's house," I tell her, "but we can't rent it again from him. He wants us out of the house by July first. Tiger was hoping to stay for the winter."

"Gladys and Russell's house will be vacant this year," Mildred says. "Maybe you should try and rent it from them."

I am terrified when I hear this and could just ignore her remark, but I don't. I'm afraid since their house is available, we'll be staying for the winter. "Thanks Mildred. I'll tell Tiger as soon as he gets back."

Tiger has been visiting Amos and when he returns, I tell him what Mildred said. I don't want to stay another winter and should have kept my mouth shut. However, it's in Tiger's best interest to stay for another winter. He is excited and we go over right away to look at the house with Mildred. She leaves us after letting us in. There isn't much to look at. It's much smaller than Jakie's.

Like most of the houses in Kivalina, it has only one room, and a storm shed. There is a kitchen table, a stove, a couple of metal chairs, and a bed in the room. The place to me is downright depressing. "The house is tiny, Tiger," I say, trying to swallow my concern about all of it—living in such a small house, staying in Kivalina for the winter. "But I guess we can make it warm and cozy. If five people lived here last year, surely two of us can be comfortable."

Tiger writes to Russell immediately to see if we can rent it. We get a letter back quickly.

"I just heard back from Russell." Tiger's voice lacks enthusiasm for some reason. "The rent is twenty dollars a month."

My heart sinks.

"Wow, that's pretty reasonable." As I say this, I wonder why he doesn't sound excited.

"It is, but there's a hitch. We can only rent it until December, and then Gladys and Russell will be back. It won't work if we can't stay all winter. It would be complicated. If we're only staying there until December, we couldn't make a big enough order of food from the *North Star* for it to be filled. We'd have to find another place to live, which won't be easy in the middle of winter."

Inwardly, I am breathing a sigh of relief, but try to share his disappointment.

"I know you're upset," I say, and then as sincerely as I can, I add, "I wish we could stay too. Is it possible you have enough information already? Have you even looked over your notes?"

"I did. I told you when I was in the hospital: I still have a lot of gaps to fill in."

Tiger puts his arm around me. "I guess I've been thinking about Plan B ever since we found out we couldn't rent Jakie's house. I kept thinking something else might come up so I didn't mention it to you. This is my plan. For the remainder of the study, we'll pitch a tent and we'll stay until October. Are you okay with this idea?"

I nod. "I guess I have to be. Anyway, I don't like staying at Jakie's house. The fire is on my mind all the time; there are too many ugly memories. Maybe it will be fun to live in a tent."

If he can't get all of the information he wants in this shorter amount of time—just a summer more here—he says he may come back by himself and spend a month in Kivalina next winter. I know I will be nervous the whole time he is here, but I also know he would have the joy of being out with a dog team again, and he could do all of the things he can't do this soon after his accident. There is so much he can't do now because of his weak lungs and hands.

I don't share my worries about living in a tent for a few months here, but I'm filled with them. What if it rains all summer and the tent leaks? What if it burns down? We can't lock it. Will I be safe when Tiger is away? By October, it will be cold and getting dark. There could be snow by then. I interrupt my chain of worries at this point, thinking of the promise I made to myself to try to be the woman Tiger wants me to be. I'm going to have to do this. I know, too, that if he were not married to me, he could just build a shack or live with one of the families and carry out the study the way he wants to. He's looking out for my feelings, and I am full of mixed emotions: sorrow for Tiger, but relief for me as well.

Now that our decision to leave before winter is made, we set a deadline to finish the study by October first. I plan to help with the study even more this year. Last year, I helped by participating with the women. This year, we'll take oral histories. In place of living like the natives, we'll focus on interviewing them to accumulate information about their lives. This is a far different method than we used last year.

I'm happy with the idea of collecting oral histories. Tiger will get to hunt and fish, which he loves, and if the people are willing to divulge their life stories, we'll get far more material than we did last year. I'm ready to help carry out the study the way Tiger wants. I'll visit the locals more, and since we're not doing a participant study, I imagine I won't have to cut up seals or fish. This is a definite bonus.

Tiger has been out on the sled, but with spring coming, it looks like I won't have a chance. Soon travel will be done by boat. I'm sorry to miss the dogsledding. Riding on the sled was magical for us both when we did it last winter. We felt like we had the whole world to ourselves when we were out. It may have been a pipe dream, but I imagined that this winter, I would learn to drive the dog team. Will I ever have a chance to go out on a dog sled again? There are probably tourist rides on dog sleds, but it won't be like the few trips I took here.

It's now early June, and the weather is beautiful—misleadingly so. We've been told that last summer's weather was unusual. Chances are, we'll have rain this year, and living in a tent will not be glamorous. But so far, the skies are blue and there is a hint of summer in the air. The ice is starting to break up.

We're in between hunting seasons right now, and everyone, including Tiger, is working on their boats. We haven't used ours since Jimmy put a hole in it. Tiger turns over his boat and decides it needs a new board, eliminating the need for fiberglass. Then, he'll paint and caulk it. He ordered a thirty-three-horsepower motor for it, and while we're here, we'll enjoy trips upriver and just boating around. We both love the country here.

Tiger's health is reasonably good right now. He's out in the sun for much of the day. His forehead is tanned where the graft is, and where there is scarring, his face is very red. It's difficult to get used to this because I remember him as he was last year—his face was suntanned, and he looked so healthy. Now, he is much thinner. His face has a slightly drawn look, but that will change once he gains back more of the weight that he lost.

Transition into village life this time has been easy. I am much happier than I was last year. I interact with the women as much as possible and get more information for the study as well.

A month from now, the repairs on the house have to be finished and our tent will be ready to live in. We plan to start shipping things we won't need back to Harrisburg.

We both look forward to a fresh start in the tent. It's hard staying in the house where Tiger almost died, and on top of that, there are rumors that Jakie's house is haunted. Villagers tell us, "Jakie's father was a mean man. Maybe his ghost wants you out of the village altogether." I shiver at the thought of a spirit haunting the place and remember wondering if we had a malevolent one in the house just before Tiger was burned. Before his accident, I was sick all the time. There was the disastrous camping trip. Now, the bed at Jakie's place is falling apart. The supports are damaged and can't hold the mattress up anymore. One of the kitchen drawers is broken. Our movie camera is wrecked. If Jakie's father is haunting the place, he is doing a great job.

Tiger has fit seamlessly into village life. He can't do much with his hands; he tires very easily, and his lungs are weak. Still, he is happy to be here. The men in the village are solicitous of Tiger, encouraging him to hunt with them, but making sure he doesn't get too tired or cold. They admire him for coming back. He went hunting the other day and was successful. He killed one bearded seal and butchered it for me, then left the skin for me to work on. I peeled the blubber away from the skin knowing it doesn't have to be perfect since we won't be using it for anything. Peeling the blubber from the skin is much easier to do this time because I had an ulu to use. I plan to give the skin to Edith to finish properly. She'll find a good use for it. In the meantime, we'll have meat and seal oil for the two dogs until we leave and for any trips we might take upriver. Except for Pepper and Lucky, we plan to give the dogs to Amos when we leave.

Before we came back to Kivalina, Tiger bought us both Canon Dial 35 cameras. They are half-frame, 35mm, and fairly easy to use. I hope to record some of the life in the village to enhance the study and have photos to show our kids—if we have any someday—what life was like in Kivalina in 1965.

I want to take photos of the children here and capture their little faces pressed up against the window, watching me. They are so cute and love to have their pictures taken. Last year, I hated it when they came to the house and just stared at what I was doing, but now I miss seeing them. They don't visit the way they used to. I guess we aren't a novelty anymore. Maybe they can't get used to seeing Tiger this way and feel uncomfortable being around him. Perhaps their parents told them they shouldn't visit so often anymore.

Amos has been keeping our dogs staked at his house. Every time we pass by there, Pepper jumps up and down wildly, pulling at his stake and growling with delight. Now that we've been here for a few weeks, Tiger thinks it's time for a change for Pepper. "Let's bring him back to the house with us," he says. Maybe we're crazy, but it's the only way we'll know if we can take him home to Harrisburg with us. He loves people. And we love him. We're determined to find out if a pulling dog can be a pet.

At first, it's amusing having two dogs in the house. This is what I had wanted when we first bought Pepper and Coco. Now we can do it, since we know we won't be staying another winter and won't have to raise dogs for a team. Pepper is like a bushy bear in the house, not at all delicate and at times, uncouth. He goes around the house sniffing at everything in sight, including my crotch. "Damn, why does he keep doing this?" I ask Tiger one day.

"It's just what the male species here does. You should know that by now."

"Well, I hate it. It reminds me that I haven't taken a bath."

Everyone in the village thinks we're nuts to consider taking Pepper home with us, but he is gentle, and he's good with Lucky. We feel guilty for not bringing Coco with us as well. Tiger favors him, and it would probably be easier to take him back to Harrisburg with us, but Coco's fur is thicker than Pepper's. He can survive in the Arctic. Amos worked hard this winter keeping Pepper alive for us.

XXXV

OUR SECOND ANNIVERSARY

I t's June fifteenth, the day of our second anniversary. We have a quiet celebration, a dinner at the house. I serve canned ham and Italian scalloped potatoes, so different from our usual fare of tuna casserole, canned hot dogs, or fish. I wanted tonight to be special. I didn't think about it before I started dinner, but we had canned ham the night of the accident. It's odd to think that we are toasting our future with the same kind of meal I planned to have the night Tiger almost died. I make an angel food cake and Tiger brings out a half-liter bottle of champagne he brought up with him. We drink to our future.

"Here's to our life together," I say, raising my glass in a toast. "We're lucky to have one. This year has taught me how much I love you." I look into Tiger's face, knowing he is not the physically handsome man I married. It doesn't matter. I love him anyway.

Tiger smiles and raises his glass.

It's hard to believe we've only been married for two years. I feel as though it's been a lifetime. I think Tiger and I both have lost our innocence.

As a young woman, I thought I was invincible and thought death wouldn't touch me in any way. I wanted my life in the Arctic with Tiger to be like a fairy tale and believed I'd learn to be happy living in a world my husband loved. But I found out life doesn't always work out that way. Life is unpredictable. Bad things can happen, no matter how much you love a person or a place.

After our anniversary celebration, we take the dogs upriver. We sit on the bank of the river, enjoying the midnight sun. Pepper is in fine form. Lucky, however, isn't so well. Last week, she started looking sick. She refused to eat and lost weight. When we took her outside, she staggered up to us with a pitiful expression and rolled over to be petted. We didn't know what to do. Tiger got the idea to put her on an all-meat diet, and he was able to get seal meat from the Swans. Still, she seems to be slipping away before our eyes. She's lost her spirit.

Suddenly, I get an idea. I remember I brought tetracycline in case Tiger or I needed it.

"I think I'll start giving Lucky some tetracycline. Maybe it'll help her."

Tiger agrees it couldn't hurt to give it a try. If either of us gets sick, the nurse's aide can give us penicillin. "Let's hope it works," he says.

At this point, we are willing to try anything. Neither of us is prepared to lose another dog. We start giving her the tetracycline and hope for the best.

A few days later, we decide to go hooking, because the fish are running. We have only one reel, but we have a net also, so it's fine. When Tiger gets a fish on the line, I net it. This is a faster method, and we lose fewer fish this way. I like this better, too, because when the fish are netted, the hook comes out in the net and we never have to take it off by hand. I'm still squeamish doing that.

After fishing for a while, we watch the two dogs. Pepper pees on every willow he sees but Lucky just lies there. It's obvious she isn't getting better despite either of the attempts that we've made to help. "Gosh, Tiger, what are we going to do?" I say, as we carry our catch into the house before we go out to tie up the dogs for the night.

"I didn't want to tell you this, Deanne." Tiger's tone is grave. "Several of the dogs in the village have been sick with whatever

Lucky has. The natives have shot them because they didn't want a sick dog on their hands."

I gasp, cover my face with both hands. "Oh no! Lucky is supposed to be our good-luck charm. Maybe we tempted fate. Let's wait a while and hope she gets better."

Tiger agrees. At this point, shooting a dog named Lucky is too much for him, too.

XXXVI

LIFE IN A TENT

In my wildest dreams, I never thought it would be so much work to move from the house to the tent. Our campsite is perched on a bluff on the beach near Amos Hawley's place. It's not really much of a bluff because the highest part of the island is only thirteen feet above sea level. The waves lapping against the shore will lull us to sleep every night. We'll enjoy the midnight sun.

Tiger pitched the tent and I stayed home packing boxes. Scrubbing all of Jakie's pots and pans was a two-day chore. They were tarnished from the fire, and I wanted to leave them in the condition we first found them in. Once this was done, we started moving our belongings over to the tent. We bought a frying pan and a pot from the supermarket in Fairbanks to tide us over for the few months until we leave. The stove is ours so we will take it to the tent as well.

Just about everything in the house is repaired, and now that the house is empty, we can clean in earnest. Soot streams from the stovepipes. Every time I think the floor is dirt-free, more soot falls and I have to start again. While I do this endless task, Tiger is outside cleaning the yard and shed. The dogs have dug several holes needing to be filled with sand. When all of this is done, the windows will be boarded up.

Both of us are happy to be so close to Amos Hawley's place. Tiger said he won't have to worry about leaving me at night because Amos will be there for me, "and if we're in trouble," Tiger said, "he's right there to help."

Tiger doesn't need to know I'm anxious about wild animals coming into the tent at night when he's away. I imagine wolves must be near the village. After all, Bubbles was half-wolf. I also worry about drunken men in the village, due to the episode last fall.

When I arrive at the tent to see how he's doing, he's stopping work.

"I was just about to come get you. Go home and pack up. Mildred Sage passed out safety cards to everyone." Safety cards are only passed out in emergencies. I hold my breath as he tells me what's going on. "There's been an earthquake in the Aleutian Islands. The coastal villages are being warned about a tidal wave."

I freeze. When we were in Anchorage, Tiger said he wanted to experience a tidal wave. Before we left to come to Kivalina, I had a dream about a tidal wave hitting. Everything was destroyed.

Tiger tells me everyone is leaving for somewhere safe. How far upriver is considered safe? Probably miles. It's so flat on this island, everything will be swept away in a minute—houses gone, dogs gone. If anyone stays, they'll be gone too.

"Should I pack for you, too?" I ask.

Tiger doesn't seem too concerned. "No, I'm staying. But I think you should go, just in case."

"I won't go without you, Tiger." Is he serious? Does he have a death wish? If he's truly worried about my safety and well-being, he'll change his mind.

I hurry to the tent and start packing for both of us in case he changes his mind. I don't want to leave Tiger behind, but I care enough about myself to go with the rest of the village. I don't want to be in this place if a tidal wave hits.

Just then, Tiger comes back to the tent.

Looking at him, I say, "Did you change your mind? I packed for you too."

"You knew I wouldn't go with you. Thanks anyway for packing for me, but it's okay now. Mildred just put out the word that the danger's passed."

I throw my arms around his neck and whisper, "Please don't try to be brave. If there had been a tidal wave, I would have lost you. I don't want you risking your life anymore."

I start to heat water to wash the clothes. I breathe a sigh of relief. The excitement has passed, and it's just another routine day in the village.

We enjoy a string of sunny days as we settle into life in a tent. The tent is a bit crowded, but apart from this, I love it. We're glad to get out of Jakie's house. It was a constant reminder of the fire, and the scars on Tiger's face and hands and his weak lungs are more than enough of a reminder already.

The tent is twelve by fourteen feet. A smaller tent sits beside this one. The honey bucket is in the smaller tent, and we keep canned goods, toilet paper, and other supplies there as well. The bigger tent gets cluttered easily, but with the stove, table, bed, chairs, and desk, it's only natural. Last year, Tiger built a desk for himself. It came over from Jakie's house. I work at the kitchen table that Tiger built as well, writing up my notes and letters to home. Tiger has hammered some boards together to make a frame for our bed. This one is not a twin like the one that we had in Jakie's house. It's more like a double or queen-size bed. With a piece of foam rubber over it, the bed is comfortable. I often sit or lie on it reading. The bed takes the place of the rocking chair and couch that we had at Jakie's place. Most of the time, we keep Pepper and Lucky outside the tent; when they come in, it's even more crowded and a bit chaotic.

Since the first few days in the tent are warm and sunny, it's fun to live like this. Soon, the beautiful weather gives way to rain, and it's windy and cold. The tent springs small leaks, making it damp inside. Everything feels moist to the touch. The rain continues day after day and tent living is no longer glamorous.

Amos comes over often and occasionally stays for dinner. His wife, Louise, comes with him sometimes. Like many women here, she is quiet and shy. We haul out the Parcheesi board and enjoy playing. Louise is delighted by the game.

Living in the tent in the rain has its hardships. On top of the space constraints, Tiger has another cold. He coughs and hacks, distressing me. With his damaged lungs, my biggest fear is that he'll come down with pneumonia. I wish I hadn't given Lucky the tetracycline. I thought Tiger could easily get an antibiotic from the assistant nurse, but the assistant nurse is out of the area for a few days.

"God, I hate it when you're sick like this," I say to Tiger one night. "Maybe we should pack up and go home. I think living in this damp tent is keeping you from getting better. I hear you hacking all night, and I worry about you all the time."

"Don't even talk about it. We're staying until I think I have enough information."

I want to leave the tent and be on my own, despite the miserable weather. But I can't go anywhere. The very reason that I want to leave is what keeps me here. I have two invalids in the tent with me—Tiger and our puppy. Lucky is no better, despite the fact I've been giving her tetracycline for a week. Her eyes are runny, and her nose is hot. I get up in the middle of the night to check on her, but she never improves.

When the assistant nurse returns, Tiger gets a penicillin injection. But after two days, there's no improvement in his health. Usually, after two days on antibiotics, he feels better. I'm concerned the penicillin may be losing its effectiveness.

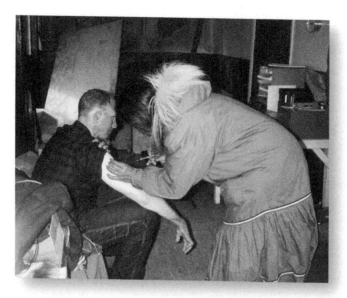

Tiger getting Penicillin

Unfortunately, there is still a lot of work to do, like hauling water, and Tiger won't accept help. "I'm not asking anybody to help me," he says when I suggest he ask a friend for help with this. "It's my job." To keep us supplied with water, Tiger has to carry bucket after heavy bucket of water to our tent, and the tent is farther away than where our house was. I get a bucket and tell him I want to help, but he refuses. "I don't understand," I say. "We did this together last year." He just shakes his head.

When he is finished and comes back to the tent, he puts on a warm sweater and lies down for a few minutes. I tell him I'm concerned about him.

"I'll be fine in a few days," he says, with a tone that means he wants to be left alone.

I thank him for what he's done and go outside to start washing clothes. I wait for a sunny day so that I can wash our clothes outside because there's not enough room in the tent.

To conserve water, we wear our clothes for two or three days before I wash them. We have once again resorted to sponge baths, as there's no room in the tent to take a bath. There was barely room for that in the house and I was always afraid someone would want to visit at the house just as we were taking a bath, so I washed as quickly as I could.

For dinner, I roast a piece of caribou. This makes Tiger feel a bit better, but then he looks at Lucky. She is lying on the ground, miserable.

"Tomorrow, I'm going to Amos's to see if he'll shoot Lucky for me. I can't do it myself."

In the morning, I decide to visit some women in the village. I want to leave Tiger alone and give him space so that he can decide whether to ask Amos to kill Lucky or whether he needs to do it himself. Whatever he decides, I will support him. Lucky can't go on suffering the way she is.

Visiting the women here is so different from last year. The women are more welcoming and seem happy to see me. I think they're starting to trust me. I watch as they go about their daily chores, and I talk and ask questions. This morning, I start by visiting Mildred. She welcomes me inside her house and is very open, answering questions about her life as a child.

When I get back to the tent, Tiger is ready to shoot Lucky, but because I came along, he decides to wait. For some reason, he didn't ask Amos to shoot Lucky. Fortunately, his attention is diverted when he hears a plane circle and land. It's not the mail plane, and Tiger decides to go out and see who has arrived. It's Nelson Walker—a pilot Tiger has chartered several times before. Tiger has wanted to hire Nelson for some time now, and he immediately charters him to fly us around the countryside. Tiger asks Amos to join us and he points out landmarks and place names. It's a beautiful day and we can see for miles and miles. The mountain range east of Kivalina is snow-covered and glistening in the cloudless sky. It's fun to fly over the Wulik River. Amos tells us it is about eighty miles long.

We went thirty miles of this distance on our camping trip last winter. The men talk about going up the Wulik to see how far they can go before it gets too shallow. They look forward to the challenge and plan to do this later in the summer.

As we fly over the land, Tiger points out where we camped last year, in the snow. Now the land around the river is green, and I can see how flat most of it is.

"Gosh, it seemed so much higher last winter," I say, marveling at the sight from high above. "Remember when I fell down it? I guess it wasn't so far after all."

Amos points out the Kivalina River. It is sixty miles long and flows into the Kivalina Lagoon. Most of the land on both rivers is flat, with some domes in the land called *pingos*. Some of these are landmarks Amos points out.

Flying over the village, I realize it's the first time I'm seeing it from the air. Every time I've been on a plane, we never got farther than the landing strip. Even walking the island last summer with Tiger didn't show how long and thin this strip of land is.

Kivalina 1965

I hoped after the flight Tiger would ask Amos to deal with Lucky, but for some reason he doesn't. Before dinner, Tiger decides it's time to end her misery. She is suffering so much, and her eyes always seem to be asking us for help. Hard as it is, I agree with his decision.

I kneel on the ground and put my arms around my puppy. She is still small because she's been so sick. "Lucky, you are such a good puppy," I tell her. This is the only way I can say goodbye, and I hold her close, tears rolling down my cheeks.

Tiger returns in tears. We are both exhausted and upset. We take Pepper out for a walk beyond the airstrip. The rainy days have ended. The sun is high, and the air is warm. Our walk with Pepper lifts our spirits.

We bring Pepper into the tent, devastated about losing our good-luck charm, and start to settle down for the night. Tiger pulls his sweatshirt over his head and puts on his pajamas. "I don't want another dog right now," he says sadly. "Please don't bring another puppy into our lives." As he says this, I nod my head in agreement. I couldn't bear to lose another dog.

XXXVII
LEARNING NEW WAYS

It's late July and the study is well under way. Living in the tent, we don't have as many visitors as we did when we were living in our house, which pleases me. Last summer, we had no privacy at all. Now, when we have a visitor, it's usually because Tiger is taking a life history.

I'm seeing the benefits of oral histories, as Tiger interviews men and I interview the women. By interviewing, we learn a lot about kinship structure and family relationships. We also learn the history of the people and the village.

We tape the interviews using a battery-operated tape recorder, and the study is progressing well. Tiger is a good interviewer. He asks the men all sorts of questions: where they were born (usually right here), what their parents and grandparents were like, and when they first started to hunt. I imagine he'll ask them personal questions later when I am out of the tent.

I notice when he is taking a life history, Tiger's tone of voice changes. He speaks better English, but at the same time, he sounds like a native. He may have picked up their inflections, but he may also intentionally try to talk like them.

For my part, I conduct interviews with the women. Between managing the recorder (not my forte) and trying to get the women to open up about their lives, it isn't easy. Over the winter, I had time to reflect on many things about our life in Alaska. White women intimidate the women here and the natives feel that we expect to be treated in a better manner than they treat each other. They didn't understand I was nervous and wanted to fit in to village life.

Many of the things bothering me last summer about native life vanished as I became more accustomed to their traditions and practices. Growing up, a girl watches her mother cutting up seals, and when she's of age to do it herself, she instinctively knows what to do. She helps her mother with several seals and watches so often that cutting up and cleaning seals is second nature to her. Looking back to the time I cut up seals with Edith, I realize she thought I could learn to cut up a seal by observing her. I remember her saying, "watch me," as she worked away. I thought she was treating me like a child, and she was: she was trying to teach me.

This time, living here, I decide to learn more from the women about tasks that might interest me more than cutting seals did. We have only three months here, and I know I won't have time to make mukluks, but maybe I can make a parka to replace the one that had been lost in the fire.

One day, before our move to the tent, I ask Tiger if he thinks I can find a woman to teach me how to make a parka. "I'd love to learn some of the creative things the women do here."

I can tell that Tiger's happy I want to do something like this. "Why don't you ask Mildred or Ruth? I think one of them would be glad to help. They'd probably be flattered."

I decide to start by asking Mildred. I don't know if she'll be a good teacher, but I know she's capable and her English is good. I walk to Mildred's place, hoping she'll say yes.

When she opens the door and invites me inside, I say, "Mildred, you did such a wonderful job sewing the parka you made for me last summer. I'd love to learn to make one. Can you help me?"

"I can help all right. I'm happy to. I made your parka from muskrat skins, but they're not easy to work on. Maybe you should use rabbit skins. They don't cost as much, either."

I want to try muskrat skins and am disappointed when she suggests rabbit. Rabbit skins will shed, but I'll do what she thinks is best.

The rabbit skin parka that she has suggested I make will be an inside shell with the fur facing my clothing. There will be an outside cover made of corduroy. Mildred helps me order the skins. They're due to arrive in a few weeks.

After the mail plane comes a couple of weeks later, I run over to Mildred's place to see if I have anything. To my delight, there is a package waiting for me. The rabbit skins!

At home, I open the box to find the skins are lovely and soft to the touch. I sweep my hand over them, feeling like I'm petting a kitten. The skins aren't big; I know they'll take a long time to sew. Good thing I have a teacher.

Mildred comes over to the house to help me get started. She's brought dental floss to use for thread. "It's waterproof," she says, and it's also very strong and easy to sew with, she adds. She shows me the stitch she uses. It's an overhand stitch, one I've used before with sewing. This shouldn't be too difficult.

"Make sure you keep them stitches close together, and try not to stretch the skins," Mildred instructs. "Watch me. I'll show you how."

After she has shown me how to sew the skins together, I give it a try, working at the skins in front of her so she can correct me as needed. I work for a while and get one seam done.

"You're doing good with them skins," Mildred says. I'm grateful for her approval. This is so different from learning how to cut up seals, and it's fun.

It's not hard sewing rabbit skins, but I run out of time to work on the skins because I have to clean the house and get ready for our move to the tent.

After our move into the tent, Ruth steps in to help me with cutting the skins. Ruth has more time, and she's a better teacher. "Be careful you don't stretch the skins when you cut them," Ruth warns as I sit down to focus on my work.

I'm nervous cutting the skins, but discover it isn't too difficult. I wish that I could have done something this enjoyable and
creative when I was here before. Last year, none of the women
seemed to think a white woman would be interested in what they
do. Because I've come back to the village after a tragedy, they
see me as a white woman who respects their culture. Ruth and
I have a special relationship too. She and my mother are even
writing letters now. After I told my mother about the importance
of namesakes here, she decided to get in touch with Ruth and
say hello. I'm glad she took the initiative.

XXXVIII

BIRTH OF A BABY

Visiting the women is easier this summer because I'm more relaxed and know what to expect. Knowing they are often quiet and uncommunicative, I'm not as uncomfortable with the silence as I was before.

My visit with Emmaline today was a wonderful surprise. Emmaline is one of the younger women in the village.

Tiger is writing up notes when I arrive home.

"Hey, guess what happened this morning."

Tiger barely looks up from what he is doing. "What?" He sounds bored.

"I went to visit Emmaline. Did you know she was pregnant? I certainly didn't. She asked me in when I knocked, and I found her lying in bed.

"Are you sick?" I asked.

"No, I just had my baby," she answered.

Now, Tiger is paying more attention.

"So, then what happened?"

I tell him that I wanted to get out of there as fast as I could. I was the first to arrive after the baby was born and I felt I was intruding on a private moment.

"She told me to stay and visit, but I couldn't. She said other people would be coming to visit, but I felt as though I shouldn't be the first. Tiger, I've never seen a baby fresh out of the chute

243

before. She was so tiny, swaddled right beside Emmaline. They looked so peaceful together."

Always ready for information, Tiger asks how long she'd been in labor. "Did you ask if she had help during the birth? Did you ask for the name of the baby?"

I realize I missed an opportunity to get some real information about birthing in the village. Now, more than ever, I want to learn more about infancy and birthing practices.

"I guess I blew it," I admit. "At least I did find out what the baby weighed: She said her daughter weighs nine pounds."

"Well, never mind. It was an interesting experience for you anyway."

I'm relieved Tiger doesn't scold me for hurrying out of there.

Back in the tent, I process what I had just witnessed, comparing Emmaline's birthing experience to childbirth back home. Some of my friends have told me about their painful labor. I can't picture any of them lying peacefully with their infant right after its birth.

At home, newborns are born in hospitals, separated from their mothers soon after they're born, and put into a nursery. They're brought to their mother only to be fed, not to be held and cuddled. Mothers are confined to a bed for about a week, and often pampered after they get home. What a contrast to the women here! Emmaline will probably be up by tomorrow and attending to chores around the house. She'll bond with her baby during these first hours of the baby's life while they lie together. I envy her. This seems so much better than being in a hospital.

After this experience, I make a point to learn about birthing in the village. I learn that, for the most part, women have their babies at home and have no problems. I haven't heard of any C-sections or other serious complications. The midwives are very competent, and if a doctor is needed, the woman is flown to Kotzebue. The doctors in Kotzebue couldn't take care of Tiger's severe burns, but they can handle a complicated birth.

The women I've interviewed have told me that years ago, there were restrictions surrounding births. Typically, a small hut—a snow house in winter, a tent in summer—was built some distance away from the family house. When her time came, the woman went by herself into the house and gave birth on her own. This practice ended by the early 1930s, and midwives were usually present during childbirth. I haven't asked yet whether husbands are allowed to witness the birth. I imagine this is taboo.

The birth of a baby is a time for rejoicing here in Kivalina. Everyone will come to visit Emmaline and show their happiness for her and her baby daughter. If her husband was out hunting when the baby was born, he'll rejoice with the rest of the village when he comes home.

Time and time again, the natives have asked why we don't have any kids. "Who's gonna take care of you when you're old?" they say. "Your kids are gonna care for you. And people won't forget you when you die. But if you don't make a kid, you really get lost there. Nobody remembers you." In Kivalina, having a child is the main reason to be married. Tiger never talked to the men about why we didn't have children. Maybe they never asked. Gladys knew about the pill and why I took it, but I don't think she understood. In their culture, marriage is meant for people to have children.

It's not unusual for a mother to breastfeed until the child is three or four years old. Nursing not only comforts the child, but it is thought to be a means of contraception. Obviously, nursing is not an entirely reliable form of birth control, as babies are frequently born a year or eighteen months apart.

For the Inuits, infant care is characterized by a single word: intense. Except when an infant is asleep, someone is constantly taking care of it. When an infant cries, the diaper is changed, and the infant is offered the breast. Before diapers, the natives used moss or lichen. I heard sealskins might have been used for diapers, but I was never able to confirm this. If the baby continues to cry, the infant is put inside the mother's—or some other female's—parka and rocked until it's quiet. I rarely see an infant crying. I love this approach. I think it's better than letting the baby cry until sleep comes, which often happens back at home.

One day, when I am working on my parka with Ruth, we talk about how babies are named.

"We know what Eskimo name the baby will have before it is born," Ruth tells me. "If we want a baby to be like another person, we might give it the name of someone who has died. We often call a baby after an animal and hope it will be like the animal. We call your husband Tuktu. He loves to follow the caribou and he also migrated to the south four years ago. Caribous migrate to the south, but they always return to the north."

"How do you know what name to give a baby before you know if it's a boy or girl?" I ask.

"The Eskimo name can be either. Then we give it an English name—often from the Bible. Sometimes the oldest son is named after his father, and then he's known as Junior."

"Do you have an Eskimo name?"

"Yes. My name is Nanuktoque."

I consider this for a moment. I like her Eskimo name. I would love for each of our children to have an Eskimo name. Of course it won't be done legally but we will tell them about their namesake. The people here have been such an important part of our lives. Forgetting to ask what her name means, I say, "Ruth, I'm going to give your Eskimo name to our first child."

Her smile turns into a huge grin. I will cherish that moment for the rest of my life.

I love visiting Ruth. She is so easy to talk to. One day, I ask her if the Eskimos would rather have a boy than a girl. (I always felt most men that I know wanted boys.) Her answer surprised me.

"We Eskimos don't care all right."

XXXIX

FINAL LESSONS

The last few days have been clear and cold. It's only mid-August, and the other night, the temperature went down to thirty-five. We're starting to light the kerosene lamps at night. They make the tent cozy, but I'll never get over the fear of lighting them. There was a light snowfall on the hills recently, and although it was beautiful, I hope it isn't a harbinger of an early fall. If it is, we may have to leave for home earlier than planned.

No matter what, our time in Kivalina is rapidly drawing to a close. Mom and Dad Burch wrote to tell us they have a farmhouse which will be vacant next fall, and we can rent it from them. I'm excited to be going home. I dream of luxuriating in a warm bath and cooking anything I want. I'll make friends with people who have things in common with me and won't have to worry about long gaps in the conversation. Tiger will be in and out of the hospital for more surgeries. It will be nice to be near the Burches, to share family time. Tiger is already planning a workspace. He talks about this frequently. Our future lies before us like a clean slate. At last, our luck might be changing.

In these last weeks in Kivalina, however, there's still a lot to be done and more information to be gathered. Tiger has collected more histories from the men than I have from the women; I have more work to do.

In interviews that I set up with a few of the women, I ask about their experience with menopause. I ask about hot flashes and depression. They scrunch up their faces, meaning no; they know nothing about hot flashes and depression. They don't even know what I'm talking about. Menopause is just another chapter in their life marked by an inability to have more children.

I wish I had the nerve to ask them about sexual practices, but I can't seem to summon the courage to do so. Asking about this would be an invasion of their privacy. Tiger doesn't have the same reluctance.

He comes home one day ready to tell me about it. "I just talked to one of the men about sexual relationships. It's interesting. When the husband gets the urge, he just does it. Wives never take the initiative. I even asked what a man would do if his wife wasn't feeling well. He told me when he wanted to do it, he just went ahead."

"And what does the wife do?"

"Apparently, she just lies still while the act is going on."

"I wish I had the nerve to ask even one of the women about it. I wonder how they feel about the whole thing. Do you think they enjoy it?"

"I think the women just try to accommodate the men," Tiger says.

"I wouldn't even know how to bring it up. You know, I think that the men communicate better than the women."

At times, language is a real barrier for me. Tiger studied linguistics, and he communicates much better with the old-timers than I do. The old-timers are harder to interview, as many don't speak English. I've been embarrassed when I can't seem to phrase a question in a way they can understand. One of the old women in the village for instance, is married to a man who is crippled. Before this, she had been married to a man many years her senior.

"Mabel," I said to her one day, "when you were married before, did you ever adopt a baby?"

She was embarrassed and insulted, thinking that I had asked if she had ever had a baby by anyone other than her husband. It took a few minutes to clear up the misunderstanding, and finally, she understood what I was asking. She never had a child of her own, but she never adopted one either. I wanted to ask her why, but I didn't. Surely a child would be a help to her in her old age. Adoption is common here, especially for those who have no children of their own.

One sunny day, I have no luck finding a woman to give me a life history, not unusual. Tiger is out fishing with some of the men. I don't want to stay in the tent and waste the beautiful day. I pick up my camera and wander out past the airstrip where there is a profusion of wildflowers. There seems to be seventeen different kinds, and I photograph them all. I'll have to wait to have them developed until we get home. I hope I have captured them; I can hardly wait to see the results.

The same night, as we finish dinner, we hear someone yell, "Belugas!"

Tiger is up and out in a flash, rushing to join the hunt. I join the women who are gathered at the shore trying to watch, but we don't see anything. We can hear the drone of the motors and the occasional rifle shot.

When the beluga is hauled onto the beach, the entire village rushes down to watch. The beluga is butchered immediately, and only the children are allowed to eat the flipper this time—not that I cared about having any. I still wonder why it's considered such a delicacy. The women tell me that more belugas have been spotted this year, but the hunt tonight isn't terribly successful. The men only managed to get one.

I have my camera with me, and I take photos of the children enjoying the flipper. I hope I have captured the look of pure delight on their faces as they eat the flipper. I'm not sure how to operate this camera because I'm new to photography, but I know what I am trying to create. The photographs could be blurry, out of focus, or not exposed properly, and I won't know until I see the final product. Still, I love freezing a moment in time—a moment lost forever if I don't seize it through the lens of my camera.

The summer continues with a string of beautiful days. One morning, we wake at around nine o'clock with the sun streaming into our tent. Tiger has set up an interview for me with Charlotte

Swan. She said she'll, "come over sometime" today. It's time to get up and get ready for her.

All afternoon, I sit around outside the tent with the usual jitters I get when I am waiting for someone to do a life history. I never know where to start the interview. Do I start with her childhood? I worry the woman I am interviewing will not open up to me. It's so different from my social work experience back in college where my clients needed help and had to talk to get it. These women are going to tell me things that perhaps they don't want to tell.

It's pleasant waiting for her. The weather is warm, with a gentle breeze keeping the mosquitoes away. By the end of the afternoon, however, I know Charlotte isn't coming. Tiger comes home, and he wants to know how the interview went. I tell him Charlotte never showed up.

Charlotte Swan

"Maybe she forgot. Ask her another time," Tiger says.

"No, I'm not going to. I get so frustrated. I wait around for ages just hoping they'll show up. I'm nervous about interviewing them. It's a waste of time and emotional energy."

"Well," says Tiger, "I wish you didn't feel that way. You're good at getting the histories from the women, but I understand if you don't want to try again."

Our time up here feels like it's spinning away like an out-of-control freight train. Tiger has completed most of the oral histories from the men, and I've gathered as much information as I can from the women. We'll have quite an impressive study. Tiger will be able to compile all the notes and the tapes. He will have enough for his thesis and probably a book as well. As soon as the Keatings come back, Tiger plans to review old papers the former teachers have written up and prepare a history of the school since its beginning. Once he writes that up, we'll head home to face all that's ahead, including a long list of surgeries for Tiger. In Harrisburg, over the next few months, Tiger will have scar tissue removed from his face and his hands. He should have his nose reconstructed, but for now he has decided not to do this. The construction of new ears will use tissue from his stomach and take several months to complete. Tiger has far different things to think about than I do when he thinks of going home. As for me, I am hoping that maybe I'll be pregnant. I am looking forward to making new friends and I will be there to support Tiger during the surgeries he has ahead of him.

XL

LIFE CHANGES

As soon as we decided not to stay for the winter, I said to Tiger, "Let's start trying to have a baby. I'm going off the pill." He didn't say much, but he didn't protest either.

Now it's August, and my period is over three weeks late. I'm convinced I'm pregnant. Maybe I'm being premature, but I have to share the news with Tiger.

"Hey Tiger, I think you're going to be a daddy."

Tiger gives me a big hug. He's as excited as I am. We start discussing names. A boy will be Daniel; a girl will be Karen.

Finally, something happy is happening.

Then, just as suddenly, I'm not pregnant anymore. Was it a hormonal imbalance? Or was I pregnant and had another miscarriage the way I did in Scotland and Chicago? I tell Tiger when we are alone.

"Tiger, I just got my period."

He puts his arms around me, consoling us both.

"Sometimes, I think nothing good is ever going to happen to us. This is just one more disappointment. Our bad luck is still following us." I say when he puts his arms around me.

"Be patient. You always want things to happen immediately. Lots of women don't get pregnant right away."

"Being patient isn't a virtue of mine. Peggy is pregnant again, and some of my friends are having second babies too. I hate being jealous."

I worry that perhaps I can't get pregnant. Perhaps Tiger is sick too much, or maybe the high fever he had last December will prevent us from ever having a family of our own. It's senseless to worry at this point, and I try not to think about it. It hasn't even been two months since I went off the pill. Tiger is right, I need to have more patience, but I have looked forward to the time when we could finally have a baby. I feel like a two-year-old—I want to be pregnant and I want it to be today, not next month or next year. Whenever I look at an infant here, my arms yearn to hold it. I never get the chance, though, because the women always carry their babies around in their parkas.

*   *   *

This summer is far more pleasant than last. We socialize more easily with people here. The other night, Ruth and Caleb came over to play Parcheesi. Neither had played before, but they were quick learners. Next, we ask Bobby and Sarah to play. We spend the evening laughing and enjoying one another's company. Playing games is far more engaging than sitting and trying to make conversation. We should have done this last summer.

In the evening, when daylight is endless, the men play ball outside near the airstrip, and Tiger joins in, though it's hard for him to catch a ball because of his hands. Still, he gives it his best. Tiger isn't as good at it as he once was, but the men are happy to have him playing. My heart aches when I think of all the things he can no longer do, but I have to focus on the things he can do and the fact that he is alive.

Tiger realizes that he almost died a few months ago, and he wants to enjoy life rather than immerse himself in his research all the time. An accident like his puts a whole new perspective on life. We fish, take trips upriver, and go on long walks with Pepper.

Today, Tiger is recording a life history with one of the men in the village. He's one of the old-timers here, probably around sixty. There are other men in the village older than he is, but this person is considered an old-timer because he knows so much about the past. He'll tell Tiger as much as he can about his life in Kivalina. He may even have tales of his own ancestors. Tiger wants to learn as much as he can about what happened in the past. Each life history is a way of bringing the past into the present.

I know his interviewee will clam up in my presence. Women don't usually listen to these types of conversations. But there's no place for me to go in the tent for Tiger to have privacy. When I realize this, I take off to wander around the village for a while. I feel the damp and cold seeping into my bones.

It's chilly, maybe forty degrees outside. The sky is studded with rain clouds, and I'm glad to be outside before another deluge passes through. I look up at the sky. There's not a hint of blue. My grandmother used to say that if there was enough blue in the sky to make a pair of Dutchman's britches, the weather would clear. I guess this won't happen anytime soon. But the air smells fresh and it is much nicer outside because everything in the tent is damp. The pounding rain has kept us inside for days.

I often think about my grandmother and the sayings she had, as well as the things that she taught me. Maybe when she talked about enough blue in the sky to make a pair of Dutchman's britches, it was a remnant of her childhood and part of her long-ago Dutch heritage, or perhaps it was a saying passed down from generation to generation. Sadly, she is in a nursing home in Ottawa, Ontario. Mom says she has severe memory loss, and I guess she doesn't know I am living with the Eskimos. She doesn't know how badly Tiger was burned either. I am happy she doesn't and wonder when she told my mother that she didn't want me to live with the Eskimos if she had a premonition of Tiger's tragedy. I miss her.

It's quiet outside. Everyone is probably inside waiting for the next deluge. I end up near Charlotte Swan's place and decide to visit her. She has tiny puppies inside the house wriggling on the floor. They can't be more than four weeks old.

"They were born in a hole and are starting to get wild," Charlotte tells me. "I'm trying to tame them."

I watch the squirming mass on the floor and wonder how many puppies there are—probably too many for Charlotte to keep.

Charlotte asks what happened to Lucky. "I never see your puppy around anymore. I remember she was sick because we gave you seal meat to try and fatten her up."

I tell her about Lucky's bad luck. She picks up one of the puppies from the litter.

"Here, she's yours, but when you come back here, no more dogs, just babies."

"Thank you!" I cry. "It's the best gift you could give me. And maybe when I come back, I'll bring a baby. I sure hope so. I want to bring my children back to Kivalina so everybody can meet them."

Charlotte is a midwife, and I think about telling her how much I want a baby and how hard it's been, but I can't. I can't tell anybody. People here and at home don't need to know we're trying to have a baby. If everybody knows, it will make things worse. The women in the village get pregnant so easily. I've never heard of a woman here who couldn't get pregnant.

I walk back to the tent with this blonde bundle in my arms. I've never seen this color of sled dog before. She is a pale yellow, the color of some golden retrievers. She fits in the palm of my hand, and her eyes are barely open. I know I shouldn't be taking her away from her mother so early, but because there were so many puppies in the litter, Charlotte has said she would have to destroy the females.

She shakes in my arms as I carry her into the tent. I'm afraid to hear what Tiger is going to say when he sees me with her. He told me no more puppies. Really, though, I couldn't turn down this gift from Charlotte. She will remind me of Charlotte, and I like the idea of taking two dogs back to Harrisburg: Pepper, the dog we raised from a pup in Kivalina last year, and this puppy, the one we'll raise in Harrisburg.

I walk into the tent and Tiger just looks at me. "What have you got there, Deanne? I said no more dogs."

Then he breaks into a huge smile and comes over to take her from me. He's just as tickled as I am to have this puppy, frightened and wild as she may be.

255

"We're crazy, you know. How do you think we are going to get all our stuff home, and two dogs as well?"

"We'll figure it out. Remember, we were going to take home two dogs before Lucky died. Your dad managed to bring Bubbles home last December, and that was in the depths of winter. Don't worry."

Tiger loves naming our dogs. "I think we should call her Fanny, after the showgirls," he says. Somehow, I don't see her as a Fanny. I hope the name won't stick.

It storms for days on end. The wind rages and the rain is torrential, beating against our tent. We're almost afraid to go outside. Our bed shakes all night, and sometimes, it feels like we're having a small earthquake.

On the positive side, the rain gives me time to work on my parka. It's almost finished. When I sew on the hood and put in the sleeves, the bulk of the work will be done. The hood will need a wolverine ruff, and I've been looking around the village to find a good one. Ruth has said that when the parka is finished, she'll make a parka cover for it. I'm touched. I ordered brown corduroy for her to use. She'll decorate it with bright rickrack trim. The parka cover will be a special gift from someone who has truly become a good friend. I'll never forget her friendship or her generosity.

Meanwhile, as the rain beats down, Fanny crouches in a corner of the tent, her tail between her legs. It's hard to train her when the weather is like this, but we try our best. She is tiny and still wild. We need to tame her. Most of the time, we keep her in the tent. Occasionally, we take her out to play with Pepper. She isn't as big as his tail, but they seem happy together.

One rainy afternoon, I'm reading a book called *Inside Daisy Clover*. Suddenly, I seize upon the perfect name—Clover.

"I've got it, Tiger! We should name her Clover. Four leaves bring good luck. She'll be our four-leaf clover. Maybe our luck will change."

"I like the name," Tiger says. "Clover," he reaches out to stroke our puppy's head. "It's a happy name, even if our luck doesn't change."

Why am I always tempting fate?

Clover --- our good luck charm

Stuck in the tent because of the rain, we write up notes for a while and then decide to play backgammon.

"Hey, you must be cheating," Tiger says when I win a game.

"I'm not. I guess I'm just better at the game than you are."

Then he challenges me to another game. He's taking time for me as well as for his study. What a change this is from last year. How much our life has changed since his accident.

XLI

MORE CHALLENGES

After days of hard rain, the sun finally peeks out from under a gray sky. Everything inside and outside of the tent is wet. I'm tired of being inside a cold, damp tent. Tiger visits Amos and they decide we'll go upriver for a bit of a getaway. The Wulik River is usually very low, and after all this rain, they want to see how far they can get before they get stuck. Amos has become a friend to me, looking out for me when Tiger is away. I'm happy he's coming with us. I feel safer when he's around. Amos is used to life in the Arctic and knows what to do in case of an emergency.

We take the smaller storage tent to sleep in, putting everything from it into the main one. We move all the cans and other items we've stored in the little tent and fit them around boxes ready to be shipped back home, and around suitcases and duffel bags. We have a supply of toilet paper, and, of course, our honey bucket. This is the last thing that we put in our bigger tent. Our main tent is now stuffed with everything we own up here. When we return from this boat trip, we'll move everything back again into separate tents.

It's nearly four o'clock by the time we are ready to leave, two hours later than we'd hoped. We're taking the small wood boat Tiger bought a year ago. He's fixed the hole Jimmy Hawley put in it and there's a new engine, making our trip faster.

Even so, because of its size, the boat isn't very seaworthy. I wish we had life jackets. It's a short way across the ocean to the mouth of the river, but it can get very rough at times.

The days are growing shorter and darkness is starting to fall as we head up the river. Some places we come to are shallow, but we don't get stuck. It will be interesting to see how far we can get before dark. The weather turns shortly after we leave Kivalina. The wind howls, and we're pelted with rain.

Tiger and Amos stop at a flat spot where there are some small willows. The willows have kept the area reasonably dry and the men decide to set up camp here. I have the luxury of just watching but honestly, I wish I knew how to pitch a tent. Sometimes, I feel so helpless. Pepper is at home with Amos's dogs, but Clover is with us, and she is one scared puppy. She sleeps in my parka like an Eskimo baby the whole way up. Native babies are dressed when they snuggle into their mother's parkas. It's different carrying a puppy around the same way—and they don't wear anything like a diaper.

In the tent, Clover becomes lively, curling herself around my neck and burrowing into my sleeping bag. Sleep is almost impossible with her antics. After a sleepless night for me, Clover seems a little less wild, even friendly. I take her outside to relieve herself. The weather is unchanged. It's still raining.

"Do you think we should head for home or try to go farther up?" Tiger asks Amos.

"Maybe up further. The weather could change all right, and then we'd be sorry we didn't try to get any farther," Amos says.

So we head out, but the weather doesn't get any better. In fact, it gets worse. Despite all the rain, the water level is lower, and we can't go any further. I breathe a sigh of relief. The weather is keeping this from being anything but a pleasant trip. We head home in a downpour, fighting a wicked wind.

"The wind is so strong, I'm afraid we'll tip," I manage to say. "Doesn't anybody here ever use a life jacket, Tiger? We'll never live in water this cold."

He looks at me, dumbfounded. "Have you ever seen life jackets here?"

"What are you talking about?" Amos asks. Tiger explains to him about flotation devices, in case there's an accident. Amos shakes his head. I imagine he's thinking, stupid white men and their ideas.

Back at the tent again, Tiger suggests I stay at Amos's place to get warm while he empties the larger tent into the smaller one. There's a lot of work to do, and I'm sure he's as cold as I am.

When I've warmed up enough, I go to our tent to help out. The bed is soaked and has to be changed. Our only other sheets are damp, but they'll have to do. We move our things around, hoping to avoid the inevitable leaks. In the beginning, I thought tent living was fun. Now, I've had a change of heart. Exciting, maybe, but not enjoyable.

That night, the torrential downpour finally stops battering our canvas tent and it's quieter than it's been in some time. It's cold and blustery and the temperature is probably about forty-five degrees, but the wind and aftereffects of the rain make it seem colder. Tiger and I huddle under the damp blankets, trying to stay warm.

Over the next few weeks, life goes on as usual despite the bad weather. Many of the women leave the village every day to go berry picking even though it remains chilly and damp. This will continue for the next few weeks. I'd love to go with them if they weren't gone all day. Fresh berries are a treat, but packing for home takes precedence. Besides, I am probably a fair-weather berry picker. I don't like the cold and damp.

Autumn seems to be closing in faster than I expected. A touch of snow is visible on the distant hills, and there is frost on the ground. We use our oil stove to heat the tent, not a Coleman stove with propane. I am happy we are not using a Coleman stove. The thought of ever using a Coleman stove again is not a palatable one.

The rain has finally stopped and it's time to do the laundry. There is a chill in the air, and I bundle up to keep warm. Just as

I finish the wash, in the late morning, Bobby and Sarah walk up to say hello. Bobby looks a bit sheepish, and his hands are in his pockets. I ask them into the tent and offer them a cup of coffee.

"I hear you guys have stuff for sale," says Bobby.

Tiger looks puzzled. "Well, no, not really. Who gave you that idea?"

"Actually, we didn't come to see if you have anything for sale." Bobby whips out a bottle of beer. "Here, Tiger, a present for you."

Tiger thanks him and takes the bottle, but he doesn't open it.

Bobby pulls out another bottle. This one is vodka. "I know you'll like this," he says.

I'm apprehensive. Now what? Tiger opens the bottle and finds some tomato juice. He fixes Bloody Marys, pours one for himself, one for Bobby, and one for me. Maybe he's hoping the tomato juice will dilute the effects of the vodka and Bobby won't get too drunk. Tiger has always been able to hold his liquor well. Sarah is drinking beer.

I'm not happy with this, and yet, I go right along with it. I've never had a drink this early. In fact, I rarely drink, and we almost never drink here. What on earth are we doing? I don't want Bobby to get drunk and create problems in the village. Tiger may be asking for trouble by pouring us all drinks. Bobby is known to be a mean drunk.

While the rest of us sip our drinks, Sarah sits nodding, looking ready to fall asleep. She can't handle her beer. She is pregnant and I'm sure it's not a good idea to drink when you're pregnant.

We are all sitting at the wooden table Tiger made last summer when we were living in the house. Obviously, the tent is more crowded, but nobody seems to notice.

Bobby has two or three drinks. He tells us about his life, talks about his family. Everything is friendly. Tiger and I could learn a lot from him right now, but we're drinking too. The stories he tells go in one ear and out the other.

Bobby and Sarah leave, and I hope Bobby doesn't have a stash at home. If he does, he could keep drinking and get the rest of the men in the village drunk too. Fortunately, the afternoon stays quiet. The vodka Bobby gave Tiger seems to be all he had.

The rain has stopped and it's a beautiful evening. We take our boat across the short stretch of ocean and head upriver with the two dogs. It's too muddy to fish, with all the rain that has fallen in these last weeks, but we enjoy the sky with its mauve and gold, colors of an autumn sunset. The moon is almost full. I can see why Tiger loves this land. I've never seen anything else like it. I'll miss this stark landscape with its rugged scenery.

After watching the sunset, we pull our boat up to the beach. It's dark now, and the air has a nip to it. We're anxious to get in the tent, where it will be warm and cozy.

"Oh, my God, is it ever cold in here. What's wrong with the stove?" I say, shivering. Usually, our oil stove chugs along and keeps the tent warm. I'm almost afraid to have him look at the stove, because of the terrible incident with our snow camping trip last year. I don't say anything as Tiger looks into what's wrong. He doesn't seem the least bit worried.

"It's full of carbon. If we want heat, we'll to have to take it outside to clean it."

"Can we get Amos to help?" I'm frightened to have Tiger do it himself. I don't trust his ability to do some of the things he thinks he can.

"No, we can do it. Cleaning a stove's easy." He picks up the stove and I help him carry it outside. We get busy, each of us with a wet cloth, and we scrape the black carbon out of the stove.

It's one of the coldest nights of the year so far, and cleaning the stove takes at least an hour. Our hands are freezing by the time we think we've finished cleaning it, and we bring the stove back inside, only to find the tent has lost any heat it had.

I hold my breath as Tiger lights the stove and all goes well. But now there's another problem. Oil is puddling on the ground inside the tent. The leak has to be fixed right away; the stove won't work without oil.

"Tiger," I say, "I'm running over to Amos's to see if he'll help."

"Don't bother. I can do it myself." Tiger says this as he tries to tighten the screws, but the leak won't stop. Finally, he gives up and shuts off the stove for the night. Thank God. I would rather be cold than risk the chance of another fire.

With our clothes on, we burrow under the blankets and try to keep warm. The icy air wakes us early, but the sun warms the tent, and we can finally feel our fingers and toes again.

Tiger goes back to work fixing the stove, which is in the tent again.

"I'm so damn sick of this stove," he says, and he goes to light it. This time, it appears as though he has had success. He plops down on one of the chairs. "I can hardly wait to get back to civilization. I'm sick of all these problems."

I can't believe what I'm hearing. I never thought I would hear Tiger say those words. At last, he's looking forward to going home.

A couple of days later, Tiger surprises me with a question. "Deanne, do you mind if I go hunting this weekend? It will probably be my last chance." Usually, he just informs me of his plans. He doesn't ask how I feel about much of anything. I feel myself trembling at the thought of being in the tent alone, as it offers no protection. Fortunately, Tiger doesn't seem to notice.

"No, go on," I tell him. "Go have fun. I'll be fine. Amos is nearby, and we both know he's the voice of the village. He'll know what's going on and will let me know if I should be worried."

After Tiger leaves, I put on my jacket and walk around the village. I run into Ruth. "Some of the men are home from Kotzebue," she says. "There is going to be drinking this weekend."

"How do you know?" I ask. This is the last thing I wanted to hear.

"Them men, they get liquor in Kotzebue and they gotta drink. Seems like they can't help themselves," Ruth tells me.

I remember the last time there was drinking in the village. Then, I could lock myself in the house or go to the Keating's place. Anything can happen. I suddenly feel vulnerable. What if someone comes to the tent drunk? What will I do?

"Ruth, I'm nervous," I say, hoping she'll understand. "What happens if any of the men come to my tent?"

"They won't dare, all right. If they do, you just scream and holler."

I toss and turn all night, listening for trouble. Tiger and Ruth said no one would bother me, but I am too frightened to sleep.

Amos comes by the next morning to check on me.

"Was there any drinking last night?" I ask, after we say hello. I'm glad to see him.

"Lots of drinking. Clarence got two of them women drunk, and they sure put on a good show. Lucky their husbands were hunting. They were doing the twist and had nothing on but their skirts. Their legs were caked with mud. They're sure gonna feel bad this morning. It was real funny to watch."

I wander over to Ruth's after Amos leaves. One of the women Amos told me about is there. She is looking like the wrath of God, and I expect she feels like it too. She's sitting at Ruth's table with her head in her hands. Her head must be pounding.

"Hi, Minnie," I say. "You feeling all right?"

She barely looks up when I say this, just grunts an acknowledgement.

Apart from Sarah, with her bottle of beer, I haven't seen women in Kivalina drink. I wonder what her husband will say when he gets home. He's sure to find out. I hope he won't be too angry with her.

XLII
ENDINGS AND BEGINNINGS

Lynn is coming soon; it's something I have been looking forward to all summer. I hope she understands what she's getting into. I worry she won't be able to cope with the culture shock and our living conditions. I have so many questions about her visit here. Is she ready to live in a tent? Have I prepared her enough for this type of living? She may not realize how cold it is with winter approaching, and her clothes may not be adequate. I'm worried, but I can hardly wait to see her.

The day Lynn is supposed to come, my heart drops when I step outside. The village is completely shrouded in fog. I can't see the ocean in front of us, I can't see any houses. No one in their right mind would fly under these conditions.

Mildred shows up with a telegram. Lynn has arrived, the telegram says, and she's been put up at the Arctic Inn in Kotzebue because pilots aren't flying in this fog.

At around seven o'clock, I hear a plane. It's probably a plane that flies in any weather. It's landing, and I hope Lynn is on it.

"If Lynn's not on this plane, I'm flying back with them to Kotzebue," I tell Tiger.

He doesn't like this idea. "No way. You can hardly see more than two feet in front of you."

"Your sister shouldn't be in Kotzebue by herself. What if she gets stuck there for the entire time she's supposed to be with us? You know she's fragile emotionally. I'm going."

As the small plane makes its way through the dense fog, my heart is in my mouth. I can't see an inch in front of me, and I can't imagine how we're going to land safely. I hate flying and I grip the side of the seat as the plane descends. Somehow, we make it, and I breathe a sigh of relief. The airport isn't far from the hotel and the pilot gives me a ride there.

In Kotzebue, I find Lynn at the Arctic Inn, a dirty, dingy place. She's been given the best room, which isn't saying much. I would hate to see what the other rooms look like.

Lynn is almost asleep when I arrive, but she wakens quickly and sits up. She looks pale, but her eyes are sparkling. "Deanne!" We embrace. "I'm so glad you came," she says. "I had visions of getting trapped here by myself for the whole time."

"I did too," I tell her, looking around. Lynn's room is small and dirty. It looks like the last person here puked all over the floor, and no one bothered to clean it up. There is dog hair everywhere, even on the beds. I don't know if bed bugs exist in Alaska, but if they do, this place probably has them. I console myself with the thought that it's better than her staying at a native's place. That would have been culture shock. At least here, there is a bathroom down the hall with a flush toilet and not just a honey bucket. "It's so foggy, you can't see at all. But I had to come and be with you. I didn't want you here alone."

Lynn turns on the light. "Even if we're stuck here four days, we'll be together." We talk until Lynn gets sleepy again. I slip on a pair of pajamas I brought and climb into bed beside her. She's asleep in seconds. I sleep after some time, relieved to be with Lynn and knowing she's safe.

We are up early, dress quickly, and go out to walk around Kotzebue. I take her to Art Fields's to taste the best hash browns, accompanied by bacon and eggs. It's the best breakfast I've eaten in months. We are filled with delicious food and ready to face the day ahead. I take her to Hanson's, the general store in town. Just before we go in, we run into Gladys, from Kivalina. Lynn knows Gladys was a friend of mine in Kivalina.

Gladys looks at Lynn and then at me. "You two sure look like sisters, all right."

I have to laugh. Lynn looks like Grace Kelly—she has fine features, porcelain skin. I've always looked like the girl next door. I take Gladys's words as a compliment.

"Thanks, Gladys," I say. "Lynn is Tiger's sister, not mine. She's going to Kivalina with me."

"Yes, I'm excited," Lynn chimes in. "I've heard so much about Kivalina."

At Hanson's, Lynn is looking at the rows and rows of calico when we run into another of my friends from Kotzebue, Mamie Beaver. I haven't seen Mamie since last August when we made our disastrous trip here. She throws her arms around me.

"I hear Tiger had to go and get himself burned," Mamie says. "It sure was too bad, but I hear he's okay now." She takes a good look at Lynn and me. "Are you two sisters?"

I tell her Lynn is Tiger's sister. It seems all women with blonde hair look alike to the natives around here.

Later, it's clear enough to fly to Kivalina. The ride is short, and we can see clearly all the way up the coast—so different from my terrifying flight last night. Tiger is there to greet us on the airstrip. He charters the pilot for a short flight to give Lynn a view of the country.

The fog is still hanging around the flats, but we can fly up the coast to Cape Thompson. It's interesting to see this place from this perspective. I remember seeing it from the ocean last summer, when I came up here with Tiger in our boat. It looks entirely different from the air. I can see more of the cliffs and have to marvel at Tiger thinking we could wander around them. From the air, they look daunting. The cliffs are jagged and rocky, and I don't see any paths. I tell Lynn about the time Tiger and I went camping there and about how the birds roost on the rocks, lining their edges.

Back in Kivalina, we walk around the village, and I introduce Lynn to several people. The natives have friends from all over visiting them. It's the first time we've had anyone stay with us.

It's wonderful having Lynn here to see Kivalina and meet some of the people we talk about. Everyone greets her warmly. What a contrast to my arrival a year ago.

The night Lynn and I arrive in Kivalina is Bobby Hawley's birthday. The whole village is there, cramped in their tiny one-room house. Cakes and pies are on the table. Lynn has her first taste of Eskimo ice cream. I'm not sure if she likes it, but she's too polite to say anything. It takes some getting used to. Tonight, I have a hard time eating it. The thought of caribou fat makes me sick.

Lynn enjoys the party, but I can tell she's getting tired. She's had a long day. Tiger and I take her back to the tent and show her to her bed: a sleeping bag with a thin mattress. She falls asleep almost immediately.

We're awake early in the morning and Lynn's eyes sparkle with anticipation of the day that lies ahead. We enjoy our usual breakfast of oatmeal, brown sugar, and canned milk. It's cloudy and cold. The women are going berry picking and Lynn and I will join them on the short expedition down the coast. I prefer the views upriver, but there will be more berries where we're headed. I hope to take Lynn upriver while she's here. We travel by skin boat, a treat for Lynn, who has never seen one before. As we near our picking spot, one of the women says, "Look, killer whales!"

Whales are jumping out of the water, almost frolicking as we make our way down the coast. No one seems frightened by these huge creatures, so Lynn and I sit back and watch as they put on a show.

Our captain, Lawrence Sage, finds a good berry picking spot and hauls the boat onshore. We pick blackberries with the other women while we talk, catching up on each other's lives. We have so much to talk about, and this is a good time to do it without Tiger here to listen.

Lynn has had a difficult time in California. But she looks good. I ask her if she's happy.

"I feel so much better than I did last year at this time," she says. "Before I met my psychiatrist, I didn't think I had a future."

I pause a moment, wanting to pretend I don't understand what she's saying, but I do. I know I have to respond somehow. In time, her words will come back to haunt me. Should I have told Tiger about this? Should I have told his parents? I had no knowledge of the depth of my sister-in-law's problems. All I know is Lynn trusts me and I'm not about to break her confidence.

"Lynn, I had no idea. You have everything going for you. You're smart, you're beautiful. What is it?"

"I don't know, and I'm not sure I can explain it to you. All I know is that I felt trapped in a deep dark place in my mind. I was on a downward spiral after I saw you in Chicago. I couldn't do anything. I couldn't read, I couldn't write letters. I received a letter from a man I really liked. I wanted to answer it, but I'd start the letter and couldn't finish it. I just sat curled up in my chair wondering what to do. I was in a nowhere land and knew I was in trouble. That's when I found Dr. M."

I'm shocked hearing this. I hope she's not pretending to like it here, and hope that being here is good for her. This place can be challenging, even for a few days.

Eventually, we stop to rest with the other women, and Lynn is introduced to dried fish. She eats it like a trooper. I'm impressed. Over the next few days, I'll see her eat the food she's served whether she likes it or not, and she never says a word about it.

After more berry picking, we head back to the village. It's getting colder. Lynn is shivering in the jacket she borrowed from Dorothy Keating. She's used to the weather in California, not to the chill of September here in Alaska.

Back in the warm tent, Lynn hauls out a bag with the hostess gifts she brought, watermelon and cantaloupe, and sets the fruit on the table. Melons are a luxury. We haven't had them all summer. I invite some of our friends over to share our special treat.

First, I knock on Amos's door. "Amos, come over and have some white man's food," I tease.

It's interesting introducing Inuits to a kind of food they aren't used to. Amos comes over and takes a cautious taste of the cantaloupe. I can see he hates it, and he's struggling to get it down. He doesn't even bother with the watermelon. It's as foreign to him as his food is to us. I find the whole scenario amusing. Next, Ruth and Caleb come over to sample the fruit. Ruth says she loves the cantaloupe, but Caleb is not as enthusiastic. It took me years to learn to eat cantaloupe, I tell them. I can understand why they might not like it.

Amos is here when we throw the rinds to the dogs. The rinds still have a bit of the juicy fruit in them. Pepper gobbles them down, but Clover will have nothing to do with them. She only likes dried fish.

"Those melons are only good for the dogs, all right, and one of your dogs won't even try them," Amos remarks and is laughing when he says this.

On Sunday, we're up early. I take Lynn to a church service in the village, choosing the Episcopalian church over the Friends church. I was here last week for the christening of Emmaline's baby. The sermon was long and mostly in the Inuit language. This week it's a communion service with Milton Swan, the priest. He notices us and kindly translates the sermon into English, which makes us feel welcome. Lynn is fascinated to find out Milton was the first native in Alaska to be ordained as an Episcopalian priest. I tell her about his ordination and how privileged I felt to be there for it. I don't tell her Tiger refused to go.

The weather is lovely after church, and Tiger and I take Lynn upriver. It's sunny without too much wind, and the temperature is in the high sixties. Indian summer may be with us for a few days before autumn arrives.

The land is starting to be tinged with autumn colors. The air shimmers with a soft light. It seems to glow as we sit on the riverbank enjoying a peaceful time together. I feel like we're in an Impressionist landscape painting. The Arctic cotton is still blooming, although it is nearing the end of its days. It's serene, relaxing for all of us. Lynn looks happy and at peace.

The setting sun bathes the land in a yellow glow and the sky is pink with streaks of lavender and periwinkle blue as we travel home. Mother Nature has given us a dazzling show to enjoy. It's Lynn's last night, and perhaps one of ours.

When Lynn leaves, as we hug goodbye, I whisper in her ear, "You were brave to come up here. Hang onto your life and see all the beautiful things that will happen."

I'm lonely without Lynn here, but I understand her eagerness to get back to civilization. I think about what she said and wonder if she was truly happy when we were teenagers. I always thought she was. But maybe I was wrong. I didn't know what lay beneath her smile—a sadness, even a despair that not even she understood?

Lynn with Clover

Two weeks from today, we'll be heading back home ourselves. I look forward to so much—running water, indoor plumbing, and fresh food. Before we leave, I have laundry to do and I need to start packing, but I think, why not put it off for another day? I want to drink in the sights of the village. I want to wander around and visit people. I want to see the women I have come to know and love—Ruth, Mildred, Lena, Charlotte, Sarah, Emmaline, even Edith. I wish Gladys were here as well.

I spend a day soaking up an experience I'll never have again. I sit with the women in their homes, talking and laughing together. I appreciate this chance to know I'm accepted as one of them. I may never see some of these people again, but their faces and their friendship will remain in my heart forever.

Two weeks pass in a heartbeat, and before I know it, it's time for us to go. On our last night, Mildred brings over a huge bowl of Eskimo ice cream as a parting gift. It's full of fresh blueberries and blackberries, and it looks delicious. After she leaves, Tiger manages to find a spoon and starts to dig in with gusto. He hands me the spoon. "Here, have some," he says. "This is probably the best we've ever tasted."

My stomach turns at the sight of the purplish sweet. "I can't eat it right now," I tell him.

"Why not?"

"I don't know. I just can't."

I do know, but I'm not saying a word about it, not yet. I am carrying our baby, who will arrive next May. I can hardly wait to share the news with Tiger when I'm sure I'm not going to miscarry again.

We wait at the airstrip with Pepper and Clover at our side. The whole village is here to say goodbye. I look around at the familiar faces—women, men, and children. What adventures I've had here, marvelous adventures, terrifying adventures, challenging adventures. I'm not the naïve young girl who came here with her new husband sixteen months ago. I'm a woman ready to face whatever lies ahead.

SUNSET

Once more, I am sitting on the deck of my cottage, enjoying the gentle waves lapping against the dock. Clouds skitter across the sky and the lake sparkles like a sheet of diamonds in the sunlight. My three children and seven grandchildren have left after a three-week visit and all is quiet. It's 2019, fifty-four years after we lived in Alaska. Tiger's ashes are scattered here, in the place we loved for so many years.

I met Tiger here at the age of fifteen and later, fell in love and married him. We went to Alaska, on a journey changing our life forever. There was so much more to our life than Alaska, but it influenced the rest of it. I reflect on that time so many years ago. A time when I was innocent and never thought tragedy would touch me.

The child I was carrying when we left Kivalina was born on May 30, 1966. Our daughter, Karen Elizabeth, was a feisty, happy bundle of joy who was indeed our light at the end of the tunnel. When she was born and I lay in the hospital afterwards for a week, I thought of Emmaline in Alaska, lying with her newborn at her side. I envied the way of birthing in Kivalina, knowing their way was a better way for both mother and child. Now, women only stay in the hospital overnight and the birthing process is so much better.

Tiger had countless operations during my pregnancy, and Lynn often came home from California to be with us. She watched Tiger's progress and saw my round belly, and all the while, I knew she wasn't content. I prayed things would change. After Karen was born, Lynn sent a short postcard. I never heard from her again.

"Lynn took her life last night," Dad Burch called on the first night I arrived with Karen in Winnipeg, where Tiger was teaching at the University of Manitoba. His voice was shaking as added, "We are in California and there will be a small memorial service for her. After, we'll come to Winnipeg to be with you."

We were shocked and heartbroken. I tried so hard to save Lynn, tried to be her confidante and help her in a way a therapist would. She would never get to see her niece grow up, never have her own family. There was no goodbye, no closure.

Our second child, Sarah Deanne, or Sarah Sunshine as we called her, arrived May 21, 1968. Tiger left for northern Canada for two months soon after she was born. He wanted to study the Inuits in the Hudson Bay area even though I wanted him to be with me, and our two tiny daughters. I spent the summer with the two little girls at the lake on my own. Returning to Winnipeg, I was content to be a stay-at-home mother, playing with my children, and making new friends. This was the life that I had longed for.

In 1969, four years after we left Alaska, Tiger was granted a sabbatical. He felt that his work there was incomplete and wanted to live in Kotzebue for ten months. I was terrified to take the young girls there, but Tiger promised that we would have electricity, a telephone, and running water. Only the promise of electricity turned out to be true.

At first, it seemed that I could handle life in Alaska as a new mom with two daughters. I loved playing with them in the newly fallen snow or just being in the house as they played contentedly together. In early January, an accident happened, marring what was beginning to look like an interesting adventure. Karen's arm was badly burned by scalding water. She spent six weeks receiving whirlpool treatment for her burned arm, which remains scarred today. Sarah became deathly ill with pneumonia and was finally admitted to a hospital intended for natives only. After that, to keep her warm and close to me, I carried her around in my parka the way the natives did and I learned firsthand how this satisfies a child, creating a strong bond between us. Life in Kotzebue with our daughters was full of hardship and joys.

When we returned to Canada, we were ready for the next big step to take as a family. We applied to adopt a child, because Tiger didn't believe in bringing more than two children into the world. Before long, on November 15, 1970, David Scott, a delightful and beautiful ten-day-old baby, became part of our family and completed it.

The house was full, with three children and our beloved dog, Clover. Clover adjusted well to her new environment after Alaska. She lived with us in many homes before dying at the grand old age of sixteen. Clover was born in a hole, lived in a tent, lived in a farmhouse and two houses in Harrisburg, as well as three houses in Winnipeg and a house in Kotzebue. She spent every summer with us at Muskoka Lake, our home in Canada and was indeed our four-leaf clover. Pepper didn't have the same longevity. Sadly, Pepper attacked a dog when we were in Canada. Worried a child could be next, we had him put down.

Kivalina beckoned again. We wanted the children to experience village life and we were curious to see other parts of Alaska. We spent four weeks there in the summer of 1976.

Looking down from the plane to the tiny village below, my heart beat faster. I'd told Charlotte when we left in 1965 that we might return with children one day, and now we were here. I was excited to have everyone meet them.

Arriving in Kivalina, in ways it was as if time had stood still. In other ways, it was very different. There were still dogs in the village, but snowmobiles were taking the place of dog teams. Many of the houses were newer and better, and most had electricity.

We were lucky to be able to rent a house provided by the government. The dogs now wandered freely around the village, and David never missed a chance to play with them. The girls made friends with others their age. We took trips upriver and enjoyed the best weather we had ever experienced in Kivalina. This would turn out to be my last trip to the village of Kivalina—a place of great adventure and challenge, terror and joy.

I remember Kivalina as I knew it in the far distant past. I think of the houses, some little more than shacks and the school-house with the barren playground. I can picture the people I knew. Today, Kivalina is a modern village. Many of the villagers we knew so long ago have died. There is electricity now, and the government has replaced many of the worn-down houses with new ones. The children enjoy a modern school and many of the residents use cell phones, watch television, and are on the inter-net. Some are on social media sites.

Sadly, the village is eroding bit by bit. Climate change has wreaked its horrors in the north. The sea freezes later in the year and breaks up earlier in spring. Temperatures are increasingly warmer. The lives of many of the people who live by hunting and fishing have changed. Five years from now, Kivalina may no longer exist. We were so fortunate to have lived there in 1964, before climate change began to erode this tiny island.

After our children were living on their own, Tiger and I con-sidered returning to Kivalina again. I knew the village would be different but felt sure I would exorcise ghosts still haunting me.

Tiger was happy to hear I wanted to go back. He promised me we'd go there soon.

I also wanted to collaborate on a book with Tiger. He would write the book—something that would appeal to the general public and not just to scholars. I would provide the photographs. After we returned from the Kotzebue in 1970, I gave up the idea of continuing my social work career and in 1976 became a pho-tographer. By the time I mentioned the book collaboration idea to Tiger, I was a well-known photographer throughout Canada and the United States. We never went to Kivalina again together, and we never collaborated on a book.

Sometimes I wish the past were a faded sepia-toned pho-tograph and the memories of the tragedies we experienced wouldn't torment me as they do today. But there are also the bright colors—the colors of joy and happiness that took us on a journey together for forty-seven years.

Watching the colors in the sky as the sun sets, I close my eyes for a minute, and think of the years that have passed so quickly. We moved to Harrisburg in 1974, never dreaming it would be our forever home. In the blink of an eye, our children were grown with children of their own. How did the years pass so quickly? Tiger has missed so much.

Tiger suffered from many things. He was always badly scarred, and remained the object of occasional scrutiny. His lungs never fully recovered from the accident, and it became more difficult for him to breathe as he aged. Before Tiger took his life in September 2010, he had heart problems, Meniere's disease, and cancer. On top of it all, he was facing a hip replacement. Both my mother-in-law (who was ninety-five at the time) and I believed he was tired of living this way. Since his tragic death, every time I think about Tiger, a knife goes through my heart. There is so much that could have been and never was.

I look at Tiger's life with deep respect. He was a man who was not afraid to face the world after he was so badly burned. Tiger adored his children and grandchildren. He was my rock and my best friend for forty-seven years.

Tiger left a legacy to scholars all over the world. Much of the Inuit's history was recovered through Tiger's fieldwork. I was fortunate to have played a small part in the massive work he produced. When his first book, *Eskimo Kinsmen: Changing Family Relationships in Northwest Alaska,* was published, he dedicated it to me. It was a small, simple dedication, but it meant the world to me. We took a long journey together, a journey that shaped our entire life.

The sun sets, and an afterglow of pinks, lavenders, and grays scatter across the sky, casting a rainbow of colors on the calm water. My thoughts stray to my life lived so long ago in Kivalina: the blue hills in the distance, the vivid colors of the sunset, and the way the light shimmered on the river's surface when we went to get water. The wind whipped my hair as we boated upriver and

I felt free—free from the dark winter months that lay behind us and the freedom to enjoy the days that lay ahead in the land of the midnight sun. I shiver, thinking of the bitter cold on my skin and the way it seeped into my bones. I remember what it was like to go out with the dog team, the great peace there was when it felt as though we were completely alone in the world, and the only sound, the runners on the sled and the panting of the dogs.

That young girl, the one who left on an unknown journey so many years ago filled with excitement and fear, will live inside me forever.

Made in the USA
Coppell, TX
13 December 2021

68387593R00164